Europe and the Andean Countries

D1178958

Euro–Latin American Relations — The Omágua Series

General Editor:

Peter Coffey, Europa Institute, University of Amsterdam

INTERNATIONAL EDITORIAL ADVISORY BOARD

Wolf Grabendorff (Director IRELA, Madrid, Spain)

Ciro Angarita (Universidad de Los Andes, Bogotá, Colombia); Claude Bataillon (Institut d'Etudes sur l'Amérique Latine, Université de Toulouse — Le Mirail, Toulouse, France); Luciano Berrocal (Institut d'Etudes Européennes, Université Libre de Bruxelles, Belgium); Harold Blakemore (Institute of Latin American Studies, London University, UK); Atilio A. Borón (EURAL, Buenos Aires, Argentina); Julien Chacel (Fundação Getulio Vargas, Rio de Janeiro, Brasil); Eduardo Ferrero Costa (Peruvian Centre for International Studies, Lima, Peru); Reinaldo Figueredo Planchart (Camara Colombo — Venezolana de Commercio, Caracas, Venezuela); Peter Flynn (Institute for Latin American Studies, University of Glasgow, UK); Gabriel Guzmán Uribe (Officina de Educación Ibero Americana, Madrid, Spain); Guy Martinière (Institut des Hautes Etudes de l'Amérique Latine, Paris France); Jorge Mendez (CEPAL, Bogotá, Colombia); Paolo Munini (Nomisma, Cooperazione Allo Sviluppo, Bologna, Italy); Fernando Murillo (Instituto de Cooperación Ibero Americana, Madrid, Spain); Paulo Batista Nogueira (Fundação Getulio Vargas, Rio de Janeiro, Brasil); Massimo Panebianco (Instituto di Diritto Publico, Universita Degli Studi di Salerno, Italy); Peter Praet (Institut d'Etudes Européennes, Université Libre de Bruxelles, Belgium); Heinz Gert Preusse (Ibero-Amerika Institut für Wirtschaftsforschung, Göttingen, FRG); Gustávo Fernández Saavedra (Genève, Switzerland); Germánico Salgado (Quito, Equador); Juan Carlos Torre (Instituto Torcuata di Tella, Buenos Aires, Argentina); Miguel S. Wionczek (El Colegio de Mexico, Mexico).

The Omágua were a civilized and peaceful Indian tribe living in the Amazon region, between present-day Peru, Ecuador and Brazil, in the fifteenth and sixteenth centuries.

Europe and the Andean Countries:

A Comparison of Economic Policies and Institutions

Edited by
Ciro Angarita and Peter Coffey

Pinter Publishers, London and New York

© The editors and contributors, 1988

First published in Great Britain in 1988 by
Pinter Publishers Limited
25 Floral Street, London WC2E 9DS

All rights reserved. No part of this publication may
be reproduced, stored in a retrieval system, or
transmitted by any other means without the prior
written permission of the copyright holder. Please
direct all enquiries to the publishers.

British Library Cataloguing in Publication Data

A CIP catalogue record for this book is available from the
British Library

ISBN 0–86187–968–6

Library of Congress Cataloging-in-Publication Data

Europe and the Andean Countries.

  (Euro–Latin American relations—the Omagua series)
  Bibliography: p.
  Includes index.
  1. Andes Region—Economic policy—Congresses.
2. European Economic Community countries—Economic
policy—Congresses. 3. Andes Region—Foreign economic
relations—European Economic Community countries—
Congresses. 4. European Economic Community countries—
Foreign economic relations—Andes Region—Congresses.
I. Angarita, Ciro. II. Coffey, Peter. III. Series.
HC167.A5E88 1987   338.94   87–29153
ISBN 0–86187–968–6 (U.S.)

Photoset by Mayhew Typesetting, Bristol, England
Printed by Biddles of Guildford Ltd.

Contents

Preface

The present volume on the relationships between the EEC and the Andean Group of Countries had its origin in a conference on the subject held at Bogota, Colombia, in the second semester of 1984. It is thanks to the joint efforts of Peter Coffey of the Europa Institute at the University of Amsterdam and Ciro Angarita of the University of Los Andes in Bogota that this edition has been possible. The original contributions have been strengthened very adequately by additional articles written by specialists of both continents.

The publication of the book in 1987 is very timely since both at the level of the EEC and the Andean Pact there have been significant new policies and strategies adopted in order to improve the global and, up to now, weak relationships so well described in the book.

In fact, as the Drekonja/Kornat article 'Western Europe–Latin America: A General Frame of Reference' well describes, despite the historical links between the two regions, the development of cooperation through the EEC mechanisms has, so far, been very much reduced. In such a sense, it is important to add that in the past few months there has been an increased effort on the part of the EEC to draft a new strategy towards the non-member Less Developed Nations, as has been voiced in the Commission's document entitled 'Role of the Community in Industrial Cooperation with the Less Developed Nations of Latin America, Asia, the Gulf and the Mediterranean'. In the same way, it is worth noting that the Cooperation Agreement between the EEC and the Andean countries signed in 1983 has finally been ratified by all Andean parliaments and has just begun to be effective.

In regard to the contents of the book, I would also like to stress the excellent idea of the editors to include parallel studies on sectoral policies in fields such as agriculture and industrial matters. To readers the dissimilarities in the agricultural strategy of the two integration processes will become quite clear. While to the EEC the Common Agricultural Policy is a key and costly element of its economic strategy, to the Andean Group common agricultural policies have been of lesser importance. As is shown in the corresponding article by Gustavo Tobón, the attempts to set up common purchases of importables have failed. In fact, if anything, the changes adopted through Decision 217 which modifies the Andean Agreement tend to facilitate the protection of agriculture in each of the countries in the face of the competition by the other members.

I would also like to point out the contrasts in industrial policies. While in the EEC some emphasis has been given to increasing competition and the promotion of technological improvements, the key has been the policies towards declining industries through aid and import controls. At the level of the Andean Group the initial efforts were guided towards the establishment of large-scale import substituting industries through an industrial programmized scheme. The instrument, however, as well indicated in Alicia Puyama's article, only showed achievements in light engineering. One of the most important changes the new regime adopted through Decision 217 was, in fact, to reduce the rigidities imposed by the programming scheme and to permit new forms of industrial programmes more adaptable to sub-sectors of member countries and to facilitate complementarities in assembling processes.

At this point, I would also like to add some comments on the Andean Foreign Investment Regime, probably the most controversial item in the Andean Integration Scheme. Such a regime — best known as Decision 24 of the Andean Group — was backed up by the economic ideologies of the late 1960s. Its focus was that direct foreign investment had to be very selective since the domestic capital investment had been chosen with priority to enjoy the benefits of the enlarged Andean market and its protective environment. Somehow, it was then erroneously thought that foreign debt was to be preferred to foreign investment. The experience is well known and it explains why one of the major changes adopted in the new regime was the change in the foreign investment regime. Decision 220 modifies aspects such as profit reinvestments eliminating restrictions; facilitates the access of multinationals to domestic credit markets and eliminates restrictions on direct investments in particular sectors. Above all, the most significant change both in economic and ideological terms refers to the obligations to convert enterprises to ones of domestic capital majority (*empresas mixtas*). While before new enterprises were obliged to become '*mixtas*' within fifteen years, the new regime establishes that the period is to be thirty years and only for enterprises that export to other members and not for those oriented to extra-Andean export markets.

Passing on now to the contributions that refer to the cooperation of macroeconomic policies, I would also like to point out the immense differences between the achievements of the EEC and the failures observed at the Andean level. The article on the European monetary system by Peter Coffey and the Hahn article on fiscal policy in the EEC not only serve to explain the EEC mechanisms, but additionally suggest procedures that could be undertaken by Latin America. In the case of the Coffey article the author outlines a very interesting scheme for a Latin American Monetary System that could be started by Argentina and Brazil under their new integration agreement. As regards the Hahn article, it serves as a good model to the Andean Group on the tax harmonization of the value added tax and excise duty. In fact, within the Andean Group it has so far been impossible to adopt a common external tariff.

One of the important reforms in 1987 adopted through the Decision 217 had to be precisely on the external tariff and the abolition of fiscal frontiers within the member countries. The general philosophy of the new regime is to make a slower, but unequivocal, approach to an external tariff and to the gradual abolition of internal duties and non-tariff barriers. Time schedules in the original agreement appeared too strict and were violated.

To conclude I would like to refer to institutional aspects. Both the EEC and the Andean Group have been adopting important institutional reforms. The EEC is preparing itself for the European Union after the approval of the single European Act. On the other hand, the Andean Group has also adopted structural institutional reforms through Decision 220, which reforms the Foreign Investment Regime, and 217, which modifies the original Cartagena Agreement. In addition, the Cooperation Agreement that was signed in December 1983 between the Community and the Andean Community and member countries has finally become effective after its approval by the different legislative bodies of the Andean countries. This all reflects an increased interest and ratifies support for the integration schemes. This book on Latin American–EEC relationships in the 1980s therefore acquires special significance.

Roberto Junguito-Bonnet
Paris, July, 1987

Acknowledgements

The editors wish to thank Mr Ben Kotmans, a secretary at the Europa Instituut, who has typed part of this work as well as the index. They also wish to thank translators of the University of Los Andes, who have translated some of the chapters of this book from Spanish into English. Last but not least, they are grateful to Mr Howard Gold, a librarian at the Europa Instituut, who has prepared the index.

The editors are grateful to the Third World Foundation, London, for permission to reprint contributions by Germánico Salgado Penaherrera and José Antonio Ocampo which originally appeared in Altaf Gauhar (ed.), *Regional Integration: The Latin American Experience*. The Ocampo chapter has, however, been updated for the present book. The copyright for these contributions remains with the Third World Foundation.

Notes About the Contributors

Ciro Angarita, a Colombian national, is Professor of Law at the Los Andes University Law School, Bogotá, UNIDROIT corresponding collaborator, member of the UN Peace Academy and the International Advisory Editorial Board of the Omagua Series and former Dean of the National University of Colombia Law School.

Roberto Junguito-Bonnet is the Colombian Ambassador to France and a former Minister of Finance (1984), Minister of Agriculture (1982) and Ambassador to the EEC (1983).

Peter Coffey, a British national, is Head of the Economics Section at the Europa Instituut, University of Amsterdam. He is also the general international editor of this new series of books on Europe and Latin America.

Gerhard Drekonja-Kornat, an Austrian national, is a specialist on Latin American foreign policies, Editor of the *Zeitschrift für Lateinamerika*, Director of Austria's Ludwig-Boltzmann Institute for Latin American Studies, Vienna, former researcher and lecturer at Los Andes University, Bogotá, Colombia.

Elizabeth de Ghellinck, a Belgian national, is Assistant Professor at the Centre de Recherches Interdisciplinaires, Droit et Économie Industrielle (CRIDE) at the Catholic University of Louvain. She is also Associate Professor of Economics at the Catholic University of Mons, Belgium.

Gustavo Tobón Londoño, a Colombian national, is Professor of Foreign Trade at the Javeriana University, Bogotá, Consultant to the Institute for the Integration of Latin America (INTAL), former Director-General of the Instituto Colombiano de Comercio Exterior (INCOMEX).

Piet van den Noort, a Dutch national, is Professor of Economics at the Wageningen Agricultural University in the Netherlands.

José Antonio Ocampo, a Colombian national, is Executive Director of the Fundación para la Educación Superior y el Desarrollo (FEDESARROLLO), national Editor of *Economic Forecasts*, member of the editorial boards of *Journal of Development Economics* and *El Trimestre Económico*, former Director of the Centre de Estudios sobre Desarrollo Economico/CEDE at Los Andes University.

Germánico Salgado Penaherrera, an Ecuadorian national, is an independent consultant, former member of the Andean Pact Junta, General Manager of the Central Bank, Minister of Industry, Commerce and Integration and Ambassador in Spain.

Alicia Puyana, a Colombian national, is a Ph.D. in Economics at Oxford University, Director of the Centro Regional de Estudios del Tercer Mundo (CRESET) and consultant to the United Nations.

Richard H. Lauwarrs, a Dutch national, is Professor of Law and Head of the Europa Instituut, University of Amsterdam.

Introduction

Since the end of the fifties and in the early sixties, moves towards economic integration have been made both in Europe and in Latin America. In Western Europe, the European Economic Community (EEC) has led to a high degree of integration between the member states which are now ready to create a real common market by 1993. In Latin America, the main move towards integration was the creation, in 1960, of the Latin American Free Trade Association (LAFTA). However, nine years later, five countries (Bolivia, Chile[1], Colombia, Ecuador and Peru), dissatisfied with the slow progress being made towards integration, and, anxious to improve their negotiating position *vis-à-vis* stronger neighbours — such as Brazil, Argentina and Mexico, signed the Cartagena Agreement which set up an economic union. Special attention was paid to industrial policy — notably, joint industrial development schemes — and preferential treatment was given to the weaker members, Bolivia and Ecuador.

In view of the friendly co-operation agreement signed between the EEC and the Andean Pact Group of Countries, the editors felt that it was desirable for both sides to know more about each other. In particular, they considered that there were certain areas of economic policy — notably agricultural, financial, industrial and monetary policies — that should be examined and compared. Therefore, three years ago, in July 1984, with financial support from the Commission of the European Communities and Columbian institutes, and under the auspices of the University of Los Andes, Bogotá, and the Europa Instituut of the University of Amsterdam, the editors organized a seminar in Bogotá on 'The European Economic Community and the Andean Pact Group of Countries'.

The papers presented at that seminar have been updated and other contributions have been added to produce this book. In reproducing Gerhard Drekonja's provocative paper, the authors wish to help to dispel some of the misconceptions that some Europeans may hold about Latin America.

In the section devoted to Agricultural Policy, the contributions by Gustavo Tobón Londoño and Piet van den Noort show that the EEC has established a much more advanced form of common agricultural market than is the case in Latin America. In contrast, when reading the contributions written by Elizabeth de Ghellinck and Alicia Puyana, it is obvious that the Andean Countries had been quicker than Common Market Countries in establishing joint industrial projects.

Turning to monetary matters, Peter Coffey considers that Latin American countries would have to conduct a much greater amount of their trade among themselves if they were to consider emulating the European Monetary System. Equally, they would have to achieve much lower levels of inflation. The collapse of intra-regional trade in Latin America is also emphasized in José Antonio Ocampo's contribution where a profound analysis is made of the source of disequilibrium in this trade, and, the LAIA Payments System, which, up until 1981, worked satisfactorily. Proposals are also made for improving the system.

In contrast with the EEC, there has been little or no fiscal integration among Latin American countries. Therefore, in this part, the contribution of Walter Hahn examines the progress made towards achieving fiscal integration in the Community.

Turning to the examination of institutions, made by Ciro Angarita and Richard H. Lauwaars, one is struck by the similarity between the institutions and their responsibilities in both groups. However, the main differences are that whereas the Andean Court of Justice has 'suffered from frustrating inertia', the European Court of Justice has been very active (though not at the beginning of its life). Also, whereas the Andean Parliament is purely a 'parliament of parliaments without legislative jurisdiction', the European Parliament is a directly elected body which will, after 1992, acquire greater power.

Looking to the future, with the chapter by Germánico Salgado Penaherrera as the point of reference, it is clear that both the EEC and the Andean Pact Group of Countries now share the desire to create a 'real' common market in each of their communities. This is the real challenge facing them and which will have to be met if Europeans and Latin Americans wish to maintain the momentum of their moves towards economic integration. It is hoped that this work will help them to formulate and adopt policies facilitating the achievement of this aim.

The authors wish to take this opportunity of thanking all their collaborators who have helped them in this venture by updating and allowing publication of their work. In particular, they wish to thank Ambassador Junguito-Bonnet (formerly Colombian Minister of Economic and Financial Affairs), who gave such encouragement to the holding of the seminar, three years ago.

Peter Coffey and Ciro Angarita
Amsterdam and Bogota,
July 1987

Note

1. Chile eventually withdrew from the agreement and that country's place was taken by Venezuela.

PART 1: RELATIONS BETWEEN THE EEC AND THE ANDEAN PACT GROUP OF COUNTRIES

1

Western Europe–Latin America: A General Frame of Reference

Gerhard Drekonja-Kornat

1. MYTHS AND CLICHÉS

Up to now, Colombian diplomat and writer Pedro Goméz Valderrama is the last in a series of authors to use Latin America's stereotyped view of Europe. Geo von Lengerke,[1] hero of his novel *La Otra Raya del Tigre*, is a German bruised by the 1848 Revolution who turns up in Bucaramanga, Colombia. He is a tall, handsome, strong man successfully dealing in tobacco and China bark. Von Lengerke tames crocodiles, sleeps with every woman and patiently proceeds to build a veritable castle in the midst of his quickly growing estate. As an ultimate feat, he even manages to carve a road through the untamed jungle down to the Magdalena River. The other characters, that is the natives, merely serve as a foil to the European who is the novel's central figure. More than any other work, this stylistically brilliant novel clearly reflects a tremendous contradiction. Whereas Latin America's concept of Europe is overly positive, Europe insists on linking Latin America to romanticism, bucolic illusions, negative images and commonplace descriptions ranging from the *'buen salvaje'* to the *'buen revolucionario'*. In other words, Europe views the subcontinent in terms of passive receptiveness.

Yet, this stereotype was not always the rule. Until the beginning of the nineteenth century, Latin America proudly lived its own hybrid lifestyle, mixing pre-colonial and colonial elements to a degree that proved to be more autonomous than concurrent developments in North America. Up to the middle of the nineteenth century, there was less violence and a greater degree of unity among young Latin American nations than in European countries shaken by nationalistic upheavals and burdened by conflict. However, when Latin America's special form of development nurtured by customs barriers began to fail, an inferiority complex set in. Great Britain's free-trade policies put an end to autonomous development — or 'collective self-reliance — as we might call it today, which was symbolized by the iron chain strung across the Rio de la Plata. In 1870, for example, a self-sufficient Paraguay under the López family was crushed by the Triple Alliance of Brazil, Argentina and Uruguay working on London's behalf. And, to add insult to injury, British free-trade ideologists and historians even sarcastically accused Paraguay of anti-modern behavior and uncivilized stupidity.

From this point on, Latin America, once a pre-industrial, quasi-autonomous manufacturer, became a dependent client for imported goods. And a rapidly industrializing Europe was quick to indulge in an illusion whereby the *buen salvaje* was supposedly being compensated for keeping imaginary free spaces open for Europeans. It was then that Alexander von Humboldt, through no fault of his own, began to influence Europe's concept of Latin America. In eighteen volumes of political commentaries and geographical descriptions compiled as a result of his travels between the Amazon region and Mexico during that fragile period prior to independence, he provides readers with information on a bucolic Latin America. Despite their scientific seriousness, these works fed the imagination of Europeans who were then in the midst of the early stages of modernization. As the Industrial Revolution spread between London and Berlin, the determinism of a society characterized by a division of labour also grew. Educated Europeans believed that Latin America had somehow escaped the constraints under which they themselves were living, and the subcontinent became a surrogate for the dreams and fantasies of an Old World confined and alienated by industrial development. Rousseau's concept of the *'bon sauvage'* materialized in the form of the freedom-loving Indian or Creole who surpassed the European in terms of happiness, wisdom and ecological equilibrium. Humboldt's scientific data, recast and misinterpreted in the melting pot of European romanticism, served to construct and crystallize the Latin American myth which, in one version or another, has haunted Europe ever since. First it was the *'buen salvaje'* and later the *'buen revolucionario'*, as defined by an eccentric Venezuelan author.[2]

Europe admired and loved her Camilo Torres, her Ernesto 'Che' Guevaras. European readers of Carlos Marighela's manual for the urban guerrilla imitated the Tupamaros, and the transitory abundance of 'Che' posters on the walls of European communes is far from a mere coincidence. Castro's comrade who was hunted down in the barren mountains of the Santa Cruz province of Bolivia, personified one of today's most attractive versions of the *buen salvaje*; and the development of this concept coincides with successive stages of European enthusiasm for Latin America.

However, Europe paid rather poorly for this psychological therapy. And, in order to sidestep her debt to Latin America, began to introduce a series of necessities aimed at Indians and Creoles who were new to compulsive consumerism. Ivan Illich reminds us[3] that Europe was bent on imposing 'masks of need' which would ultimately determine Latin America's status as a consumer. It began with the Catholic Church marketing salvation to the Indians and has led up to the modern development expert who defines people as 'underdeveloped people' and suggests that their lot could be improved through the purchase of industrial hard and software. Latin America has been transformed into an alternatingly underdeveloped, incorrectly developed or even retrodeveloped area revolving around the industrialized nations. Rafael Gutiérrez Girardot, a caustic Colombian critic, remarked that, ever since the colonial period, Latin America has been an active but exploited partner in the capitalistic world. In other words, its actions merely echo decisions made by the central countries and, although ruled by the law of progress, Latin America merely limps along behind.[4]

Gutiérrez is also well aware of the fact that Latin Americans are hampered by an inferiority complex. They even fall prey to their own myth and often think of themselves as the *buen salvaje*, which automatically makes those on the other side of the Atlantic supermen. Yet, one must be careful. Paris, the symbol of the European *par excellence*, ruthlessly dropped the hero of Eduardo Caballero Calderon's *Buen Salvaje*[5] once he failed his studies and spent his last cent. As final proof of bureaucratic charity, this shipwrecked young writer is sent home, thereby transferring him from one vacuum to another. On board the plane which carries him back, the novel's hero reflects on the price of his disastrous European adventure: *'Dentro de mi no hay nada, fuera de un tremendo vacio. Es como si me hubieran extraido las muelas de los recuerdos, las illusiones, los sentimientos, las esperanzas, las ideas y tuviera la encia de la memoria monda y lironda.'*

2. LATIN AMERICA AND EUROPE WITHIN THE AMERICAN SYSTEM

The clichés survived, and were even reinforced — primarily owing to the fact that at the beginning of the twentieth century the United States steadily began to dislodge European influence in South America and the Caribbean. In 1902, gunboat activity off the Venezuelan coast marked a turning-point in European authority. From then on, the United States moved to consolidate its influence in Latin America. The Kemmerer Commission had opened the door to South America even as early as the 1920s. A few European strongholds, like those of the Germans, remained intact, but were later eliminated during World War II.

The year 1945 brought with it more than just a renewal of interrupted relations between Europe and Latin America. Both regions were now an important part of the American System, whose universal nature had deprived the Allies of their classical sovereignty and reduced them to the status of clientele states. If the partners in this astonishingly novel empire failed to recognize its true features in the beginning, it was because this 'creation'[6] included a series of pacts and alliances (i.e. the OAS in the political sector and the TIAR in the military sphere as applying to Latin America) between participating nations (Latin America, Western Europe, Japan and parts of Asia) which gave the impression of being a coalition among equals.[7]

Having gained strength during World War II, Latin America attempted to pit its own form of regionalism against Washington's universal approach. However, the experiment did not succeed and the basis for the global American System was established between 1944 and 1948. Several of the political elite, like Alberto Lleras Camargo, the Colombian statesman and first Secretary-General of the OAS, enthusiastically supported the United States. The International Trade Organization, a major element in Latin America's envisaged line of defense, was discussed in La Habana in 1948; yet, only fragments of the original design (like GATT) eventually materialized and were accepted by the United States.[8]

Latin America's only attempt at protest failed because of the lack of allies. Péron's Argentina had been toying with the *'tercera via'* concept but retreated in 1945–46 when faced with possible exclusion from the newly established United Nations. There was no Third World to ally with. Japan was in ashes and Europe, exhausted after World War II, sold its railroads and other public investments in Argentina and sneered at Evita Péron's Rainbow Message. Washington falsely branded Péronism as 'nazi-fascism', thereby damaging any chance *tercera via* may have had of development. However, Péron's gesture of opposition, vague as it may have been, did somehow formalize a desire to expand the influence of Latin American and Western European medium powers within the American System. This topic has come up again and again during the last thirty years and has meant some difficult moments for the United States alliance. Still, in 1945 it was simply too early for this type of initiative to take hold. As a result, the American System was swiftly implemented and eventually succeeded in reaching unsurpassed heights within the unique framework of the 1950s.

It was essential that the client states should first become aware of their own particular situation. In Latin America, Cepalismo[9] was the first to diagnose the asymmetry. In 1948, CEPAL established its intellectual headquarters in Santiago de Chile (as far away from Washington as possible and notwithstanding some North American opposition). In the early 1950s, a new generation of Latin American economists and technocrats brought together by the Argentine, Raúl Prebisch analyzed (unlike the classical economic theory) the asymmetry of the American System, thereby paving the way for Latin America's theory of dependence. This analysis, although perhaps not very precise or sophisticated, proved to be considerably more productive than theories put forth by North American and European writers who at best defined Latin America as a 'regional subsystem' with potential for future autonomy.[10]

Western Europe, itself a regional subsystem which later experienced a high degree of integration, lived at an astronomical distance from Latin America during the 1950s. Except for banks and some European firms which reestablished relations interrupted during World War II (these were never high priority), the subcontinent remained in the hands of anthropologists, ethnologists and the archeologists: heirs of the late nineteenth-century *'naturalistas'* who had given Europe sound geographical descriptions of Latin America. Occasionally, a traveling European writer would describe his impressions in a flurry of adjectives. From a European point of view, Latin America was not the surrealistic *'Tloh, Uqbar, Orbis Tertius'* of Borges, but rather *'La Voràgine'*, *'Huasipungo'* or *Cangaceiro* folklore which confirmed the exotic expectations of European readers who had previously indulged in the metaphysical orgies of Count Keyserling's *South American Meditations*.[11]

Slowly but steadily, this concept began to change towards the end of the 1950s. Latin America was discovered — for the fourth time.[12] This cannot be attributed to any one specific event, not even the Cuban Revolution in 1959, despite the fact that Fidel Castro, the *'buen revolucionario'* par excellence, had a strong effect on Europeans.[13] After having thrown its colonial ballast overboard, Europe optimistically subscribed to a development policy. This was the real reason behind a rediscovery of Latin America. In view of the events of the early 1960s and demands made by the new development policy, traditional connoisseurs of Latin America — archeologists and ethnologists — just could not do the job. Owing to a tremendous demand for expertise, Europe witnessed an amazing growth in the number of Latin American institutes (almost always public and founded both in and outside the universities). Based on several classic Latin American organizations such as London's Canning House, the Institut des Hautes Études de l'Amérique Latine in Paris and the excellent Ibéroamérika-Bibliothek in Berlin, new regional institutes and Latin American professorships expanded to meet the needs of Development Ministries which were also created at the time. The early 1970s witnessed even a modest degree of institutional cooperation between new Latin American centers in Western and Eastern Europe in the form of CEISAL.[14]

However, the Europeans paid the price for this particular form of institutional expansion. Inevitably, Latin America was seen in the light of development policies: not as a potential political partner but as an underdeveloped, dependent continent characterized by the usual stereotypes such as bloated bellies, slums, exploitation, oligarchs, generals and revolutionaries. A substantial portion of European literature on Latin America published during this period consists of research directed towards development policy or aimed at programming technical projects. On the other hand, those aspects most cherished by Latin America in its persistent quest of Europe such as partnership, cultural links and political cooperation designed to outweigh North American influence went unnoticed.

3. EUROPEAN ECONOMIC COMMUNITY AND EUROPEAN INTEREST IN LATIN AMERICA

The Treaty of Rome was signed on 1 January 1958. In accordance with its content, the six founders of the European Economic Community were bound to the creation of a common market and a political union. Latin America was disappointed by the careless treatment it had received from individual EEC members, yet it set great hope on Brussels in the assumption that Europe, as another regional subsystem within the American alliance, would offer some kind of preferential treatment in its own political interest. After all, international theory forecast a strengthening in the trend towards autonomy as a result of interaction between regional subsystems.[15]

Latin America did not have to wait long to see its hopes diluted and this disappointment has been a constant factor in relations ever since. For Eurocrats, Latin America has never been more than an export market seen in a Third World context and therefore subordinate to development policy. The Latin American 'contact group' which established itself in 1963 discussed a few points with Brussels but was never allowed to touch on real political issues. Italy's special interest in Latin America initially led to some insistence on initiatives in this respect. However, for the most part the first ten years of relations between Latin America and the EEC proved to be little more than a *'dialogo entre sordos'*.[16]

This situation finally began to change, owing to a political initiative on the part of the Latin Americans. A new generation interested in foreign policy, and one whose efforts were coordinated by Gabriel Valdés, a Christian Democrat in charge of the Chilean Ministry of Foreign Affairs (1964–1970), succeeded in transplanting the French Gaullist experience and that of the Non-aligned Movement, thereby developing a basis for the concept of a *'poder negociador latinoamericano'*.[17] This group used the Comisión Especial de Coordinación Latinoamericana (CECLA) established in 1963 as a vehicle for dialogue with Brussels. As the first collective bargaining entity representing the subcontinent, CECLA[18] edited the 'Carta de Buenos Aires' in 1970 which voiced Latin America's demand for an economic and political dialogue with Brussels. The document was a success, particularly since Brussels had also called for an effort to encourage neglected relations with Latin America.[19]

Despite this auspicious beginning, 1971 marked the first, and up to now the last, 'Latin America Year' for the EEC. A much celebrated 'mechanism for dialogue' was established which provided for at least one yearly meeting between Latin American ambassadors and their counterparts at the Charlemagne Building. The political nature of mutual relations was accepted by Brussels and Ralf Dahrendorf (who as a member of the 'Commission' was in essence Minister of Foreign Affairs for the EEC) enhanced relations by visiting Brazil, Argentina, Chile and Peru in the fall of 1971. Beginning with Argentina in 1971, Brussels simultaneously initiated negotiations with several Latin American countries concerning the establishment of bilateral, non-preferential trade agreements. Brussels also demonstrated an interest in the integration scheme adopted by the Andean Group which had a structure similar to its own, thus offering the potential for a special dialogue with Lima.

However, the good fortune of several farsighted statesmen handling Latin American affairs in Brussels was not to last for long. Ralf Dahrendorf clearly saw contact with Latin America as a matter of politics and outlined prospects for autonomy through cooperation with the EEC.[20] But the dry Eurocrats in Brussels left little room for doubt that the future of mutual relations would bring anything other than marginal improvements with no real qualitative advancements. (A typical example is the Multifibre Accord, under which Argentina, Brazil, Guatemala, Haiti, Colombia, Mexico, Peru and Uruguay voluntarily agreed to limit their exports to the EEC.) Brussels created a global Third World policy in the early 1970s, thereby depriving Latin America of the last hope for a special status. Preferential treatment (i.e. the Lomé Agreement) was granted only to former colonies of the EEC countries. Against the backdrop of a decline in the percentage of Latin American trade with Brussels, mutual relations in the late 1970s were eventually limited to:

(a) Non-preferential bilateral trade agreements with Argentina (1971), Brazil (1973) and Uruguay (1973).
(b) Agreements for economic cooperation with Mexico (1975) and Brazil (1980).
(c) Bilateral agreements with Argentina (1963) and Brazil (1965) concerning the peaceful use of atomic energy.
(d) Technical assistance in integration (with the former ALALC, the Andean Group, the Central American Common Market and the Latin American Integration Institute (INTAL) in Buenos Aires).
(e) Export promotion.
(f) Technical and financial aid.

And what of the political nucleus of this cooperation? What had happened to the autonomy which, according to theory, should have materialized as a result of interaction between two regional subsystems tied to a larger whole?[21] Obviously, Europe, after having experienced a tremendous economic expansion during the 1960s, and given its dedication to a strong foreign policy in the early 1970s, abandoned these initiatives because of its resource vulnerability and loyally fell into line behind Washington. Latin American foreign policy, whose *'autonomia periférica'*[22] had first peaked around 1972-73 also began to change. The *'tercer-mundistas'* lost ground to the *'occidentalistas'*. And, more importantly, Western Europe began to put its own economic interests ahead of all else as a result of a global crisis beginning in 1973. It adopted a defensive position and lost its taste for cooperation with Latin America which had become decidedly *'tercermundista'* in terms of the North–South dialogue.[23]

In the end, only marginal improvements were made. For tactical reasons, Brussels renewed its dialogue with Latin America at the end of the 1970s and established contact with the Sistema Económico Latinoaméricano, SELA, in Caracas. (SELA issued Resolution No. 44 of 1979 calling for a *qualitative* improvement in relations between the two regions and threatened asymmetrical countermeasures if Latin American demands were not heard.[24] In 1980, a more ambitious attempt to formalize relations with the 'democratic' integration group, i.e. the Andean Pact, failed with the Bolivian *coup d'état* of July 1980. (This was actually an attempt to adapt the ASEAN cooperation model to South America.) Since then, dialogue concerning a future global agreement between the EEC and the Andean Group has been suspended. The political crisis in the

Andean Pact has led to an embarrassed silence between Brussels and Lima. Meanwhile, Argentina is very concerned about growing EEC restrictions on agricultural imports and is reconsidering an extension of its 1971 bilateral trade agreement. The melancholic remarks of a Venezuelan observer sum up the situation:

Ahora bien, cuál fue el papel desempeñado por Europa? Sin duda, no asumió un papel protagónico ni independiente, sino que básicamente fue un partenaire *de los Estados Unidos en sus relaciones con América Latina, como segundo socio comerical, segundo centro financiero y segunda zona proveedora de tecnologia y de inversiones directas. No se perfiló, o al menos no suficientemente, una concepción politica y una estrategia económica que se diferenciara con nitidez de la de los Estados Unidos.*[25]

Latin America's young critics began to see a growing difference of interests between the two subcontinents. Latin America forced the political question while Western Europe — where individual countries were neither superpowers nor possessed sufficiently ample internal markets — favored the economic issue. This was a dominant factor prior to 1973 and has become even more so ever since — all of which has led to an even greater divergence of interests.

Prior to 1973, Latin America was a major, although not decisive, customer for Europe. Latin America was an important supplier of raw materials and proved to be a profitable area of operations for private Western European investment. By the end of the 1970s Bonn had concentrated 64 percent of all its private investments for developing countries in Latin America. However, the Federal Republic of Germany was the only European country to place priority on investments in the region. France, Italy and Great Britain (economically, politically and ideologically the 'hard core' countries) were more diversified. This kept Latin America at a level of secondary importance. All authoritative texts on the relationship between Europe and Latin America reflect this phenomenon and authors inevitably lament the decline percentage-wise in trade between the two regions.

Interest in industrial exports and investment continued after 1973; however, Europe, now clearly identified with First World interests, was leaning in another direction. The Middle East became of the utmost importance because of its oil. At the same time, Western Europe's security needs forced it to rely on Washington's (nuclear) arms umbrella more than ever before. In this context, Europe, characterized by its status as a medium power with limited internal markets, resource vulnerability and growing economic difficulties, had little room for a 'special relationship' with Latin America. Instead, a set of global rules was developed for the Third World, offering relatively expensive concessions in the areas of export agreements, financial aid and institutional cooperation (i.e. Stabex, Lomé). The 'old order' of 1945 which, after all, had provided Europe with considerable gains, was not subjected to a drastic revision. Consequently, there remain a number of overlapping and contradictory elements with regard to Western European interests:

(a) Industrial export interests continue to dominate on a global level and are reinforced by free-trade ideologies.
(b) Strategically, Western Europe continues to be characterized by Western Bloc interests.
(c) There are a number of special overlapping interests on the national level which have as a common denominator the search for partial autonomy and a defense of the status quo (life-style, material well-being, social market economies, party democracy, etc.).

However, these elements are increasingly opposed to the political-ideological-humanistic demands being made by Western European parties, trade unions, churches and political ideologies, most of which do not coincide with any of the economic-political interests noted above. On the contrary, owing to contradictions that have continued to grow since 1973, antagonism has increased and attitudes have become polarized. One faction favors a 'stability alliance' between Western Europe and Latin America emphasizing exports, European transnational business activity, investment, safe and secure supplies of raw materials and Western bloc interests. The other advocates an ideological power field which would reflect and reinforce demands for human rights, democracy based on popular support, the New International Economic Order and social justice.

The impact and success of these transatlantic cross currents will be the decisive factor in determining whether or not Europe's stubborn economic orientation continues to dominate in the years ahead or if persistent Latin American demands for a political dialogue will be heard by the 'other Europeans'.

4. THE GESTURE OF GAULLISM

Under the presidencies of Charles de Gaulle (1959–1969) and his successor Georges Pompidou (1969–1974), France began to deviate politically from Washington. This *'autonomia periférica'* was better known as 'Gaullism', a metaphor for France's effort to create its own maneuverability within the American System, particularly with regard to foreign policy and military matters. Paris began its experiment after having tackled the Algerian situation and its decolonization problems. De Gaulle first sought a fresh, different approach to French foreign policy and second a new view of the Third World and an alternate definition of France's role on the international scene. De Gaulle's concept of a powerful Europe, one capable of acting on its own, thereby replacing classical bipolarity with new power centers (which is exactly what J. Galtung[26] hoped to avoid) seemed ideal to Latin Americans who during the early 1960s had also begun their first intellectual experiments with a semi-autonomous foreign policy. They still placed great hope in Europe and, under the circumstances, De Gaulle's two trips to Latin America in 1964 were extremely symbolic.[27] It could even be said that France took the offensive in Latin America at this particular point in time.[28] De Gaulle played with the principle of *'latinité'*, a concept which (as clearly opposed to *'hispanidad'*) emphasized similar cultural traditions and the vision of a great destiny for all 'latin' nations.

Though still very much oriented towards Paris, the Latin American elite were honest enough to realize that their own reality could scarcely be explained within the context of Malraux or Proust. Once the initial enthusiasm had passed, reaction was mixed. Of course, Latin Americans would have liked to have given De Gaulle's *latinité* real political substance and to have used it as the basis for an alliance among the medium powers within the American System. But their interest cooled when it became evident that De Gaulle had little more in mind that a *'beau geste'* and had rather unscrupulously subordinated *latinité* to French economic and cultural interests. The gesture was never followed by practical offers. In 1973, when Argentina (in the midst of the second wave of Péronism) took the Gaullist metaphor literally and gave it a decidedly anti-American turn on the basis of *'geopolitica de la liberación'*, De Gaulle's heirs assumed a noncommittal attitude.[29] When Chile's Christian Democratic President Eduardo Frei made his pilgrimage to Paris he at least had De Gaulle's rhetorical support in his quest for independence. Yet some years later, even this was denied to a left-wing Péronist Argentina. Meanwhile, it was quite clear that France, rather than accepting Latin America as a serious ally, only sought a tactical advantage. In 1966, when atomic testing was begun, France had little regard for South American countries bordering the Pacific and took no notice of their protests. One of history's ironies is that at the same time (1967–68) France began to sell the first Mirages to Peru, thereby making her first inroad (via arms technology) into the North American sphere of influence. Brazil, Colombia, Venezuela, Argentina and Ecuador were subsequent clients for French combat planes and tanks. Everyone understood that there could be no question of either *latinité* or any specific European–Latin American cooperation at the moment: the export interests of French public enterprises were all that really mattered.

Despite initial expectations, De Gaulle's Latin American initiative proved to be a disappointment in the end. The handy formula of *latinité* was of little use in resisting the 'American challenge'. In 1978–79, it was energy-rich Mexico which assumed a 'Gaullist' profile[30], while President Giscard d'Estaing rather modestly traveled to Mexico City as a customer. On second thoughts, Régis Debray and *Les Temps Modernes* seem to have done more for the Gaullist design than the statesmen at the Elysée by attempting to eliminate the asphyxiating bipolarity via cooperation between Latin American and European clientle states within the American System. However, in 1981, with François Mitterand as French President and Régis Debray, the novelist turned presidential advisor, the Gaullist heritage had reappeared in a socialist context. Not all Latin American countries acclaimed the Franco–Mexican alliance of the summer of 1981 when both countries recognized the armed opposition in El Salvador. However, all of

Latin America definitely understood that finally a Western European nation was prepared to dissent from Washington on the basis of an alliance with a strong Latin American partner.

5. CULTURAL POLICY AND IDEOLOGY TRANSFER

In 1959, the United States was forced to revise the organizational structure of its Latin American sphere of influence as a result of the Cuban Revolution. This led to an ambitious initiative known as the Alliance for Progress which, despite its failure as a whole, did produce some lasting effects. Through the empirical social sciences and working within the framework of a science policy begun in the 1950s, the United States succeeded in creating an elite corps of technocrats which was designed to dislodge 'corrupt' oligarchs from the newly established planning offices, land reform agencies and development projects. Having regained its strength, Europe was urged to take part in this enterprise. Yet the Old World was not as concerned about Fidel Castro as Washington was. Only Bonn, the United States' most loyal European ally within the American System, broke off relations with La Habana. Europe offered Latin America a series of cultural policies, but little else.

The difference in attitudes between Europe and Washington was striking. Whereas the United States provided intense training in the reform-oriented social sciences, European countries offered only their own traditions and cultural values. France, working within the scope of Gaullism, mobilized a well-organized and well-financed chain of Alliance Française institutes which provided Latin Americans with an opportunity to read Proust in the original — just as before! The Federal Republic of Germany opened its cultural doors via the Goethe Institutes where pupils took crash courses in German. From the mid-1970s on, a further aspect of their duties has been to deny the existence of the Herder Institutes (the cultural arm of the German Democratic Republic). Great Britain, with its overseas bureaux of the British Council, made a modest attempt to exert its influence since the teaching of English was already dominated by the more agressive and better equipped American centers. Rome, with its over-bureaucratic Dante Alighieri Institutes, played a similar role. In other words, Europe offered whatever cultural elements it happened to have in stock: language study, literature, self-representation. Oftentimes, these efforts were directed more towards Europeans living abroad than Latin Americans themselves. Dozens of *colegios alemanes* financed by Bonn insisted on conveying a traditional image of a Germany that had little bearing on the new reality of the Federal Republic in the 1970s. Consequently, in 1972–73, with prompting from the social liberal coalition, Bonn took advantage of a redefinition of priorities and froze financial aid to German cultural programs in Latin America where older Germans did not agree with Bonn's current view of the world.

The best thing to be said about Europe's cultural policy in Latin America is that it did little harm because of its inefficiency. In any event, its effect was limited when compared with the massive American science policy which produced thousands of Ph.Ds (now ironically referred to as *'los másteres'*)[31] and a new corps of elite technocrats.

On the other hand, an exchange of experiences through informal channels established between Latin America and Europe proved to be much more effective. In the early 1960s, the Old World, left with the obsolete theories of archeologists and anthropologists at a time when it had embarked on development policies, was forced to train its own experts. This gave way to the establishment of a variety of Latin American institutes, referred to previously. Yet, Latin America could not be understood in terms of European history and civilization. Europe's young 'latinamericanists' were therefore eager to use tentative solutions coming from within the region itself, the foremost of these being the concept of *'dependencia'*. Its attractiveness obviously had something to do with the revolutionary approach. A popularized version of this theory reached Europe's academia around 1970 where it was quickly accepted and still holds a prominent place even today. We might go so far as to say that the theory of dependence monopolized European discussions on Latin America to the extent that other variations and schools were excluded. Darcy Ribeiro, author of *The Process of Civilization* barely passed through this barrier. Orlando Fals Borda's 'action research'[32] is used only by outsiders, and the work of an important Peruvian philosopher, Augusto Salazar Bondy (*Para una Filosofía de Valor*) was totally ignored. Unfortunately, as pointed out by H.A. Steger,[33] Europe's enthusiastic reception of the theory of dependence overlooked the concept's most basic element: an insistence on the structural impossibility of solving Latin American problems with European revolutionary logic. Régis Debray stumbled into this trap, as he later recognized in *La Critique des Armes*. Had he clearly understood *dependencia* he might have spared himself, and Latin America, his disastrous focus theory.

After 1970, Europe became more receptive to the Latin American literary boom: Gabriel Garcia Márquez: literary metaphysicians from Buenos Aires to Mexico City; the manifold authors of 'dictator' novels; and finally just about every more or less suitable and translatable author were all marketed by European publishers.

Psychologically, it would have been difficult for Europe, which controlled Latin America along commercial and technological lines, to play a recipient role. This made it convenient for Europe to offer ideologies, the reception of which seemed to confirm Latin America's passivity. Two variations of this 'ideology transfer' appeared after World War II: the Christian Democratic and the Social Democratic. The Christian Democrats were responsible for Europe's first offensive move in Latin America since 1945. They are historically credited with the reconstruction of war-torn Western Europe and were able to provide an ideological incentive by adapting the formula of 'reconstruction' to one of 'development'. This initiative was first evident in the form of reading material for young intellectuals who, having outgrown conservatism and prior to the invasion of American empiricism, devoured Toynbee, Papal Encyclica, Luigo Sturzo, Oswald van Nell-Breuning, Ludwig Erhard and French philosophers of any color. The fact that Maritain[34] finally surpassed Maurras as a favorite among Latin American readers is due to the influence of strong European political father figures like Adenauer, de Gasperi and Schumann who gave postwar Europe its democratic stamp. Maritain's Christian Humanism and Gabriel Marcel's Christian Existentialism, both specific European responses to a new beginning after World War II, proved to be fascinating to Latin America's national Catholics, partly because their message was so abstract.

On the other hand, Latin America's fledgling Christian Democratic movement got its chance only when the United States needed an alternative revolutionary formula to play against the Cubans. Chile's 'Revolution in Liberty', which achieved a sensational victory under Eduardo Frei in the 1964 elections, was the movement's first test. An increasingly compromised Europe felt that if things in Chile turned out well, all of Latin America might be Christian Democrat within ten years!

However, in order for Frei to win the elections, solid organizational work had to be done so as to adjust a rather abstract Catholic social doctrine to the requirements of a cadre party within a Third World context. Italy's Christian Democratic Party, spiritually supported by the European and North American Catholic Church, saw this as the opportunity for a modern-day mission and provided organizational support. The Catholic University of Louvain assumed the task of familiarizing Christians in general and young theologians in particular with the tools of (Christianized) positivism and the empirical social sciences, thereby enabling them to work among the *marginados* as caretakers of the body as well as the soul. Some extraordinary tactical work was done by the Belgian Jesuit Roger Vekemans who built the multi-financed Centro para el Desarrollo Social de América Latina (DESAL) in Santiago de Chile from where he spread the gospel of European cooperativism. The result was Latin America's Christian Democratic *'comunitarismo'* which achieved some important inroads during the late 1960s and early 70s (i.e. Rafael Caldera's victory in the 1968 Venezuelan elections; a strengthening of the Catholic cooperativist movement in Central America). Yet, from an operational point of view, *comunitarismo* was no rival to Marxist ideology. Put to the test, Christian Democratic youth sided with Christian radicalism and unhesitatingly sacrificed the formal elements of democracy.[35] While Europe merely sustained a 'dialogue' with the Marxists, young Latin Americans within the Christian Democratic movement easily succeeded in collaborating with the *'Fidelistas'*, Marxists and Trotskyites. In 1965–66, it was Louvain-trained Camilo Torres, Latin America's most famous guerrilla priest, who led the way in this respect.

The year 1970 marked a turning-point for Latin America's Christian Democratic movement. The Unidad Popular triumphed in the Chilean elections with the unhesitating support of the radical Mapu Christian Democrats. Yet, the Unidad Popular exceeded the limits to Latin American reformism granted under the American System, and the Christian Democratic ideology imported from

Europe became the 'Kerenski' formula.[36] Latin America's Christian Democratic movement never recovered from this turn of events. After 1970, only the anticommunist and antifidelist CD-centrist parties survived. And today, they appear to be unable to achieve a decisive breakthrough despite improved organizational cooperation.

Twenty years after the Christian Democratic experiment, the Social Democrats (successors to the Christian Democrats in Western Europe as a leading political force) initiated their own 'ideology transfer' to Latin America. Though organized in June 1951 at Frankfurt-on-Main as the Socialist International, SI, Western Europe's Social Democratic movement had been inactive for quite some time. There was some contact with Latin America, yet it proved to be sporadic and sometimes so orthodox that even political allies were attacked (i.e. Péronism was labeled a *'dictadura totalitaria'*).[37] A transfer of ideology was offered only after Western Europe's Social Democratic parties had established themselves in government and settled a series of urgent local matters. The Austrian Hans Janitschek, a former Secretary-General of the SI (1969–76), was instrumental in getting things started. He established contacts which led to a meeting between Social Democratic party leaders from Europe and Latin America in Caracas during May 8 1976. In the years that followed, the SI (organizationally framed by the ILDIS Institutes of the Friedrich Ebert Foundation of the Federal Republic and inspired by Willy Brandt's international prestige) succeeded in building a tight network of affiliated parties, although occasionally some 'headhunting' for associates was unavoidable.[38] Meanwhile, the Socialist International's Latin American initiative which had lent a Social Democratic turn to the Gaullist design, developed into one of Europe's most successful political-ideological efforts since the end of World War II. Nevertheless, there remains a certain degree of mistrust among Latin Americans who are uncertain as to just how far Europeans will go towards risking Washington's disapproval in Central America and Grenada.[39] After all, in contrast to their ideological deviations, Western Europeans are still the United States' most reliable allies in the strategic field. No wonder Latin Americans occasionally denounce European double-crossing, and several Latin American labour parties have refused to be enlisted as SI allies.[40]

6. MARKINGS

Twenty years of interplay: clichés, generalities, understandings and misunderstandings, half-hearted attempts at dialogue, gestures and the transfer of ideology have fostered what is today the sharpest dissent ever witnessed within the Atlantic Alliance regarding Latin American affairs. Heirs to the Christian Democratic transfer of ideology to Central America (which led to a radical leftist Catholicism tied to a local criollo Marxism) challenged the harsh stability of the American System, thereby receiving the passionate support of the Socialist International. This in turn caused alarm in Washington where European partners are expected to guard the flank rather than provoke divergencies.[41]

The cases of Nicaragua, El Salvador and Grenada in 1981 are proof that the European–Latin American encounter after World War II has been plagued by too much improvization, too much emotion and too many diverse ideologies. To begin with, Europe took no notice of the fact that Latin America's importance as an active partner on the international scene has increased tremendously since 1973. At that time, the international system suddenly became an 'energy social system'[42] as a result of cooperative action on the part of oil-exporting countries (whose OPEC organization would not exist in its present form were it not for the tenacious efforts of the Venezuelan, Juan Pablo Pérez Alfonzo). Nation states and geopolitical competition regained status and Western Europe lost maneuverability while Latin America's *'poder negociador'* increased substantially. By the mid-1970s at the very latest, Latin America should have been much more important for Europe than being a mere márket for goods and ideologies. But London, Brussels, Paris, Bonn and Rome had no clear understanding of the transformation that had taken place.[43] It was up to Latin America's new foreign policy to make full analytical use of this sudden change and to diagnose Western Europe's 'strategic dependency'.[44] The logic inherent in this process should have encouraged Europe to adopt a more balanced approach towards cooperation with Latin America, a continent rich in raw materials and energy resources. However, Europe continues to dwell on her traditionally over-officious way of doing business.

Europeans were definitely successful in establishing some remarkable inroads into what had previously been strictly American territory in Latin America.[45] The transfer of arms technology is one example. By the late 1970s, this area was dominated almost exclusively by Europeans (including Israel). European firms consolidated their positions in Argentina, Brazil and Mexico in certain fields of selected technology. Their influence was also felt in Central America with regard to politics and ideology. And last but not least, Western Europe managed to break Washington's monopoly in the nuclear sector. The atomic agreement signed in 1975 between Brasilia and Bonn might have caused even more dissent within the Atlantic Community than it actually did were it not for the fact that Brazil was forced to partially pull back on these projects owing to financial, administrative and managerial shortcomings. Nevertheless, the case in point is conclusive. While Bonn's representatives initiated atomic cooperation with Brazil as good, i.e. normal business, their counterparts interpreted the step as an eminently political initiative, an expansion of *'autonomia periférica'* which seemed appropriate for applying Gaullist principles within a Latin American context. In this respect, Brazil's military government even went so far as to modify the 'Brazilian model'. *'Distensão'* and *'abertura'* appeared; scientists who had emigrated after 1964 were called back and rehabilitated; and European experiences were introduced in order to free Brazil's system of higher education from its unilateral fixation with American standards.[46] The fact that such forceful strategic moves are usually met with evasive tactics on the part of the Europeans naturally brought about trouble in the end. In discussing the basis for a new foreign policy, Latin Americans have created the concept of *'clase media de las naciones'*,[47] or even more unconditionally, that of *'paises intermedios'* which is an hispanic adaptation of the Nics-concept (Newly Industrializing Countries) whose followers want to independently force their way into the OECD group.

Today, Latin Americans are much more self-confident in their behavior towards Europe, and are prepared to collect on old debts. Despite their adherence to 'Christian civilization', the former automatic alignment with Europe can no longer be guaranteed, as Willy Brandt discovered when his Report was dismantled and criticized during two Latin American evaluation seminars.[48] The fact that the Brandt Report, though credited with the very best intentions, could be interpreted as a delaying, maneuvering tactic directed against Latin America as part of the Third World, demonstrates that Latin America's best brains are on the verge of losing their patience.

In summary, during the 1980s Latin America will give the Old World credit only where credit is due. Europe must be prepared to offer substantial concessions in terms of finance, commerce, politics and diplomacy if it is to profit from relations with Latin America.

Will a social democratic Western Europe make a difference? Particularly with France under Mitterand who might 'socialdemocratize' the Gaullist tradition? A prominent observer, Constantine V. Vaitsos, remains pessimistic because of Western Europe's resource vulnerability, export necessities, growing economic difficulties, unemployment and the ever-increasing contradictions existing between countries of the North. These factors may impose restrictive attitudes regardless of the political parties in power.

Within this framework, the emergence of progressive political forces close to or within the power structures of Western Europe, have shown themselves to lend support and political weight in favour of some important internal causes for change in developing nations. Yet, in the external sector (which is intimately related to the internal changes in the Third World), the nature of Western Europe's own interests might mitigate against any serious contribution for economic development in developing nations, regardless of what parties find themselves in power in Europe.[49]

On the other hand, the Franco–Mexican alliance of the summer of 1981 in favor of El Salvador's opposition forces is basically what Latin America's intellectual avant-garde has been hoping for ever since 1945: a political alliance between Latin American and medium Western European powers aimed at weakening the rigid structure of the American System. By now, time has told us that this kind of bilateral initiative was not successful and did not increase the autonomy of both regional subsystems — the Latin American and the European one. The Central American and Caribbean political crisis *vis-à-vis* the Reagan Administration in Washington was necessary to persuade the Western Europeans that new, unorthodox steps were necessary in order to survive the 1980s. First of all, both regional subsystems had to overcome the traumata of the South Atlantic war of 1982 which left all hopes for a special Euro–Latin American relationship in ruins. Second, both Western Europe and Latin America began to understand during the 1980s that a new kind of associative diplomacy was urgent to prevent the outbreak of open war in Central America (after both regional subsystems stood idle as the United States intervened in 1983 in Grenada). Since them, indeed, a couple of steps have been taken in the right direction: the European Communities and the Andean Pact finally signed the long-delayed cooperation agreement. Brussels, furthermore, entered the tortured Central American arena through a series of meetings with the foreign ministers of Central America and Contadora states in order to offer a special European contribution to *all* the five Central American republics (San José I; San José II; 1984 and 1985 respectively). And IRELA, the new Euro–Latin American Institute established in 1985 in Madrid under the directorship of the German, Wolf Grabendorff and the Chilean Alberto Van Klaveren, will do its best to foster a new and more productive relationship between the two regional subsystems which share so much in hope but leave so much in doubt in reality.

NOTES

1. Pedro Gómez Valderrama, *La Otra Raya del Tigre*, Bogotá–Mexico: Siglo XXI, 1977. The novel is based on German immigration to Santander in the nineteenth century with historical data provided by Horacio Rodriguez Plata, *La Immigración Alemana al Estado Soberano de Santander en el Siglo XIX*, Bogotá, 1968.
2. Carlos Rangel, *Del Buen Salvaje al Buen Revolucionario*, Caracas, Monte Avila, 1976.
3. Ivan Illich, 'The New Frontier for Arrogance: Colonization of the Informal Sector', *International Development Review* (Rome), **22** (1980), 2–3.
4. Rafael Gutiérrez Girardot, *Horas de Estudio*, Bogotá, Instituto Colombiano de Cultura, 1976.
5. Eduardo Caballero Calderón, *El Buen Salveje*. The manuscript was awarded the Premio Nadal, 1965. Many editions since then.
6. Dean Acheson, *Present at the Creation. My Years in the State Department*, New York, Norton, 1969.
7. William H. Riker, *The Theory of Political Coalitions*, New Haven: Yale University Press, 1967. According to Riker, coalition leaders (United States or the Soviet Union as prototypes of the new imperial system) tend to overspend in the process of bargaining with minor participants. They disburse more in side payments than the spoils of victory are worth, which supposedly explains the instability of today's international system.
8. Reference is made to a series of conferences held in Chapultepec, San Francisco and La Habana. See Manual Casanova 'El Sistema Económico International de la Postguerra: La Participación de América Latina', *Estudios Internacionales* (Santiago de Chile), **12** (1979) 46.
9. Cepalismo was one of the first and most persistent advocates of the 'European connection', designed to achieve greater independence from Washington. Compare the two Cepal reports from 1953 and 1980: *'Cepal, Estudio del Comercio entre América Latina y Europa'*, Mexico: February 1953 and *'Cepal, The Economic Relations of Latin America with Europe'*, Santiago de Chile, 1980.
10. As to the discussion on the adaptation of the political subsystem in Latin America, see W.H. Agor and A. Sùarez, 'The Emerging Latin American Political Subsystem',

Proceedings of the Academy of Political Science, August, 1972. The limitations of Latin America as a political subsystem are clearly outlined by José A. Silva Michelena, *Politica y Bloques de Poder*, Mexico: Siglo XXI, 1976. See Chap. 6 in particular.

11. Graf Herman Keyserling, *Suedamerikanische Meditationen*, Stuttgart, 1932. This volume was required reading for every educated German.

12. Reference is made to Alfons Goldschmidt, *Die dritte Eroberung Amerikas*, Berlin: Rowohlt, 1929. The respected German professor sees three discoveries or 'standardization phases' for Latin America: (1) the old indians; (2) the Spaniards and (3) the United States civilization at whose materialism the author sneers in disgust.

13. In my opinion, the impact of the Cuban Revolution on Europe is exaggerated by Harold Blakemore, 'Europe and Latin American Studies: A Synoptic View', Working Paper B-13, London, Institute of Latin American Studies, 1978.

14. CEISAL, *Consejo Europeo de Investigaciones Sociales sobre América Latina.* Established in 1971. A survey on many, but not all European Latin American Institutes is found in 'Latin American Studies in Europe', Carmel Mesa-Lago with the collaboration of Sandra E. Miller and Shirley A. Kregar, Latin American Monograph and Document Series, University of Pittsburgh, Center for Latin American Studies.

15. Karl Kaiser, 'The Interaction of Regional Subsystems: Some Preliminary Notes on Recurrent Patterns and the Role of Superpowers', *World Politics*, October, 1968.

16. On the early relationship between Latin America and the European Common Market, Gerhard Drekonja, *'América Latina y las Comunidades Europeas: Politica Comercial o Politica Exterior?'*, Revista de la Integración (INTAL — Buenos Aires) May 1974.

17. Used for the first time by Marcelo E. Aftalión, 'Poder Negociador Latinoamericano', *Foro Internacional* (Mexico) No. 60, April–June 1975.

18. Gabriel Valdés, 'América Latina y la Politica de Nuevo Mundo: El Papel de la Comisión Especial de Coordinación para Latino-América, CECLA', H.H. Godoy y D. Uribe Vargas (eds), *Politica Mundial* Siglo XXI, Bogotá, 1974. Also by the same author, *Conciencia Latinoaméricana y Realidad Internacional*, Santiago de Chile: Ed. del Pacifico, 1970: 'Europa es el fruto más perfecto del hombre occidental; América Latina es el inmediato desafio al hombre occidental' (p. 123).

19. *Comunicación de la Comisión al Consejo,* 'Las Relaciones con los Paises Latinoamericanos' del 29 de julio de 1969.

20. Ralf Dahrendorf, 'Möglichkeiten und Grenzen einer Aussenpolitik der Europäischen Gemeinschaften', Europa-Archiv (Bonn) **4**/1971.

21. Disappointment must be measured against expectations. After all, Britain, France and Germany 'are middle powers in a global system characterized by loose bipolarity, détente and tendencies towards multipolarity'. James N. Rosenau *et al.*, *World Politics*, New York–London, The Free Press, 1976.

   Not even Latin America's rich mineral and energy resources motivated a stronger interest on the part of Brussels. See Miguel S. Wionczek, *'Las Relaciones entre la CEE y América Latina en el Contexto de una Crisis Económica Global'*, Comercio Exterior (Mexico) **31** (1981), 2.

   The idea of a complementary relationship based on cooperation between Europe and Latin America is tempting, even more so if founded on democracy: 'Probablemente, lo más interesante que tiene la idea de mirar a nuevas formas de cooperación entre Europa y América Latina, es que comienza a dibujarse, al menos en la imaginación, la perspectiva de una relación diagonal entre los dos continentes, que se aparta de las formas tradicionales de vinculación vertical u horizontal.' Francisco Orrego, 'Europa y América Latina: Hacia un Rol Internacional Complementario?', *Estudios Internacionales* (Santiago de Chile), **14** (1981), 53. However, I do not see any evidence of this.

22. This creative concept was coined by Helio Jaguaribe, *'Autonomia Periférica y Hegemonia Céntrica'*, *Estudios Internacionales* (Santiago de Chile), **12** (1979), 46.
23. See the case study by Manfred Nitsch, 'Rich Country Interest and Third World Development: The Federal Republic of Germany', Paper, ILDES-RIAL-FES, Brazil, 1980.
24. *'América Latina ante la CEE: Bases para una Relación de Nuevo Tipo'*, SELA en Acción, *Boletin Informativo* No. 5, Febrero 1979.
25. Juan Mario Vacchino, *'América Latina y la Europa Comunitaria: Alcances y Perspectivas de las Relaciones Reciprocas'*, *Comercio Exterior* (Mexico), **31** (1981) 2.
26. Johan Galtung, *The European Community: A Superpower in the Making*, Oslo, 1972.
27. De Gaulle's Mexico visit took place in March 1964. Visits to Venezuela, Colombia, Ecuador, Peru, Bolivia, Chile, Argentina, Paraguay. Uruguay and Brazil were made in September/October 1964. See Frank Schwarzbeck, *'Frankreich und Lateinamerika in der Gaullistisches Ära'*, *Vierteljahresberichte* (Bonn), No. 66/1976.

    The fact that De Gaulle enjoyed enormous prestige, even among radical students, is demonstrated in a 1965 interview-study done in Colombia. De Gaulle was at that time rated far ahead of Castro, Nasser and Frei. See Mario Latorre, *'Politica y Elecciones'*, Bogota: Universidad de los Andes, 1980 (Chapter: *'La Universidad de Espaldas al Sistema'*).

    Conservative Latin America always remained Francophile and Gaullist. *'Nos interesa Francia, avanzada Latina'*, says the editorial of *Vision*, dated 20 March 1981: *'El ejemplo francés es particularmente interesante para los latinoamericanos, desde el momento que Francia es el más avanzado de los paises latinos: en ella, en cierto modo, miramos nuestro propio futuro.'*
28. In this sense, France becomes a 'foreign power' in Latin America. See H. Goldhamer, *The Foreign Powers in Latin America*, Princeton, 1972.
29. Carlos J. Moneta, 'La Politica Exterior del Peronismo: 1973–1976', *Foro Internacional* (Mexico), **20** (1979) 2.

    In Péronist writings of the early 1970s, Europe as a political alternative appears as a recurrent theme. As an example, see Norberto Ceresole, *Geopolitica de la Liberación*, Buenos Aires, 1972. Also, E.J. Uriburu, *El Plan Europa: Un Intento de Liberación Nacional*, Buenos Aires, 1970.

    The topic is introduced again in a European version by B. Lietar, *Europe + Latin America + the Mulitnationals*, Westmead, Farnborough, 1979. The Belgian author sees Latin America as the last and only logical area for significant European diversification. A massive resource and technology transfer is advocated through European transnational firms in order to create a strong interdependence between Western Europe and Latin America, with mutual benefits for both.
30. 'López Portillo Stakes His Claim as Latin America's De Gaulle', *Latin America Weekly Report* (London), 8 August 1980.
31. *'Los masteres'* are constantly referred to in Jorge Child's *Informes Semanal de Economia* (Bogotá).

    To a certain degree, Latin America's new technocrats, capable of handling the modern social sciences, became 'the functional equivalent of a ruling class'. This at least is the result of a study on the impact of international development agencies in developing countries. See International Legal Center (ed.), *The Impact of International Organizations on Legal and Institutional Change in the Developing Countries*, New York: 1977. The excellent chapter on Colombia was written by Fernando Cepeda.
32. Orlando Fals Borda's thesis on *'sociologia subversiva'* was amply discussed during 1969/1970/1971 in the journal *APORTES* edited in Paris by Luis Mercier Vega. *APORTES* made some very important contributions towards lending a more

professional nature to budding Latin American Studies in Europe.

33. Hanns-Albert Steger, *'Siete Tesis Equivocadas en la Relación entre Europa y América Latina'*. Paper, Alpbach (Austria), June 1979.

34. Jacques Maritain's decisive influence on Catholic thinking in Latin America is confirmed by Eduardo Frei, *América Latina: Opción y Esperanza*, Barcelona: Pomaire, 1977. See also Edward J. Williams, *Latin American Christian Democratic Parties*, University of Tennessee Press, 1967. On the Charles Maurras reception in Latin America see *Le Monde Diplomatique en Español*, Novembre, 1980. On the formation of the European Christian Democracy, J. M Meyeur, *Des Partis Catholiques à la Démocratie Chrétienne*, Paris, A. Colin, 1980.

   See also Jaime Castillo Velasco, *Las Fuentes de la Democrácia Cristiana*, Santiago, Ed. del Pacifico, 1967.

35. Darcy Ribeiro feels this was inevitable: *'La Democrácia Cristiana de Chile, aunque tenga algunas potencialidades reformistas, es principalmente un esfuerzo de restauración del patriciado con un nuevo ropaje. La de Venezuela, todavia más tibia, apenas aspira ser un partido de tecnócratas capaces de conquistar algunas ventajas en el trato con los norteaméricanos.'* D. Ribeiro, *El Dilema de América Latina*, Mexico, Siglo XXI, 1971, p. 209.

36. Reference to a hateful pamphlet by Fabio Vidigal Xavier da Silveira, *Frei el Kerensky Chileno*. The Spanish version was printed in Argentina (Ed. Cruzada, 1968) and widely distributed to decision makers in Chile and throughout Latin America.

37. 'Mensaje a los Trabajadores de América Latina' (1955), In K.L. Guensche and K. Lantermann, *Historia de la Internacional Socialista*, Mexico, Ed. Nueva Imagen, 1979.

38. 'Latin America: Socialist Headhunters', Latin America Political Report (London), 22 December 1978. The list of Latin American members and associate members of the London-based Socialist International in 'La Socialdemocrácia en América Latina', *Le Monde Diplomatique en Español*, junio, 1980.

39. The fact that the Development Fund of the European Community is considering co-financing the construction of a jet airport on revolutionary Grenada led to a clash of opinions with Washington in April 1981. Washington fears that Cuba will take advantage of the new Port Salines airport as a 'bridge' to Africa.

40. See Anibal Quijano's violent denunciation in *'La Doble Táctica de la Actual Ofensiva Imperialista'*, Economia (Quito), No. 67, diciembre, 1976.

   Leading Latinamericanists of the Soviet Union discuss the role of the Socialist International in Latin America in *América Latina* (Moscow) (1978), 4.

   In Brazil, Luis Inácio da Silva, better known as 'Lula', keeps the Partido dos Trabalhadores outside the social democratic camp and leaves this 'European connection' to Leonel Brizola's Partido Democrático Trabalhista.

41. Wolf Grabendorff, 'Die Beziehung der USA und Westeuropa zu Lateinamerika: Gemeinsamkeiten und Unterschiede', *Zeitschrift für Lateinamerika*, Wien (Vienna) (1980), 17.

42. Samuel Z. Klausner, 'The Energy Social System', The Annals of the American Academy of Political and Social Science (Philadelphia), July 1979. According to the author, 1973 and the years following witnessed a metamorphosis in the international system favoring anew nation states which, if they possess energy resources, are gradually assuming control of the transnational petroleum distribution network.

43. The Iran crisis shook Western Europeans out of their complacency. Fearing other 'Iranisations', Bonn began a complete revision of its cultural policies. On this point, see Manfred Mols, 'The Relationship of the Federal Republic of Germany with Latin America', Paper, Mainz: October 1980.

44. 'Strategic dependency' — the dependence of advanced capitalistic countries on foreign sources for the supply of cheap, critical minerals essential to their economies and national defense. Heraldo Muñoz, 'Strategic Dependency and Foreign Policy:

Notes on the Relations Between Core Powers and Mineral-Exporting Periphery Countries', Vierteljahresberichte (Bonn), No. 80, Juni 1980.

45. Gustavo Lagos (ed.), *Las Relaciones entre América Latina, Estados Unidos y Europa Occidental*, Santiago: Instituto de Estudios Internacionales de la Universidad de Chile, 1979.

46. Barbara Freitag, *Escola, Estado e Sociedade*, São Paulo: Coleçaõ Educação Universitaria, 1979.

47. Francisco Orrego (ed.), *América Latina: Clase Media de las Naciones?*, Santiago: Instituto de Estudios Internacionales de la Universidad de Chile, 1979.

48. In Canela (Brazil), August, 1980 and in Villa de Leyva (Colombia), October 1980. There is a basic mistrust of the Brandt Report among Latin Americans. They fear being coopted into the First World via the Nics concept (Newly Industrializing Countries) and through the Latin American monetarists — the 'Uncle Toms' of the subcontinent. See 'El Informe Brandt y América Latina: La Lucha Contra el 'Tio Tom' Latinoaméricano', *Desarrollo y Cooperación* (DSE — Bonn) (1981), 1.

Costa Rican ex-President Oduber (a member of the SI) cannot hide his doubts about renewed European interest: 'The European countries that made us poor and then abandoned us are again turning their attention to our Caribbean Basin, and seek it as an alternative to the Middle East to guarantee their way of life. As the Middle East and Persian Gulf crises become more acute, our territories will become more and more an area fought over for the advantage of others, but never for our own development.' Daniel Oduber, 'Toward a New Central American Dialogue', *Caribbean Review* (Miami), Winter 1981.

Gabriel Garcia Marquez is also unsure about European interest in Latin America. He feels it will be easier to establish a dialogue with the people of a partially 'hispanoamericanized' United States than with the arrogant Europeans. 'Durante la década de los sesenta, los intelectuales europeos se colocaron en la primera linea de la solidaridad con nosotros, nos desbordaron con un alborozo idealista que sin embargo no resistió el primer embate serio de la realidad. Su análisis tenia, y sigue teniendo un rezago colonial: sólo ellos se creen depositarios de la verdad. Para ellos sólo es bueno lo que ha probado serlo en su propia experiencia. Todo lo demás es extraño, y por consiguiente, inaceptable y corruptor.' Garcia Marquez in his weekly column published by *El Espectador* (Bogotá), 13 September 1981.

49. Constantine V. Vaitsos, 'From a Colonial Past to Asymmetrical Interdependences: The Role of Europe in North–South Relations', in 'Europe's Role in World Development', EADI Conference, Milano, September 1980, Milan, 1981.

PART 2: AGRICULTURAL POLICY

2

Agricultural Policy and Integration — The Andean Case*

Gustavo Tobón Londoño

1. INTRODUCTION

Just a few short years after the Montevideo Treaty was signed, the initial symptoms of difficulty began to appear. Potential agreements under the complex system of negotiations established by the Treaty diminished with the dwindling range of products that were easily granted owing to their low importance in the national economies. Above all, the experience of LAFTA showed the Latin American countries' tremendous difficulty in adjusting their economic structures to conditions of open trade competition when it entailed the rivalry of productions with marked differences in their levels of efficiency. It should, however, be noted that precisely because of the minimal country commitment and scant significance of the trade induced by LAFTA, during the period of the Treaty there was no clear idea of the complications beyond that regarding equitable distribution of the benefits within the territory integrated. The response to LAFTA's premature lethargy was the creation of the Andean Group, made up of countries whose national interests had been insufficiently upheld by the Montevideo Treaty. The very signing of the Cartagena Agreement is, however, a reassertion of Latin America's interest in the idea of integration. It is also a challenge to our countries' ability to carry out a joint effort to overcome their backwardness and underdevelopment. The broader scope and increased commitment by the countries of the Andean subregion, compared to the LAFTA agreement, were based on the conviction that if Latin American integration was to emerge from its sluggishness there would have to be a greater intertwining of the national economies as well as simpler and more automatic procedures. This, of

* This paper was prepared with the collaboration of economists Mauricio Pérez and Luiz Yezio Hoyos

course, was the outcome of a diagnosis based on the brief experience of LAFTA and other integration schemes. It was therefore evident that a fair formula for the distribution of benefits would require some consistency among the economic policies individually adopted by each country, and a differentiation among countries on the basis of their relative degree of development.

It seemed apparent that granting preferential treatment to lesser developed countries would entail no major difficulties other than setting the expiry date of such concessions. The matter of consistency among national policies is much more difficult, largely because such policies, as instruments of the concept of development, are particularly sensitive in long-term agreements. Initially, the idea of Latin American integration appears as an extension of the original idea set forth by ECLA for the region's development, transferring the national terms of 'inward development' to the broader context of a group of countries. Its acceptance has been largely a result of this organisation's influence on the governments of the area at that time. The agreement with ECLA's diagnosis and acceptance of its main formulas of economic policy greatly stimulated the integration process. It should be no surprise, then, that the basic strategy of the Cartagena Agreement is based on that organisation's theoretical output, showing a marked preference for industrialisation and planned allotment of resources.

During the life of the Subregional Pact, there has been an evident reorientation of national policies which have gradually strayed from the ECLA development model toward more eclectic and varied approaches, as a result of the performance of the national economies. This trend has been underscored in recent years owing to the effects of the economic crisis hitting the industrialised countries, and reflected at the Andean level in policies to protect national production, affecting even intra-subregional trade.

Seventeen years after signing the Agreement, the Andean Group portrays some positive results as regards increase in subregional trade, which was satisfactorily active throughout the seventies; and a relatively important market was established, which in the specific case of Colombia became the leading buyer of its non-coffee exports. Although this cannot be largely attributed to the use of preferences, it did result in part from the *rapprochement* generated by the integration process. Nevertheless, achievements have fallen quite short of the original objectives. For example, customs unity has not been improved; industrial programming was limited to the approval of three programmes presently being reviewed; and save for the early definition of the statute on capital, also being revised, no significant steps have been made to harmonize economic and social policies.

The automatic advance of the Exemption Programme, without the least consistency in national policies, has led to non-fulfillment of commitments on the part of some member countries — due also to the recession in their economies and the critical reserve situation in the majority. This has led some sectors to question the viability of the process in its present form.

The existing situation requires alternative solutions that will preserve the trade currents already established and even increase them, taking into account the complex panorama of our economies characterised by their enormous vulnerability to crises in the developed countries. The experience gained during this process shows the impossibility of considering rigid rules resulting from a single development model for the subregion. The countries have been realising the need to be pragmatic and flexible in their actions, combining the implementation of existing instruments with all types of cooperation aiming at a greater economic interrelationship and new points of *rapprochement* among member countries. It is perhaps necessary to admit that the greatest obstacle to integration is the ineffectiveness of the mechanism designed to handle very different situations. The rigidity of the safeguard instruments, and the orthodox way they are interpreted, make their application extremely difficult. We seem to have built a structure without earthquake protection in a region affected by constant tremors.

2. THE AGRICULTURAL SECTOR IN THE CARTAGENA AGREEMENT

It has become a truism to speak of the special treatment granted the farm sector in the different integration schemes, considering the special problems involved in its development. Its extreme sensitivity to competition, its leading role in the economies of underdeveloped countries and the strategic function assigned by industrialised areas to the production of food and raw materials, all call for unique approaches to the integration of the farm sector.

In Latin America, ECLA's initial statements regarding integration already mentioned the need for special treatment of agricultural products, under a scheme granting national production a certain measure of protection so as to avoid the damage caused by open competition between the most efficient and the most backward producers. LAFTA incorporated this concept formally by adopting a special scheme that provided specific escape mechanisms in the liberation of farm products and some provision on the advisability of coordinating the policies on development and trade of such products, although it stated that such coordination should not 'disarticulate the usual productions of each Contracting Party'. Be this as it may, the Exemption Programme adopted by the Montevideo Treaty allowed some flexibility in granting preferences, leaving each country free to choose the sectors that it wished to protect for a longer time. ALADI, which replaced LAFTA, refers to the sector only briefly, considering the possibility of making Sectorial supplementation Agreements that may be based on 'temporary, seasonal, quota or mixed concessions, or on contracts between state or para-state agencies', bearing in mind the social and economic features of production in the countries involved.

Treatment of trade

Essentially, the Cartagena Agreement adopts a scheme for the agricultural sector very similar to that provided by LAFTA, but characterised by the decision to set up a speedier and more active integration system, involving less reciprocal protection for this sector's production and the risk, in some cases, of destabilising it.

The treatment agreed upon for agricultural trade was largely a result of the influence of theories prevalent in the sixties, which attached great importance to the need for industrialising our economies in view of the equivalence established between industrialisation and economic development. At the same time, the sketchy analysis at the time identifies an international division of labour with our countries specialising in the production of commodities, with the comparative advantage in our favour. This notion is reflected primarily in the degrees of protection against outside countries established by the Minimum Common Outside Tariff Schedule. A document of the board of the Cartagena Agreement,[1] shows that the original version of the Minimum Common Outside Tariff Schedule set an average tariff level of 25 per cent for farm products — that is slightly over half of the nominal protection assigned to industrial activities. A later revision of the Minimum Common Outside Tariff Schedule, which lowered the general average protection, corrected this discrimination, although not significantly. Nevertheless, the tariff differentiation between the sectors mentioned was only slightly less than that set individually by each of the Andean countries at the time they were established.

In the different implementations of the Exemption Programme, both the products of this sector and the inputs and capital goods used in farm production were included in the list for automatic lowering of duties. They have been free from para-tariff restrictions since 31 December 1970 and their total exemption was scheduled for late 1983. A few products, which do not belong to this scheme, receive the treatment granted to the LAFTA Common List, for which all duties and non-tariff restrictions were eliminated as of 14 April 1970. Under the preferential treatment granted to countries of relatively lesser economic development, imports from Ecuador and Bolivia have been granted full exemption by the other Andean Group countries since 31 December 1973, while being allowed to begin the Exemption Programme, though not before 1983.

In order to avoid the detrimental effects that could potentially arise from the implementation of a free-trade scheme for the regional exchange of agricultural products, the Agreement preserved the special safeguard mechanism established by LAFTA for this sector. By virtue of this mechanism, the countries may, in trading in farm products that are of considerable importance to their economies, apply corrective measures to limit imports to the minimum necessary to cover the gaps in domestic production and to level the price of imported goods to the level of domestic goods. Its implementation is very broad and flexible, owing to the wide range of causes making it applicable, its expedite use, the absence of time limits to the duration of the corrective measures, and the fact that the Commission alone can decide on the legality of the measures adopted.

Despite the foregoing, the safeguard can only be invoked to affect imports from Ecuador and Bolivia under a special procedure restricting its use to cases previously defined by the Board, which entity must verify serious damages resulting specifically from such imports. In practice, this last restriction has become a seriously limiting factor in the application of the safeguard, as the Board, when examining the cases brought up to it, has taken the notion of damages to mean damages actually incurred, attaching no value whatsoever to the risks foreseeable by observing the market conditions. Additionally, the range of products covered by the safeguard scheme for farm goods is limited to a list defined by Decision 80 of the Commission and this list time has shown to be inadequate.

The creators of the Cartagena Agreement, and those involved in developing its initial instruments, probably considered the farm sector eligible for subregional competition. This idea is supported by the manner in which the Lists of Exemptions were drawn up, excluding agricultural products. It was not until Venezuela's membership that some of these products were considered eligible for exception. Although national productions did not complement each other, no major complications arose until early this decade, as the detrimental effects of free trade were largely offset by unilateral provisions. These unilateral provisions were, of course, violations of the Agreement, but there were no national or subregional legal provisions to restore normal conditions.

In recent years, the substantial exchange modifications in the majority of Andean countries have given rise to a significant increase in agricultural imports from the subregion. The difficulty in adopting appropriate corrective measures, owing to internal legal provisions enforcing strict compliance with international treaties, has made it necessary to consider adjusting the trade mechanisms for agricultural products in the Cartagena Agreement to make them consistent with their specific production and marketing situations. This idea implies recognising the existence of a divorce between the characteristics of the agricultural sector and the system of absolute, irreversible free trade among the Andean Group Countries in the exchange of their products.

The evidence that the scheme adopted by the Agreement is inconsistent with the nature of farm production is to be found in the continuous violation of the Exemption Programme which member countries are forced to commit. In addition to the total failure to fulfill commitments on the part of Ecuador and Bolivia — a well-known fact — there is also the role of government trading houses which act, in practice, as agents influencing domestic demand, contrary to the principle of free trade, and neutralising subregional preference.

The need to adjust the mechanisms for subregional trade of agricultural goods was accepted in principle by the Ministers of Agriculture of the Andean Group at their Fifth Meeting, in Resolution 17 which, recognising the special characteristics of the farm sector, its tremendous economic, social and political importance in each member country, and the obvious need to allow for coherent management of domestic sectoral policies, felt it pertinent to recommend adjustment of the subregional mechanisms regulating trade. The reform of the scheme for the agricultural sector has been included as a priority topic in the renegotiation of the Cartagena Agreement, which began in 1984.

Scheme for the agricultural sector

The Agreement established, in Chapter 7, a scheme for the farm sector which, while wholly excluding the treatment of aspects regarding exchange, does state the need to adopt a common policy and an indicative subregional plan. Harmonisation of national policies and coordination of development plans should take into account the following objectives, among others: improvement of living conditions in the rural sector; increased production and productivity; specialisation in terms of better use of production factors; subregional import substitution; export diversification and increase; timely and adequate supply of the subregional market. In order to attain these objectives, it was decided that the Commission would periodically adopt measures regarding: joint farm development programmes by products or product groups; common marketing systems, and agreements on supply between the respective state organisms; encouragement of agreements between national organisms involved in planning and implementing agricultural policy; initiatives regarding export promotion; joint programmes of applied research and technical and financial assistance for the sector; and common standards and programmes involving animal and plant health.

In view of the difficulty in formulating a Subregional Indicative Plan for the sector, and of even designing a Common Agricultural Policy, countries have directed their efforts mainly at the formulation of specific projects to increase production and productivity of those products for which there is an overall deficit in the subregion. Also, projects have been designed to improve the marketing infrastructure and some action is being taken to strengthen and harmonise sanitary controls. This action seeks to attain results at two levels: first, steps towards consistency among policies so as to allow joint programming; and second, implementation of investment projects designed, among other things, to increase production and productivity and for the development and adoption of new technologies, training of human resources and creation of mechanisms for joint negotiation on the outside market.

Although the actions of interest to the countries were defined at the first Meeting of Ministers of Agriculture of the Andean Group, held early in 1974, the balance to date has not been entirely satisfactory. Results portray just a few studies, none of which have gone beyond the feasibility stage, either because their content lacked due approval or because investment resources were lacking. Additionally, there is a lack of consistency in the objectives of such studies. Although they are supposed to be projects of interest to the countries since they seek to increase production in deficit areas or to solve specific problems of infrastructure, this is inadequate if the aim is to set the bases for future harmonisation of sectoral policies. This is a very indirect and impractical approach, as it is impossible to isolate the performance of a given product from the general economic context. Although it is possible with some restrictions to develop certain joint policies to develop and stimulate a product or product group, it would be well-nigh impossible, using this approach, to coordinate national policies in more definitive areas such as credit, prices and trade with outsiders.

Even leaving aside subregional considerations, the efforts made to identify and formulate projects have come up against financial obstacles. A project requiring investments by the private sector normally needs financial resources to support it unless it is highly profitable. Unless there is close coordination among the pre-investment activities and subsequent attainment of funds, many of the designed studies will probably remain unimplemented.

The scene is quite different when it comes to the adoption of common standards and programmes on animal and plant health. Since the action here is more punctual and markedly beneficial to the countries of the subregion, it has been relatively easy to move along in the formulation of a uniform and dual purpose health policy aiming to diminish the economic impact of pests and diseases affecting farm production, and to remove obstacles to intra-subregional trade of products in the sector. In this respect, the record to date has consisted of the preparation of a health register, the compilation of a basic catalogue of pests and tropical diseases and an Andean Register of health norms — all being constantly updated. Equally, reference should be made to the programmes for the prevention, control and eradication of coffee tree rust, African swine fever and banana black mould.

Despite the afore-listed achievements, the Andean Organisations have not overlooked the desirability of drawing-up an agricultural policy for the sub-region. Here, mention should be made of the plan to achieve this through the setting-up of specific projects for products. Prior to this plan, in 1977, the junta presented a number of basic options to the countries for their consideration. These options which would form the framework for the process of agricultural integration in the medium-term were based on the idea of product specialisation. These proposals did not receive the support of those countries which did not wish to give up their sovereignty in the field of agriculture — preferring to encourage inefficient self-sufficiency.

Also, intentions have been expressed to set up an Andean System of Agricultural Planning. As a result, a three phase programme has been proposed — the final one being the drawing-up of an Indicative Plan for the sub-region. So far, i.e. since 1977, it should be pointed out that we are still in the first phase — being occupied with the compilation of information about planning systems in the countries and knowledge of the economic characteristics of the national agricultural sectors.

Lastly, it should be emphasised that aside from the commercial treatment provided in the general mechanisms and the adoption of a particular safeguard clause, the Cartagena Agreement set no definite strategy for the farm sector. Chapter 7 of the Agreement only states some general objectives to be borne in mind in harmonising national policies and formulating an Indicative Plan, and states some measures that should be taken periodically but without setting any compulsory deadlines. Development of an agricultural scheme should be a subject for analysis and decision-making by the institutional organisms of the Andean Group. However, if we examine the Agreement in its entirety and determine the priorities chosen in terms of the schedule of commitments, we shall find that the agricultural sector was not of primary concern to the countries of the subregion. This has changed in recent years and ought to be reflected in the revision of the Agreement.

The point of departure agreed to being an irreversible scheme of free trade for reciprocal exchange, it should be asked whether the right conditions were created for the adoption of a Common Agricultural Policy or whether, on the contrary, that initial definition seriously limited any possibility of agreement on the consistency of sector policies. It may be inferred that the activities carried out on the basis of the chapter on the Agricultural Scheme of the Cartagena Agreement can be taken as a complement to trade freedom but can in no way serve as a basis for a true subregional agricultural policy. At first glance, the assignment of resources and specialisation of production in the farm sector based on the free play of market forces would seem to be incompatible with the idea of state intervention, or at least would reduce the efficacy of the latter. With time, it is not even clear whether the countries wish to discourage any area of production for the benefit of specialisation.

3. THE VIABILITY OF A COMMON AGRICULTURAL POLICY IN THE ANDEAN GROUP

When the European Economic Community decided to adopt a common policy for its farm sector, it had a powerful cohesive force: the need to create mechanisms whereby the risks of un-supply would be diminished. Even so, they admitted that they were not prepared to accept the contingencies of a market free of state intervention. The Community's essential interest in connection with agriculture called for encouraging the development of domestic production based on a reasonable amount of protection *vis-à-vis* outside countries and on balanced competition within the Community. Both conditions were achieved through the adoption of a variable tariff on imports from the rest of the world and a complex system of prices for the output from member countries. Its basic mechanisms were improved and perfected during the course of seven years and its management difficulties are explored at each round of multilateral negotiations in setting domestic prices, in the handling of surpluses and the application of corrective measures for exchange fluctuations.

It is not by chance that its efforts have been centred on the definition of an internal price system guaranteeing farmers an adequate income. Agriculture, more than any other economic activity, is subject to continuous fluctuations in the price of its products. Essentially, this sector is characterised by disorderly and uncontrollable supply which transfers its own instability to the market. The complexity of the system adopted by the Community, and the periodic difficulties it faces, are largely a reflection of the diversity of elements that come into play in agricultural pricing. It is surprising, then, that the Andean Group countries should be committed to a scheme of free trade for such products, shutting out any possibility of control over reciprocal trade, when price regulation is an essential variable in the management of the farm sector. The Cartagena Agreement's approach to the agricultural sector seems to ignore the characteristics of that sector and their specific weight in the economies of the countries of the subregion.

Agricultural goods cannot be considered as a homogeneous group with standardised performance; it can be said, rather, that the demand for most farm products is generally inelastic. This statement applies equally to the price elasticity and income elasticity. The low price elasticity of agricultural products implies that a relatively small increase in supply generates disproportionately large reductions in the final prices of the goods, since consumption will remain stable. Additionally, price reduction will tend to discourage production. On the other hand, a decrease in supply caused by an outside factor such as adverse weather conditions may, because of the price inelasticity of demand, generate undesirable price increases. Because of low income elasticity, growth in the overall demand is only partially reflected in increased effective demand for agricultural goods. Both in the short and long term, inelasticity of demand makes the agricultural sector highly vulnerable to extreme price fluctuations resulting from small increases in supply, and this has been an obstacle to the sector's sustained growth.

Furthermore, supply in the agricultural sector is subject to other risks that are unforeseeable and outside farmers' control. The close dependency on random biological and weather conditions, duration of the productive cycle and breakdown of production into a large number of economic units unrelated to each other and distanced from consumers by a long chain of intermediaries, are just some of the basic features of the agricultural sector, making it an uncertain activity, slow in responding to market signals and with a supply that is difficult to organise. Despite technological advances that aid in reducing risks and to a certain point facilitate control of supply by individual producers, on the aggregate there is still uncertainty as to the behaviour of agricultural and livestock production, since a large percentage of farmers lack the conditions to apply the necessary techniques and procedures and because many natural factors are beyond human control. Thus, marked fluctuations in production are added to the instability inherent in farm product prices because of the low elasticity of demand. Inadequacies in the marketing systems obstructing the transmission of market signals are another source of instability and risk for the sector. For this reason, a central concern of domestic agricultural policies has been to assure price stability. Although many policy instruments used, such as credit incentives or input subsidies, have a direct impact on the price of the final product, they are no substitute for an explicit price policy aiming to diminish price variability either through direct intervention in the market, through support prices, production restrictions, accumulation of inventories or through foreign trade policy. In this connection, there are two main approaches:

(a) The majority of industrialised countries and some developing countries seek through various means to establish prices that are incentives to producers.

(b) Other developing countries give priority to supplying the needs of the population, especially food, at moderate prices. The drawback of this approach is that if the prices set are not consistent with production costs, supply is discouraged and inflationary pressures may later arise owing to the non-supply that must be corrected through imports.

The two approaches described are, of course, subject to broader economic policy considerations, such as priority attached to the agricultural sector, existence of comparative advantages, availability of production factors or ability to import agricultural goods when deficits occur. However, short-term instability of prices for agricultural goods makes it essential to have a definite policy if the destabilising effects on production and supply are to be avoided.

The above considerations are particularly relevant to the make-up of an enlarged market within the framework of an integration scheme. If member countries lose their autonomous control over import or export trade flows of farm products, the inconsistent management by different countries of the policy instruments determining the price structure for the agricultural sector will generate distortions. Freeing trade makes it necessary to adopt a common policy in these matters, unless the countries adopt the exclusive use of the mechanisms of free play of supply and demand as a policy objective.

Formulation of a common policy requires that definitions be adopted at community level regarding its determination and application. There must be consensus on the purposes of intervention, on whether it should favour producers or consumers, and in what ratio. Since consistency of development measures or price interventions imply the transfer of resources not only within each country but also between countries, it becomes necessary to define the means and procedures of such transfers and the origin of the respective resources. Price harmonisation will obviously be affected by fluctuations in exchange rates, especially if these take the form of massive devaluations. In the short term, variation in exchange rates may cause the mechanisms to stray from their set purposes, and appropriate remedial measures must be established. Lastly, competent institutional mechanisms would have to be developed to implement the community policies.

To the extent that these conditions are met, the essential elements characterising national agricultural policies could be reproduced on a supranational scale. Otherwise, freeing trade among the countries without adequate consistency in their policies will produce no benefits, since the action of market forces would tend to offset inconsistent national policies rather than help to attain the purposes of agricultural development.

Assessment of the characteristics of the agricultural sector within the Andean Group leads to some interesting conclusions on the viability of agricultural integration in the terms conceived in the Agreement. The agricultural sector in the Group represents about 17 per cent of the Gross Domestic Product, occupies 32 per cent of the economically active population and accounts for 15 per cent of all exports. These indicators (for 1984) give an overall idea of the importance of this sector in the subregion, although it does not show the outstanding cases, such as generation of 50 per cent of all employment in Bolivia and 47 per cent in Ecuador, nor the 68 per cent share of total exports in Colombia. It should also be pointed out that there are large differences as regards the sector's share of the domestic product in each country: in Colombia, it is 25.4 per cent while in Venezuela it is only 6.9 per cent and in Peru 15 per cent (see Table 2.1).

Table 2.1: Some indicators of the subregion's agricultural position, 1984

	Farm GDP US$m 1973	Farm sector's share of GDP %	Agriculture GDP per capita (1973 US$)	Farm sector's share of AEP %	Share of subregional Agric. %
Bolivia	0.483	21.5	77.9	49.9	3.8
Colombia	7.172	25.4	255.2	29.5	56.5
Ecuador	1.075	15.9	118.1	47.0	8.5
Peru	2.398	15.0	124.9	33.7	18.9
Venezuela	1.559	6.9	92.2	19.8	12.3
Subregion	12.687	16.7	159.6	31.9	100.0

Source: JUNAC, 'Principales Indicadores Socioeconómicos del Sector Agropecuario del Grupo Andino, 1980–1984'.

In the make-up of the subregion's Gross Agricultural Product, the share corresponding to the different countries varies widely. In 1984 Colombia's share was 57 per cent of the production value, while Peru and Venezuela together accounted for only 31.2 per cent, the remainder corresponding to Ecuador and Bolivia, as shown in Table 2.1. It is interesting to note that, in the period from 1950 to 1984, the structure mentioned has varied only slightly, including a seven-point increase in Colombia's share and a five-point increase in Venezuela's, while Peru went down four points compared to 1950.

Although the rural population portrayed an absolute increase of almost 3 million persons in the period between 1970 and 1984, its percentage share of the total population went down from 42.6 per cent in 1970 to 33.7 per cent in 1984. The per capita Gross Domestic Product, which in 1970-80 grew by 9.4 per cent for the rural sector and by 10.9 per cent for the urban zones, decreased considerably in 1980–84 as a result of the virtual stagnation of the gross product, in constant 1973 US dollars, while the population increased by 10.7 per cent.

The subregion's agricultural production, which grew at an average rate of 3.7 per cent for the first five years of the seventies, declined to 0.5 per cent in the next five and portrayed a negative rate of 0.7 per cent between 1980 and 1983. In 1984 the trend was reversed, with a growth of 2.5 per cent compared to the previous year. Estimates by the Board of the Cartagena Agreement show that the demand for food grew at an annual rate of 4.6 per cent during the decade of 1970–80 and by 1.5 per cent during 1980–83. It is evident, therefore, that agricultural growth was not significant enough to improve internal supply, which had to be met in part by imports, especially of food. The sluggishness observed in this sector has been largely due to low price levels on the world markets, although we must not underestimate the impact of domestic policies adopted by practically all countries of the subregion, which tended to depress prices for producers in order to lower the prices for consumers.

The Andean Group as a whole shows a positive trade balance for the agricultural sector during 1983 and 1984. However, this has not always been so. In general, it may be said that the balance depends on the size of Venezuela's deficit and Colombia's surplus. In 1984 the former country's share of the Group's sectoral purchases was 56 per cent, while the latter provided 61 per cent of all sales. The share of total trade was 12.5 per cent for exports and 5.4 per cent in the case of imports. It should be noted, however, that the low sales figure is considerably biased by the inclusion of oil in these estimates (see Table 2.2).

Table 2.2: Importance of the agricultural sector in foreign trade, 1984

	Total farm exports (US$ 000s)	Total farm imports (US$ 000s)	Agriculture trade balance	Farm sector's share of total exports %	Farm imports share of total imports %
Bolivia	28,142	151,592	−123,450	3.6	31.2
Colombia	2,353,660	552,045	1,801,615	67.6	12.3
Ecuador	733,966	231,968	501,988	19.4	13.5
Peru	559,963	489,436	70,527	17.9	22.9
Venezuela	151,239	1,816,353	−1,665,114	0.1	23.5
Subregion	3,826,970	3,241,394	585,576	14.9	19.6

Source: Calculations from JUNAC, 'Principales Indicadores Socioeconómicos del Sector Agropecuario del Grupo Andino, 1980–1984'.

Contrary to what might be assumed, the mutual exchange of farm products is small and takes place mainly between neighbouring countries. Only 3 per cent of the total subregional farm imports came from member countries, while 2.6 per cent of the agricultural exports in the area were shipped to Andean Group countries during 1984 (see Table 2.3). During that year, 39.7 per cent of overall trade took place between Venezuela and Colombia and 24.2 per cent between Colombia and Ecuador. The scant share of intra-subregional agricultural trade is largely due to country productions that are not complementary. However, trade possibilities were also affected by unilateral restrictions motivated by the need to protect domestic production. Likewise, the fact that a large part of the imports from outside countries took place through government agencies enjoying tariff franchise was a discouragement to subregional trade when international prices were below Andean prices.

This brief statistical synthesis is enough to show that, despite the notable

Table 2.3: Indicators of subregional trade in farm products, 1984

	Agriculture Balance with the subregion (US$ 000s)	Share of Intrasub-regional farm exports %	Share of Intrasub-regional farm imports%	Farm exports to ANRG %	Farm imports to ANRG %
Bolivia	3,831	5.8	1.9	20.2	1.2
Colombia	−18,453	32.7	51.8	1.3	9.0
Ecuador	28,426	37.4	7.9	5.1	3.4
Peru	7,804	21.4	13.3	4.1	2.6
Venezuela	−21,608	2.7	25.1	1.7	1.3
Subregion	—	100.0	100.0	2.6	3.0

Source: Calculations from JUNAC, 'Análisis del Comercio Agropecuario Intrasubregional y Propuestas Preliminares para su Reactivación, Documento J/DA/87, October 1986'.

differences, the agricultural sector plays a leading role in the subregion's economic context. However, unequal production performances gave rise to government policies that differed with regard to the priorities of stability and income distribution.

The following analysis of price matters made by the Board is illustrative of the above:

Price policy has been decisive for the sector. Traditionally, it has tended to depress prices for producers in order to cheapen consumption of basic products. It has been the mechanism to transfer resources from agricultural producers to other sectors of the economy and has conditioned traditional peasant agriculture to the supply of traditional foods and cheap labour for the rest of the economy.

One exception is Colombia, which has been using support prices to stimulate production since 1945, defending its food security with this policy. Lately, Venezuela and Ecuador have also tried to promote production on the basis of support prices for farmers, while Peru and Bolivia continue to set official prices for the defense of consumers only. Here farm product prices are set by the Ministry of Economics and Industry. These contrary agricultural policies result in very different price levels in the Andean markets.[2]

4. CONCLUSIONS

Given the basic principles of integration and the present economic situation of the Andean countries, it is worrisome to see that importations of agricultural products from outside the subregion have grown more rapidly than production of the same in recent years. This indicates the need to conduct a careful revision of agricultural policies and their role in integration.

In the regional integration schemes, LAFTA and ALADI, the agricultural sector was treated very briefly. Although the Andean Group set broader goals, it did not provide the mechanisms to make feasible the creation of a community agricultural policy. In the crucial aspect of the trade regime applicable to products from this sector, the treatment established differed little from that set for industrial products.

The fact that this is not an adequate solution to the problem is shown by the divergence between what the Agreement envisions and what happens in actual fact in the member countries. The exemption programme has not begun in Bolivia and Ecuador. In Venezuela it is subject to the discretionary management of government authorities. Although the exemption programme is in effect in Colombia and Peru, the major role played by state marketing agencies makes the subregional preference margin simply theoretical in many cases.

If integration is actually to contribute to the purpose of agricultural development in the subregion, the needs and characteristics of the sector must be taken into account. In this connection, the experience of the European Community is illustrative. It has an extended market for agricultural goods, the operation of which is made possible only by the effects of a common agricultural policy, through which the countries reach joint agreement on the objectives sought and ensure standard and consistent application of their mechanisms throughout the community. This is a vital condition considering that the operation of market forces, when national instruments differ, leads to arbitration operations resulting in the neutralisation of the purposes of such instruments.

The Andean Group's difficulties in creating a common policy similar to that of the European Community are evident. In the first place, national priorities in this matter vary widely, reconciling them would demand substantial changes in the national policies of member countries, and policies depend on the varying roles of the agricultural sector from one economy to another. There is no doubt that an Andean agricultural policy would require — as occurs with European agricultural policy — very large financial resources. We all know that such resources are not available.

The limited results of efforts towards agricultural integration on the part of member countries come as no surprise. Since the attainment of a real and effective extended market would require an apparently unattainable degree of consistency among policies, consideration should be given to the possibility of adopting a framework other than that of the Cartagena Agreement, as admitted by the Ministers of Agriculture of the Andean Group in Resolution 17 of 1983. Under the reform of the Andean Group being studied, all member countries have agreed on the need to grant priority consideration to the topic of agricultural integration. The government of Colombia has suggested the possibility of adopting a managed trade scheme with the double aim of increasing the subregional trade of agricultural products and avoiding detrimental effects of such trade on the production of member countries or on the effectiveness of their national agricultural policies. Managed trade could take the form of schemes of surpluses and deficits, allowing free trade but ensuring unconditional automatic safeguards or, alternatively, the creation of mechanisms so that state agricultural marketing agencies may channel trade among themselves.

This approach is not to hinder the maintenance and strengthening of the specific projects being carried out in the Andean context, but their conceptualisation must be adjusted so that they will produce concrete results and not be left on the shelf. In this connection, their administration should be centralised and better use be made of the existing infrastructure in the field of agricultural research in each of the member countries. If agricultural integration of the Andean Group is to be successful, the countries must profit from the vast experience of the European Community. However, such experience can only be useful if we are aware of the immense differences between the two groups. A mechanical imitation is not the same as the transmission of knowledge.

NOTES

1. JUNAC, *'El Sector Agropecuario y el Mercado Ampliado', Estudios* 3, 1982.
2. JUNAC, *'El Sector Agropecuario y los Instrumentos del Comercio'*, COM/XL-E/dt., 7 November 1983.

3

The Common Agricultural Policy – Key to European Integration

Piet van den Noort

WHY AGRICULTURAL PROTECTION IN THE EEC?

All capitalist countries have agricultural protection in one form or another and for various reasons. One of the best reasons is the free market's inability to reach stability and to achieve income parity for farmers. There are also other reasons. Switzerland and Sweden have protected their agriculture so that, in times of war, in which they prefer to be neutral, their agriculture and food supply can be independent. Also, the conservation of agricultural topsoil and landscape can be a reason for agricultural protection; for example as in Norway or Austria. There are countries with a long tradition of agricultural protection, such as France and Germany, but most other countries have only had such policies since the great Depression of the 1930s.

Now, we could say that, just as each individual country has protection for its agriculture, so the EEC has such a policy for itself. This seems to be a logical explanation, but it does not explain all the problems. Why is there no common policy in other fields where each country traditionally had its own far-reaching policy measures? Why is agriculture a lone forerunner in the field of common policies? Given the ideal of unity underlying the EEC, we might have expected common social, fiscal and monetary policies and also common policies in the fields of research, energy, environment or transport. Other cases of economic integration (Benelux, EFTA, LAFTA, CACM, ACM) have no common agricultural policies.[1]

So there must be an additional factor. It is useful to remember that economic integration was a third attempt to reach political integration in Europe; that is, to agree on a policy for achieving a stable, democratic order in Europe, with reconciliation between France and Germany, no wars or revolutions, but peace and security. The earlier attempts at unification were the Marshall Plan, and the European Coal and Steel Community. The third attempt should have been the

European Defence Community but this treaty was not ratified by the Frenc. National Assembly in 1954.

Integrating the economies in Europe, however, was also a means of achieving more stability and peace. Germany was all in favour of this policy, not least because it has much to gain from a large industrial market. Unlike Germany, France believed that its comparative economic strength was in agricultural production. Post-war France could therefore only agree to join the integration policies provided it could expand its markets for agricultural products in Europe, in exchange, as it were, for German industrial expansion. The participation of France was essential: its government was prepared to play it hard (it had already refused to ratify the E.D.C. Treaty), so the other countries involved thought it wise to humour France. This 'grain deal' would give France access to the European agricultural markets, Germany could expand its industrial markets, and political integration could proceed. The deal had, of course, its 'conditions'. The United States, as a traditional grain supplier, agreed to retreat a little for the greater good of political integration, but was unwilling to relinquish a considerable part of the European Market. The consumers and taxpayers implicitly agreed to use more French grain provided the policy did not become too expensive, i.e. prices did not rise too high. Farmers in Germany, on the other hand, were willing to co-operate, providing their losses were made good. It is therefore not surprising to find these provisos in the form of 'goals' in the Treaty of Rome; in principle the deal was simple, but its implementation was only achieved by much hard work on the part of the politicians.[2]

It is clear that France wanted to expand its agricultural production throughout the Euro-market and therefore demanded a market policy for agriculture and not an income-deficiency payment or social measures for farmers. To have a market means nothing without price guarantees, so the second aim of the common policy proposed for the EEC was a price policy. The aim was for the price of French wheat to a least meet the level of production costs in France, as otherwise a Common Market would not be an interesting proposition for the French. The EEC member states were to give preference to French wheat: this was done by creating an artificial price difference with the world market by means of imposing a levy on imported grain ('community preference').

It was difficult to arrive at a common acceptable price level and therefore at a common tariff or levy on grain. The French national price level was not acceptable to the Germans and the German level was not acceptable to the other member states or to traditional overseas suppliers. So the conclusion was that the common price level should be somewhere in between and should be found during a transitional period of some twelve years!

Within the EEC, France directed its political attention to securing a watertight guarantee of the grain deal by attempting to secure detailed regulations for agricultural markets. Outside the EEC trade policy was paramount for France: for example, during the Kennedy Round, when the EEC (and also the individual member states) negotiated about tariffs, mainly on industrial goods. France, however, was not prepared to accept an attractive deal in this area unless there

Table 3.1: The EEC market regulation scheme

Commodities	Target price	Threshold price	Sluice-gate price	Free at frontier price	Import levy	Supplementary levy	Import duty	Provision for market intervention	Provision for export refunds	Quota	Quality standards	Producers' Organization	Initial date	Date for unification[10]
Grain and grain products	●	●		●	●			●[1]	●				1- 8-62	1- 7-67
Rice and rice products	●[1]	●		●	●			●	●				1- 9-64	1- 9-67
Pigs and pig meat			●	●	●	●		●	●				1- 8-62	1- 7-67
Eggs and poultry			●	●	●	●			●				1- 8-62	1- 7-67
Milk and dairy products	●[2]	●		●	●	●		●[9]	●				1- 8-62	1- 8-62
Beef and veal				●	●		●	●	●	●[4]			29- 7-68	29- 7-68
Sugar and sugarbeet	●	●			●			●	●	●[5]			1- 7-67	1- 7-68
Oilseed	●		●[3]	●				●	●				1- 7-67	1- 7-67
Olive oil	●	●		●	●			●	●				1-11-66	1-11-66
Fruit and vegetables			●[6]				●	●	●	●[7]	●	●	1- 7-68	1- 7-68
Wine							●	●	●	●[8]	●		1- 8-62	1-11-69

1. In France and Italy; 2. Only in the case of milk; 3. Guide price; 4. Levy-free import quota for frozen beef; 5. Production quota; 6. Reference price; 7. Import quota applicable only through a safeguard clause procedure; 8. Import quota; 9. Applicable for butter and skimmed milk powder; 10. Since the dates mentioned the EEC has been unified. This means that for the inner EEC trade there are no import levies any longer and, furthermore, that for the trade with third countries there are uniform import levies and export refunds.

was also an agreement about the tariffs on agricultural products (and in fact also about the common price in the EEC). The stand taken by France was extremely effective and the EEC countries also agreed on the common price of wheat (106 'Units of Account' per ton). This, combined with the detailed market regulations, gave an almost complete common agricultural price policy (see Table 3.1). It was set up as a system of protection with in fact unlimited guarantees. The most important flaw was that no agreement had been reached over the wheat price in years to come. Politicians played on this weak spot during prolonged negotiations (marathon sessions). No wonder France was in favour of an automatic procedure, a so-called 'objective method', for fixing future prices. Although such a method was adopted, it never became a really automatic procedure. Thus, the common agricultural price policy was necessary to obtain French co-operation, without which European integration could not proceed.

RESULTS AND PROBLEMS

The EEC has a common market policy and a common price level for many agricultural products, but if we look at the price level in national prices (applying exchange rates) we will see that the price levels and their trends differ greatly between member countries. The differences are as great as before the Treaty of Rome. These differences can exist because of a system of special levies and subsidies between the member states called Monetary Compensatory Amounts. The various price levels, however, have always been above world market price levels and were attractive for France. France could, therefore, profit from the grain deal: it could increase its share of the European market (see Table 3.2). In exchange for German industrial expansion, the French did indeed obtain a larger agricultural market, although they were faced with some competition from the Dutch who had high agricultural productivity and an excellent geographical position. Because of German political pressure the price level was high, which also prevented the French from having a larger market share.

It is said that the CAP has only one instrument — the common price level — whereas the Treaty of Rome lays down many targets. Formally, the CAP is therefore an illogical construction; it would be logical to have a separate instrument for each target or political end. But should we look at the CAP in this way?

Table 3.2: The expansion of the French agricultural market share

	1960	1967	1980	
Grains	23	32	48	m. tons
	(33)	(36)	(40)	
Sugar	19	12	26	m. tons
	(33)	(20)	(32)	
Milk	23	27	32	m. tons
	(26)	(28)	(28)	

(n) = relative share of Euromarket

The real and primary target of the CAP was to obtain French co-operation in European policy. Market and price policies have realised this goal, though with some clashes of interest. The so-called goals of the CAP, for example as formulated in article 39 of the Treaty, can better be seen as limiting conditions, indicating other interests to be considered in realising the agricultural policy.

Consumers, for example, were apprehensive of too high price levels for agricultural products. Is it true that the CAP has consumer's interests at heart and that prices are not too high? The facts are that prices at the farm gate have risen less than retail prices or retail prices for all consumer goods. Without the CAP, the purchasing power of consumers would have been higher. They have been paying about 2.3 per cent of national income as income transfer to farmers (see Table 3.3), but without CAP there would have been a similar (national) transfer to income, so we should only look at the additional aspects, which are difficult to estimate. Consumers also had some interest in supply and in self-sufficiency. The achievement of self-sufficiency has increased considerably since the inception of the EEC, often to figures exceeding 100 per cent!

As a consequence, ample supplies have been available for consumers, but in their role as taxpayers consumers have also paid out large sums. This has taken place in a period in which all countries have been experiencing serious problems with government finances. So when EC expenditure reached the limits of 'own resources' (see Figure 3.1) we had a problem but also a political chance of

Table 3.3: Recent estimates of EC transfers and costs as a result of agricultural support in relation to gross domestic product and on a per person basis*

Period	Cost to consumers	Cost to taxpayers	Total cost to consumers and taxpayers	Cost to the economy (deadweight losses)
	As a percentage of gross domestic product			
	%	%	%	%
EC–9				
1974–trough	0.6	1.1	1.7	0.16
1978–peak	1.8	1.0	2.8	0.48
EC–10				
1983	1.2	1.0	2.2	0.32
Average				
1973–83	1.3	1.0	2.3	0.30
	Per person (in 1982 values)			
	ECU	ECU	ECU	ECU
EC–9				
1974–trough	48	84	132	12
1978–peak	163	85	248	43
EC–10				
1983	112	90	202	29
Average				
1973–83	112	86	198	27

* After allowance for the estimated effect of EC support policies on world market prices for major agricultural products.

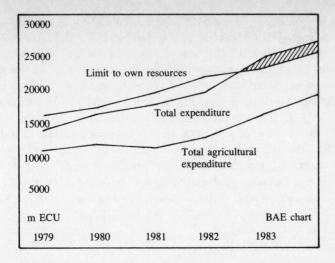

Figure 3.1: EC own resources: limits and expenditure commitments[3]

changing the CAP. Foreign consumers have benefited from this, because food has become cheap and this may have improved the standard of living in some countries, but foreign exporters have suffered: they complain of dumping. For developing countries the repercussions are mixed: industrialisation policies benefit, but those countries that give priority to agricultural development have suffered.[4]

Some politicians and economists were afraid of the high real costs of protection: too many resources in agriculture, a bad structure and low productivity. According to article 39, this should be prevented and in this the agricultural policies have been successful. Since the Treaty of Rome was signed, there has been an enormous outflow of agricultural labour (about 4 per cent per year), an increase in farm size and a rise in technical productivity (by between 3 and 5 per cent per year): this rate is as good as can be found in industry.

It is true, however, that as a consequence of price protection labour (that could better have been employed in other parts of the economy) was retained in agriculture — at the expense of the domestic product of the EEC. So there are real costs involved with the CAP. These are not more than 0.5 per cent of domestic product — see Table 3.3. In the period of growth 1965–75 this was not a large burden, particularly when it is remembered that without the CAP we would have had national price policies that would also have had their real costs. The additional real costs of the CAP are therefore around 0.2 per cent of domestic product. The real benefits of free trade between member states were according to Scitovsky[2] perhaps 0.1 to 0.5 per cent of domestic product. In comparison with these benefits the costs of agricultural protection were high. This could only be accepted because the political and 'dynamic' benefits were considerable. It is not surprising that protests against the CAP become serious again in the 1980s when the economic growth, the dynamic benefits of integration and even the political benefits seemed too small.

The real cost of the CAP should not be confused with the budget cost, which is impressive indeed in absolute terms (see Tables 3.4 and 3.5), but in relative terms it is not more than 0.9 per cent of national product,[5] which can be not such a burden as is sometimes suggested. Farmers were afraid of a loss in their position. In general the relative position of farmers increased. Farmers' income grew considerably in the 1960s and 1970s but there is still a disparity of incomes.[6]

So there really have been problems: real costs, income transfers, budgetary costs, income disparity, disturbance of international trade or development policies. Nevertheless, the EEC has obtained six new members: Greece, United Kingdom, Eire, Denmark, Spain and Portugal. The recent entrance of two new members (Spain and Portugal) will lead to additional problems in all these areas.

SOLUTIONS AND PROSPECTS

Looking back, we can say that the European policy to arrive at peace, stability and democracy in Europe has been a priority. The policies of economic integration can be seen as a means of achieving this goal. The agricultural policy is part of this policy and is also a concrete example of a complicated and costly means of achieving that goal. The situation is now very different from that of the 1950s. We are no longer concerned with reconstruction and reconciliation; East–West relations are also different. We are concentrating more on daily, technical problems than on dealing with high ideals. Nevertheless, we have grave social and economic problems and it is surprising that there is not more common action against unemployment, environmental destruction, energy problems, or in favour of scientific research and strategies of development. The entry into the EEC of Spain and Portugal was a reminder of the idealistic desire to strengthen democracy in Europe. But again, even these important policies are over-shadowed by a large number of more or less technical problems concerning vegetables, grain, wine, money and all kinds of foreign relations in the Mediterranean.

I believe that France and the northern areas of the EEC are now in a similar position to that of Germany in 1957. Spain and Portugal have special agricultural interests, just as the founder EEC members now have industrial interests. It is indeed interesting to 'swap markets'. It is even questionable whether France did in fact have such a large economic interest in grain exports as was said at the time;[7] but nowadays even France is an industrial nation and should give Spain a chance, in exchange for participation in large industrial markets. The CAP has the historical role of improving and accelerating economic and political integration and should not become a brake on these policies.

Many proposals for new policies have been put forward and some have indeed been incorporated into the CAP. I believe it is unwise to continue changing policies each season. There are still many alternatives open to the CAP. Let us consider some major examples.

Table 3.4: Guarantee expenditure by economic category

Year	Storage*	Aids**	Others†	Co-responsibility receipts from milk	Export refunds‡	Total guarantee expenditure§
	m ECU	m ECU	m ECU	m ECU	m ECU	m ECU
1979	1658	3779	116	−94	4982	10441
	(15.9)	(36.2)	(1.1)	(−0.9)	(47.7)	(100.0)
1980	1617	3928	298	−223	5695	11315
	(14.3)	(34.7)	(2.6)	(−2.0)	(50.4)	(100.0)
1981	1631	4343	436	−478	5209	11141
	(14.6)	(39.0)	(3.9)	(−4.3)	(46.8)	(100.0)
1982	1818	5468	603	−537	5054	12406
	(14.6)	(44.1)	(4.9)	(−4.3)	(40.7)	(100.0)
1983	2893	7281	712	−527	5560	15930
	(18.2)	(45.7)	(4.5)	(−3.3)	(34.9)	(100.0)
1984 (supplementary budget)	3583	7942	1130	−972	6718	18401
	(19.5)	(43.2)	(6.1)	(−5.3)	(36.5)	(100.0)

* Includes rebates on storage of, for example, butter for pastry-making and skimmed milk used in animal feed — in accordance with the budget nomenclature.
** Aids to producers, processing aids, marketing aids for products, MCAs for intra-EC trade and guidance premiums (195m ECU in 1983).
† Distillation and withdrawals.
‡ Includes MCAs for extra-EC trade.
§ Including the common organization of the market in fisheries. There may be minor differences in total expenditure in various tables owing to the different treatment regarding payment of previous years' accounts.

Note: Figures in parentheses are proportions of total guarantee expenditure.

Source: Commission of the European Communities (1983a, 1984c, 1985a).

Table 3.5: Community revenue and expenditure

Item	1974 m EUA	1975 m EUA	1976 m EUA	1977 m EUA	1978 m EUA	1979 m ECU	1980 m ECU	1981 m ECU	1982* m ECU	1983*** m ECU	1984† m ECU
Revenue											
Customs duties	2737	3151	4064	3927	4391	5189	5906	6392	6815	6989	7884
Agricultural levies‡	330	590	1164	1778	2279	2143	2002	1747	2228	2295	3172
Value added tax						4738	7259	9188	12000	13699	14377
Other	1969	2473	2765	2779	5507	2532	899	1122	197	1783	1816
Total	5036	6214	7993	8484	12177	14602	16066	18449	21241	24766	27249
(Change§	(5)	(23)	(29)	(6)	(44)	(20)	(10)	(15)	(15)	(17)	(10)
VAT percentage						0.79	0.73	0.79	0.92	1.00	1.00
Expenditure											
Agriculture											
— Guarantee Section¶	3278	4821	5365	6167	9279	10434	11306	10988	12406	15898	18333
— Guidance Section	128	184	218	297	324	403	601	576	548	688	675
Social Fund	238	136	256	317	285	596	735	746	1019	1431	1644
Regional Fund	—	91	277	373	255	513	727	799	2988	2431	1455
Co-operation with developing countries	169	324	137	216	265	405	508	858	791	981	897
Research and energy investment	78	116	118	143	192	254	290	359	454	1441	1740
Reimbursements to member states	284	354	422	665	662	900	1222	2394	1068	1120	1155
Other sectors	5	9	24	31	36	88	78	128	35	106	539
Administration	337	375	420	497	677	773	820	944	701	760	811
Total	4516	6411	7238	8705	11973	14367	16290	17792	20012	24871	27249
(Agriculture's share‖)	(75)	(78)	(77)	(74)	(80)	(75)	(73)	(65)	(65)	(67)	(70)

* Out-turn. ** After supplementary budget no. 2 for expenditure. † Amending and supplementary budget, 1984.
‡ Includes sugar levies. § Figures in parentheses are percentage changes from previous year. ¶ There may be minor differences in total expenditure in various tables due to the different treatment regarding payment of previous years' accounts. ‖ Figures in parentheses are proportions of agricultural expenditure in total expenditure.

Sources: Commission of the European Communities (personal communication, December 1983; 1985a); Office for Official Publication of the European Communities (1984b).

One of the oldest alternatives is a structural policy. Price levels could be lower if we had a modern, well-structured agriculture. Thus, in the late 1960s, Commissioner Mansholt proposed a plan to achieve this in agriculture. The idea was to accelerate the outmigration of rural labour and the modernisation of agriculture. This plan ran into much opposition because of its flaws. For example, it had a low rate of return, needed a large budget, did not consider the unfavourable social consequences of migration and it disregarded the vested interests of the agricultural lobby. Today we could also use a better organised agriculture, but a new Mansholt Plan would be an unwise policy because an additional outflow of labour from agriculture would be unprofitable owing to unemployment, and the modernisation of agriculture would also lead to more production and more surpluses, which is also unprofitable. Additional structural measures are therefore not the solution.

An effective measure is to decrease price levels or levels of protection. The high price levels are the real cause of surpluses. Many would gain from lower prices, but farming and some agribusiness would not. The income position of farmers is an important aspect of agricultural policies in Europe and this policy line is therefore not generally acceptable in real politics; for example, when applied to cereals in 1985, it created much political tension in the Community. Comparable proposals that have been considered have involved increases in import prices, especially of feedstuffs, which have always led to an intensive political debate with no results.

To retain the advantages of low prices but also income protection and the social position of farmers, Professor van Riemsdijk proposed a direct income payment system in which the loss of income resulting from the lower prices would be compensated for by direct income payments to farmers. These payments would only be made for a limited period of time — at most twenty years — and only to farmers up to 65 years of age. This would give a stimulus to improve farming, since after that transitional period low prices would rule the agricultural economy and, to survive, farmers would need large and modern farms. This plan was also debated but rejected, because it also had a low rate of return, needed a large budget and would have led to large migration, with all its social and political repercussions. Today, all these problems would still follow such a policy to an even greater degree, because an additional outmigration is not at all profitable and any increase in the budget for agriculture would meet great political opposition.

Another method is to restrict production by imposing production quotas per country and per farmer. There is a wide range of possibilities in this field. The super levy system now in use in the dairy sector is perhaps the best-known example. It is a purely technical measure. It restricts production and therefore decreases the budget costs of the CAP, but without the basic systematic improvements that the above-mentioned alternative policies promised to give. The restrictive measures that have in fact been taken for sugar and milk have changed the CAP system from an unlimited guarantee to a limited one. This is already a considerable change when we realise how strongly the farmers are organised compared with all other interest groups involved.

Other interesting proposals involve taking marginal land out of agricultural production and using it for timber production or for recreation. The difficulty with this proposal is in fact to find this marginal land. In the Netherlands, for example, you cannot find any large area of this type of land and it is said that timber production is not profitable and therefore not an attractive alternative to milk production. But in several other regions it could indeed be a splendid idea, to increase alternative production. The problem with labour-extensive products like timber is that you have to find new means to protect employment now found in the CAP. This would require an additional social policy. It is interesting to note that such policies of new uses for agricultural land have a positive effect on the environment.

Each of these measures has its variations. So, in the theory, there are many alternative proposals for solving the CAP problems. Among economists there is a strong tendency to try to find the optimal instrument in that series of solutions by estimating the total net effect on welfare of the Community that each instrument has, and selecting the highest-scoring measure. The difficulty with this procedure, based on Professor Tinbergen's theory of economic policy,[8] is that there is in fact no social welfare function or no such function can be specified and estimated. So it is no use looking for an instrument or measure that will lead to the maximum value of this function.[9] This method can only be applied to individual or partial preferences but will not indicate the *social* preferences of a nation or the Community as a whole. The real selection can therefore only be made by other, that is political, means. This conclusion is too often overlooked by economists. It is a pity that political science has no empirically tested theory on political decision-making at this level. So they too cannot explain why some policies are applied or rejected. What we can say is that the political selection process in Europe is dominated by the 'unanimity rule' in the Council of Ministers (this is a result of President de Gaulle's policy towards the EEC in 1965). This Council is a kind of coalition government of the EEC: ten ministers working towards common decisions. The bartering of votes between them is an obvious way to reaching agreement. To reach unanimity will require more strength and more exchange or trade-offs than simple majority rule would require. Since, in practice, this Council only deals with agricultural affairs and not all types of other affairs (as a national cabinet must do), the political bargaining will lead to ever more measures in the agricultural field, each time making agricultural policy more expensive. So if we could find more common policies (e.g. for energy, environment, unemployment, research) and if we could really apply majority rule we could get easier and cheaper political solutions for agriculture too. The CAP has a very introvert character, because it mainly contains the representatives of farmers and of the ministers of agriculture who are involved in the decision-making process in Brussels. The only opportunity for others to influence the process is in case the 'own means' of the Community fall too short. We see new proposals for financing the Community or to reform the CAP, but they hardly succeed in really changing and improving the situation.[10]

An enlarged EEC cannot continue with its agricultural policies in the same way as it did before the entry of Spain and Portugal. Continuing to increase price levels is leading us into grave problems. We must also realise that small farmers, with only small means of production (of which there are many, especially in Southern Europe) can never be given a reasonable income by price policies alone. High prices also lead to large income differences within agriculture and have a tendency to lead to high rents and land prices. We will need a freeze on prices and production for some time. To prevent social problems, we could try to secure a reasonable income for farmers by introducing, for example, income deficiency payments. This social measure could even be part of the national social policy and therefore be completely financed out of the national budget. If this is done we will have reached the watershed between the economic and the social aspects of agricultural policies. In future, the social aspect could better be dealt with separately. This idea has become part of the new proposals of Commissioner Andriessen to reform the Common Agricultural Policy as formulated in his Greenbook. These proposals are now at the start of the political decision-making process. Experience with previous reform proposals shows that it will not be simple and easy. (In fact the German government started such a policy, to be effective in the second half of 1987.) But this time it must have positive results, otherwise the Common Agricultural Policy will become the breaking point in European policies.

NOTES

1. S.J. Wells, *International Economics*, Allen and Unwin, London, 1973.
2. Tibor Scitovsky, *Economic Theory and Western European Integration*, London, Unwin, 1958, p.67.
3. 'Agricultural Policies in the European Community, Their Origins, Nature and Effects on Production and Trade.' Policy Monograph No.2, Canberra, Bureau of Agricultural Economics, 1985.
4. L. Spaventa, L. Koopmans *et al.* 'The future of Community Finance', CEPS-Papers No.30, Brussels, 1986.
5. M. Tracy, *Agriculture in Western Europe, Challenge and Response*, London, Granada, 1982.
6. G. Meester and D. Strijker, *Het Europese landbouwbeleid*, Voorbij de scheidslijn van zelfvoorziening, Wetenschappelijke raad voor het Regeringsbeleid, Den Haag, 1985.
7. D.R. Harvey, 'National Interests and the CAP', *Food Policy*, August 1982.
8. J. Tinbergen, *On the Theory of Economic Policy*, Amsterdam, North-Holland, 1952.
9. P.C. Van den Noort, 'The problem of optimum policy choice in European agriculture', *Netherlands Journal of Agricultural Science*, **31** (1983), pp. 93-7.
10. J. Pelkmans (ed.), *Can the CAP be reformed?*. Maastricht, IEAP, 1985.

PART 3: INDUSTRIAL POLICY

4

The Community's Industrial Policy

Elizabeth de Ghellinck

1. THE CONCEPT OF INDUSTRIAL POLICY

Following Swann (1983:3), 'industrial policy can be defined as the attitude of governments towards the industries for which they have some form of responsibility or which lie in their constituency'. Whilst not conforming to the actual general acceptance, this quite obvious definition has the merit of throwing light on the fact that there could be as many industrial policies as people sharing different views about the role that industry has to play in an economy. Therefore, this explains the confusion surrounding this concept.

More commonly, industrial policy is seen as a series of objectives and measures aimed at influencing the structure of the economy. In this framework, its task is to create optimum conditions for the necessary structural transformations to be carried out. The need for transformation arises from changes occurring in the process of industrial development: technological changes, shifts in demand, maturing and declining industries, and so on. The required adjustments take time, so that industrial policy is essentially long-term. Divergent views concerning aims or the means used lead to the distinction of two basic types of industrial policies.

The *market-oriented* policy is based on the rationale that an automatic and continuous process of industrial adjustment is realised by a decentralised competitive system. Industrial policy is then seen as the instrument intended to allow competition to function totally efficiently. One of the main instruments of such industrial policy is competition policy. Its aims are to create and maintain objective conditions ensuring the development of a competitive process. Likewise, the commercial policy will seek to promote competition and abolish all restraints domestic agents or foreigners have imposed on an arms-length competitive process. This market-oriented policy does not exclude some state action in order to slow down the pace of structural changes in order to obtain what is thought desirable. But it rests soundly on the constraints of the competitive process. Private enterprises, by their investment and production decisions, remain the main protagonists in industrial evolution. In turn, public authorities facilitate efficient decisions and ensure an environment propitious to healthy functioning of the decentralised system. The limits of this system are numerous and we will be limited to distinguish between two types, one at the domestic and the other at the foreign level.

At the domestic level, the market economy is beset with important failures. The regional imbalance and differences in development are less and less tolerated but could be accentuated by the free circulation of people, assets and capital. As shown by J. Meade (1976), if different citizens start with different endowments of factors of production, then the forces of competition can lead to greater inequalities in the absence of any governmental intervention to make the winners compensate the losers. The social costs, combined with the mobility of resources, and especially of employment, are often considered to be intolerable to such an extent that only the mediation of the state is capable of safeguarding a minimum of organised institutionalised mobility.

The price system may fail to emit correct signals on economic scarcity in cases of non-renewable resources, externalities and public goods; furthermore, even if correct signals are emitted, economic agents may fail to react to them if they are short-term profit maximisers, reluctant to bear high risks, cannot divide investments over time, and fee unable to appropriate the fruits of their work if it turns out to be successful.

At the foreign level, the limits of the international division of labour present a threat. This division is confronted with the advantages of a minimum level of national autonomy below which national security would be threatened. The oil crisis, the tendency of the countries producing raw materials to reduce their supply and to transform the materials at home, the hazy character of the industrial list of initial and anticipated comparative advantages, the necessary structural adjustments and the transformation of entire sectors — all these make less realistic, at least at the socio-political level, a system that would leave to market forces the solution of such problems.

In the light of multiple criteria and in a dynamic perspective, the acceptance of a model of free exchange and of the Pareto-optimality character of its implications is much less evident. As long as there exists no mechanism to ensure that world cooperation — leading to a maximisation of the common surplus — is possible and would be stable, in as far as this solution also gives more to certain partners and is not reinforced by systems of international redistribution of profits (side-payments) effecting transfer from the more favoured to the less favoured, it is understandable that states hesitate to accept a specialisation leading to the maximum degree of international openness. They could be tempted to adopt individual policies of the 'maximum' type — with the risk that these latter would lead to results that could be fatal for the collective equilibrium.

According to a more *interventionist conception*, industrial policy is seen as a number of means used by the public authorities to channel industrial activity in the framework of a general economic programme towards a number of pre-established objectives.

The means employed to achieve this are many and can be coercive in nature or able to stimulate changes. In the first case, preference is given to systems of quotas, to rationing, or to imposed prices. In the second, one attempts to make profitable the adoption by economic agents of the policies desired by the public authorities. For this subsidies, allowances, or relief from taxation are used. In particular, if the government is more neutral towards risk than the private investor, it subsidises the projects in order to further the level of investment. Such neutrality could be justified as long as the total cost of risk-bearing of an independent project is make negligible by the spreading of the risk over the entire population of taxpayers. This is where the various forms of contracts for restructuring and encouraging business management come in. They ensure that, in exchange for the subsidies transferred by public authorities, the enterprises agree to contribute to the achievement of the sectoral, technological and regional objectives of the plan. The state might also influence industrial structures directly by taking on productive activities, whether in collaboration with the private sector or alone.

Competition and commercial policies are then instruments, among others, that authorities may use in order to maximise their social welfare function. Contradictions among the different instruments will be avoided only if the ranking among the different socio-economic aims is well established. The limits of this type of policy can be summed up by the following dilemma: should one submit to the demands of efficiency generally linked with international conditions of competition and risk losing the means of control linked with the responsibility of public interest; or should one fix public objectives with the danger of misguided actions or the creation of big 'white-elephants'?

More precisely, the choices for industrial redevelopment are not self-evident and — apart from some general themes such as the move towards products of great value added, depending on an advanced technology and incorporating little energy — exact criteria are lacking. Public authorities are too often confined to the role of giving social assistance to enterprises in difficulty. Furthermore, public industrial initiative can become a kind of 'corporatist' system, with nomination of employees for political reasons, lacking a sense of responsibility and initiative, and not subject to the discipline of competition and of profitability (public enterprises which are badly managed do not usually disappear by way of bankruptcy courts).

The choice between market and directive industrial policies depends on the social welfare function of the state and on the confidence authorities place in the virtues of competition to reach socio-political aims such as technical progress, increasing standards of living . . . But as we shall see in the European context alterations in the general environment impinge on this social welfare function, by affecting the relative importance attached to the different aims and hence lead to a change in the orientation given to the industrial policy. Furthermore, the contrast between the two types of policies appears, to some extent, theoretical, especially in the case of mixed economies such as the European ones. In fact, there is a *continuum* in the degree of interventionism. In each European country, some industrial sectors are affected by public micro-economic measures to prevent or to promote a structural change, while simultaneously other sectors are freely submitted to the market system. Similarly, when comparing two countries such as Germany and France, the two corresponding industrial policies are officially quite different, the first one being of the market type and the second one of the interventionist type. In fact, they are very similar in everyday practice, particularly if the differences between the national industrial structures are taken into account.

2. THE INDUSTRIAL POLICY OF THE COMMUNITY: GENERAL FRAME

When analysing the policies adopted in the context of the European Economic Communities, it is useful to compare the role assigned to industrial policy respectively in the Treaty of Paris, which in 1951 established the European Coal and Steel Community (ECSC) and the Treaty of Rome which in 1957 laid down the foundations of the European Economic Community (EEC). Whilst pursuing both an objective of economic integration on the basis of competitive trade in order to:

contribute . . . to economic expansion, growth of employment and a rising standard of living in the Member States [article 2, Treaty of Paris], and promote throughout the Community a harmonious development of economic activities, a continuous and balanced expansion, an increase in stability, an accelerated raising of the standards of living and closer relations between the states belonging to it [article 2, Treaty of Rome].

The general tone of the two treaties differs quite a lot. Roughly stated, the Paris Treaty has a more *dirigist* character than the Rome Treaty. In entrusting to the high authority powers of supranational management, the member states have permitted the creation of a common strategy in the fields of coal and steel. In the Rome Treaty, the abolition of internal tariffs and trade barriers and the crea- tion of a common internal market were thought to provide such a competitive impetus as to reduce a natural adjustment of the structure of productive capacities. Along with the conventional theoretical wisdom, free trade was hence a sufficient device for an optimal allocation of resources.

Two factors might explain this difference. On the one hand, the ECSC was conceived against a background of uncertainty and some fear about the impact that international free competition would exert on these historically highly cartelised sectors. On the contrary, the EEC was elaborated in a context of expansion and influenced by the fact that the ECSC seemed to have had fewer problems in meeting international competition then had been foreseen. On the other hand, the ECSC covers two relatively homogeneous sectors sharing common characteristics such as a high level of capital investment, a high degree of concentration, and cyclical fluctuations in demand, whilst the EEC's industrial structures are much more heterogeneous, confront problems of a very different nature and call therefore for a differentiated treatment.

The drafters of the ECSC were aware that the lumpy nature of investment in the coal and steel industry could lead companies left to themselves to develop investment plans which collectively could create excessive production capacity. If capacity is chronically excessive, competition will be ruinous and will act against the achievement of the general objectives of the Treaty as stated in article 2. Hence, article 5 of the Paris Treaty specifies: 'The Community shall ensure the establishment, maintenance and observance of normal competitive conditions *and exert direct influence upon production or upon the market only when circumstances so require.*' This direct influence might take the form of production quotas (article 58), maximum or minimum prices (article 60) under circumstances described as a 'manifest crisis' (article 58) or 'serious shortages' (article 59). Several instruments are thus available in the ECSC Treaty for the implementation of a *dirigist* industrial policy.

In the Rome Treaty, on the contrary, no such reference to a direct influence upon production appears. Article 3 states that, in order to promote the goals mentioned in article 2: 'The activity of the Community will establish a regime assuring that competition within the Common Market is not falsified.' The industrial policy, implicit in the Rome Treaty, is hence a market-oriented one, based on the creation of a competitive internal common market. The instruments of this policy, after the abolition of the internal tariffs, consist of those designed to assure a common market, namely the competition policy, the common external policy and authority to favour harmonisation of member states' laws.

The aims of the competition policy are, as stated in the Eighth Report on Competition Policy: 'To prevent the unity of the Common Market from being jeopardised by actions which have the effect of re-erecting the internal barriers.' Hence, agreements between firms or concerted practices (article 85), abuse of dominant positions (article 86) and public aid to companies (article 92), which may affect trade between member states, are prohibited. However, and contrary to other competition laws such as the American one, competition is not a goal *per se* but, as stated in article 3, a means to achieve the general objectives of the Treaty. Its maintenance is therefore justified as long as these objectives are better reached through a competitive process than by the means of other forms of control such as more or less detailed public regulation, cooperation between the public and private sectors, and so on. Along this line, article 85 (3) states that prohibited agreements or concerted practices can be exempted under the following conditions:

(i) if they contribute towards the improvement of the production or distribution of goods or promote technical and economic progress;
(ii) if they allow consumers a fair share of the resulting benefits;
(iii) if the restriction is necessary for the attainment of the objective;

(iv) if the firms concerned are not enabled to eliminate competition in respect of a substantial part of the product in question.

Alongside this, the provisions governing state aid offer extensive powers in the industrial policy field. Article 92 (3) specifies the categories of aid which may be regarded as being compatible with the Treaty.

(i) aid to areas with an abnormally low standard of living or serious unemployment;
(ii) aid to remedy a serious disturbance in the economy of the member states;
(iii) regional or sectoral aid, provided that trading conditions are not unduly affected.

Furthermore, any aid policy that distorts or threatens to distort competition must be part of an overall policy. The Treaty also provides the Commission with more general powers which can be exercised in pursuit of industrial policy objectives, namely through the European Investment Bank, The European Regional Fund and via the provisions that spell out clearly the goal of harmonising member states laws.

The high degree of openness of the European Community (in 1983, total imports from third countries amounted to 12.8 per cent of the GPD of the ten member countries and total exports to third countries represented 11.9 per cent) implies that the degree of competition within the integrated area depends not only on the ease with which industries and firms in each member state can sell in the markets of other member states but also on the extent to which the integrated market can be penetrated from outside. The establishment of a common external tariff (CET) implies that member states cease to be free to unilaterally determine the level of tariff and quota protection *vis-à-vis* third countries and that the level of tariff constitutes one of the key variables in the Community's commercial stance towards the rest of the world. The Commission is entrusted with negotiating the conditions of entry for imports from all over the world. It handles anti-dumping actions and negotiates self-limiting arrangements.

3. TOWARDS THE IMPLEMENTATION OF A EUROPEAN INDUSTRIAL POLICY

During the 1950s and 1960s, the European Community benefited from an unprecedented period of growth and prosperity which eased the establishment of an internal integrated market. Openness and cooperative economic relationships were felt to increase both national and world welfare.

In the 1970s, however, the general economic environment changed substantially. The European economies were confronted with a rise in the real price of raw materials inputs, the expansion of newly industrialising countries (NIC) into their traditional exports — steel, shipbuilding and textiles — and the increasing competitiveness from Japan and the United States in the field of advanced technology. All these factors revealed a need to adapt the industrial structure to sources of competition unforeseen in the 1950s. As recession and unemployment replaced expansion, growing scepticism about the virtues of competitive adjustment developed. The member states were induced to react to the problem of overcapacity in a defensive and inward-looking manner. This led to increasing interference of states in order to protect national interests by the means of aid, national regulations in the field of technical standards, and so on.

At the theoretical level, too, the optimality of free trade has come under serious challenge as imperfect competition in international markets is integrated into the analysis. Factors governing imperfect competition at the international level are: reduced number of firms, product differentiation or governmental practices. Hence scale and scope economies and barriers to entry combine to limit the number of firms in industries such as the aerospace, the automobile construction, the semiconductor and the computer industry. In such oligopolistic industries where equilibria allow pure positive profits or rents, it is in a country's self-interest to capture more of these profits by an appropriate trade policy.[1] If such a policy is in general not optimal from a world welfare point of view, Dixit and Kyle (1985) have shown that in markets where the world game is characterised by threat and dominance, precommitment by the government to sustain a domestic productive capacity by means of a subsidy or a tariff protection might be beneficial even from the world welfare point of view to the extent that it determines the decision of domestic firms to enter the market.

The efforts made by the Airbus consortium to compete with Boeing in the market for intermediate-range commercial jets is one well-known instance of such strategic behaviour, even if, as stressed by Dixit (1986), 'in the absence of serious empirical tests, the scope and significance of these theoretical results must remain doubtful', there seems to exist some scope for positive government intervention in the field of industrial policy.

Confronted with this evolution, the Commission responded along two lines; on the one hand by redirecting available instruments, namely the competition and commercial policy, towards the achievement of industrial policy objectives and, on the other, acting as an initiator of policy by making various proposals favouring more positive actions in the field of a European industrial policy. We shall first consider some of these attempts and the level of achievements they have attained.

Proposals for a positive European industrial policy

In fact, the first manifestation of an industrial policy goes back to 1964, when the idea of a 'medium-term economic programme' was introduced. Since the publication of a second programme, prepared in 1965, and covering the period 1968–70, the Commission insisted on the necessity of public intervention to improve the industrial structures of the Community and set up a Directorate for Industrial Policy and a Directorate for Science, Research and Development, which are responsible for the preparation of orientations for the Common industrial and research policies and the coordination of the intervention of the member states. Besides this, sectoral cooperation with the industrialists, trade unions, and national experts are occasionally organised in various sectors, such as aeronautics, shipbuilding, data-processing, paper and textiles.

About 1970 the necessity of defining a general industrial policy was clearly and publicly asserted: such is the aim of the Memorandum of the Commission to the Council, entitled 'The Industrial Policy of the Community' EEC Commission, Brussels, 1970. The objective chosen by the authors was: 'to allow industry to derive the maximum advantages from the existence and size of the Common Market' (p. 9). The way in which they hoped to establish this industrial policy included the following:

— The achievement of a unified market by the elimination of technical obstacles, the opening-up of the public sector and the abolition of fiscal frontiers.
— Common procurement of technologically advanced products.
— The unification of the judicial, fiscal and financial laws.
— The restructuring of enterprises through the elimination of obstacles to the formation of transnational European enterprises, using to this end public credits for industrial development in the sectors of advanced technology.
— The organisation of changes and adaptation by facilitating changing jobs, industrial exploitation of innovation, improvement in management of enterprises, and in the recruitment of their managers and directors.
— The extension of Community solidarity in economic relations with third parties, in particular by way of the common commercial policy.

In spite of its qualities, the Memorandum gives an impression of dissatisfaction. There is a clear contrast between the wealth of information that it gives on the situation of the Community's industry and the absence of a precise political engagement. The quarrel concerning the enlargement of the Community, the absence of a political consensus on the part of the member states on the orientation to give to industrial policy and the insistence on the principle of 'juste retour' delayed the governments' support to this loose industrial policy until the Declaration of Paris in October 1972.

On the basis of the Declaration of Paris, the Commission produced, as from May 1973, the 'programme for industrial and technological policy', also called the Spinelli Report, which is a simpler version of the 1970 Memorandum where the rare positive instruments contained in the 1970 document such as common procurement policies of technologically advanced products, development contracts primarily given to firms willing to carry out technological development on a transnational basis, are dropped or watered down.

The report emphasises the need to create a single market, to facilitate business integration and to promote enterprises of European scale. Since 1973, some progress has been realised among others in the field of harmonisation of national regulations, the opening-up of national markets for purchasing by public and semi-public sectors by forbidding any 'preference' or reservation for national production and cooperation between small and medium-sized enterprises. In the field of science and technology, the need was stressed for the coordination of national science and technology policies, joint execution of projects of Community interest, more effective flow of scientific and technical information, technology forecasting and the creation of an effective organisational structure.

In a communication to the Council,[2] the Commission stressed once more the need for the Community to implement specific policies favouring structural adjustment. Besides measures designed to facilitate product standardisation and the growth of truly Europeanwide corporations to take advantage of Europe's inherent economies of scale, the main proposition of this document concerns the suggestion to add an element of 'Community preference' in all cases where industrial development involves the participation of public authorities, such as the setting of technical norms and standards, the public procurement policy, the R & D policy, etc.

Despite the willingness of the Commission to engage in positive actions, the member states have not until now endowed it with new powers. Consequently, the European industrial policy remains a competitive-oriented one based essentially on negative actions.

Use of the competition and commercial policy for the achievement of industrial policy objectives

We will successively consider the case of declining sectors and progressive industries. Let us first remark that the proposals made by the Commission to the Council emphasised the importance of new industry elements and placed the stress upon labour mobility, application of new technologies and improved effectiveness of business management. They did not even discuss the specific techniques to be applied to industries in decline. In fact, the problems involved in coping with industries in decline are a major preoccupation of the Community's industrial policy.

Declining industries. Given that the Community does not have the power (or the financial resources) to step in and rationalise industries in difficulties, any intervention will emanate from member state governments. It is therefore not surprising to observe that nine-tenths of all industrial policy in the EEC takes place at the national level. But the Community can exert three forms of leverage: it has the power to regulate state aid (article 92), to encourage desirable forms of cooperation between firms (article 85 (3)), and is in a position to control or influence imports from third countries.

It is important to stress that the entire action of the Community rests upon the need to promote an industrial structure that can face up to worldwide competition.[3] Within this framework, the Commission explicitly recognises the role of state aid in speeding up the response of the private enterprise system to new opportunities, to correct serious regional imbalances, to permit smooth cutbacks in certain activities where it is desirable for social reasons, or to neutralise, at least temporarily, certain distortions of competition due to action outside the Community. The aims, forms and conditions relating to such aid, justifiable in that they facilitate the orderly development of industry structures, must not conflict with the Community's general objectives[4] and must be designed in such a way as to entail a minimum of distortion of competition. Therefore, aid should be transparent, selective and temporary. Furthermore, in cases of industries that encounter structural problems across the Community (ship-building, textiles, man-made fibres, steel), specific guidelines have been developed which lead to the specification of the following principles:

— production aids should be conditional on action by the recipient which will facilitate adjustment;
— rescue measures should be limited to cases where they are required to cope with acute social problems;
— aid should not be given to investment projects which would result in capacity being increased unless they applied to more buoyant areas of activity.

As regards private restrictions to competition, the Eighth Report on Competition Policy states (p. 11): 'Although the Community competition law operates by banning certain practices, the possibility of exemptions gives it a certain flexibility. The Commission has made ample use of these derogations to encourage desirable forms of cooperation between firms'.[5] This refers to specialisation, patent licensing, selective dealings agreements, and so on. Furthermore, in cases of structural problems where demand for products manufactured in the Community shows a sharp and persistent downward trend, contrary to the expectations of forecasters and investors, the Community:

is inclined to accept that under certain conditions agreements between firms aimed at reducing structural excess capacity may be authorised under 85 (3) but only where the firms have not simultaneously, whether by agreement or concerted practice, fixed either prices or production or delivered quotas.[6]

This is the answer to an attempt, sustained by the DG IV (industrial affairs), by the man-made fibre industry, to introduce a crisis cartel regulation similar to the one contained in the ECSC Treaty.

As regards the trade policy, the Community has negotiated agreements aimed at providing temporary external protection when the need for a breathing space enabling the industry to make progress in its restructuring efforts was felt. This concerns the textile, steel and shipbuilding industries.[7]

Progressive industries. There were various attempts by the Commission to develop and pursue some sectoral policies under Commission control, for example in the field of aerospace and data-processing, which have been swept away by national actions. As the experience in the framework of Euratom has shown, member states desire to retain programme control in their hands and implement it through national firms.

The action of the Community is now mainly guided by the need to promote the development and diffusion of new technologies. Henceforth, Community policy in pacemaking sectors has taken the form of:

— Provision of information of value for the Community as a whole by stimulating exchanges of information or experience, by setting up multinational groups comprising R & D teams from several member states or by working on the establishment of integrated network informations systems (Euronet-Dyane, Insis).
— Promotion of European norms, European patents and trade marks, which aims at easing the access of firms to the whole European market.
— Opening-up of public procurement markets, e.g. in the field of telecommunications.

Coordination at the European level is promoted when EC has a comparative advantage in reaching international agreements to prevent escalation at national levels, e.g. in the fields of technical standards and health or safety norms.

Cooperation on a transnational basis is favoured in order to avoid the development of big national champions sustained and protected by national authorities by allowing funds to international teams or researchers. A first realization is the five-year European Strategic Programme for Research and Development in Information Technologies (ESPRIT), agreed upon by the Council in May 1984. Its aim is to develop an alternative to the next generation of computer projects under way in Japan and the United States. The idea is to overcome fragmentation of the industry around the ten member states by inducing collaboration across national boundaries within a programme which has specific priorities. This stress on collaboration between companies focuses on 'pre-competitive' research designed to lay the foundations for the different commercial policies each participant will adopt when it comes to the product development stage.

Similar programmes in the field of telecommunications (RACE), biotechnology and industrial technology (BRITE) have been approved in 1985. Even if the funds available for such a policy are rather limited,[8] EC spending undervaluates EC contribution as EC often finances only part of the total value which it is sponsoring and as the EC contribution is merely one of coordination.[9]

These developments affected the implementation of both competition and trade policies. In the anti-trust area, a more flexible approach was adopted in 1985 with regard to constructive forms of cooperation between firms. Agreements which favour the dissemination of new technology (block exemption for patent and know-how licensing) and agreements which allow to diminish the cost of R & D, to increase the size of risk that can be afforded and save time in the technological cooperation (block exemption which covers agreements providing for joint R & D and joint exploitation of results) are now exempted under article 85.3. At the external level, duties on products, mainly chemicals, medical supplies and products of the electronics and aircraft industries have been temporarily suspended in order to ease the introduction of foreign technology.

4. PERSPECTIVES

Confronted by a tendency to generalized national protectionism which could cause the disintegration of the European Community and in the absence of a political consensus on a coherent and specific European industrial policy, officials of the Community are led to adopt a policy based on selective, supra-nationally supervised and negotiated agreements.

The potential drawbacks of such an orientation are a transformation from a Common Market towards a cartel organization and an absence of coherence in the implementation of the different policies. Concerning the former, the experience of the steel industry does not give the impression of a real desire for common policy but rather for cartel arrangement implying all the problems of instability and inforcement, since the temptation to cheat is strong (because the returns from cheating are substantial) and the degree of control is weak. On the contrary, the case of aerospace has shown the ability of the Commission and member states to work in pursuit of a viable aerospace capability.[10] Concerning the latter, the absence of well-defined priorities among different goals favours the tendency for conflicts to be solved through internal negotiation between the different divisions of the Community. Besides the problems of power conflicts and inefficiencies, this mechanism increases the feeling among citizens that Europe is more a technocratic organization than an executive entrusted with the carrying out of a policy, the guidelines of which have been set by the Parliament,[11] and therefore hampers any political willingness in favour of more integration. Europe has to show its ability to solve problems in a better and easier way than member states separately.

Whilst some success, in terms of the organization of the cut of overcapacities and of modernization of production facilities, seems on the way to be achieved in sectors such as steel and textiles, the Commission has difficulties in resisting the pressure on the Common Market to become fragmented in industries where national aid and national limits on imports from outside the Community remain substantial (e.g. the automobile sector). In progressive industries, the action of the Communities is slowed down by the sluggishness member states show in harmonizing their national regulations and their reluctance to increase the financial means of the Commission. Hence, it was only on 12 November 1984 that the Council adopted two recommendations — based on proposals made by the Commission in 1980 — on the harmonization of standards in the field of telecommunications and on the first phase of the opening-up of public tele-communications procurement contracts. In order to avoid delay in the field of harmonization of technical standards, the Commission now favours the mutual recognition of type-approval procedures against the adoption of uniform standards which was systematically blocked by recourse to the rule of unanimity. Concerning the financial means, let us notice that, although the need to increase the proportion of Community resources devoted to finance priority Community research and development activites was asserted several times during the year 1984, it was only on 19 December 1984 that the Council did approve the proposals of the Commission and agree upon the appropriations necessary for the implementation of the different programmes. These appropriations amounted to one-third of the amount originally estimated by the Commission. In the case of the ESPRIT programme, for example, one might question the probability of success of such a project when observing that the total funding over the five years does not even approach IBM's R & D budget for 1984 alone. Furthermore, the development of the EUREKA project, with the aim of favouring high technological cooperation within Western Europe, which is under direct control of national governments, is once more a clear example of simultaneous tensions between national and European authorities and convergence of interest. As in the case of Esprit, a Eureka project has to be transnational, to use advanced technology, and to offer adequate financial commitment by the companies involved. However, at the Hanover summit of November 1985, European governments were not able to take any specific decision on the site of the Eureka secretariat, its link with the Commission and its future powers;[12] bigger countries want to keep extra bureaucracy at its minimum, smaller countries are suspicious that, without adequate channels of information, they and their industries will be bypassed.

Finally, one might ask if in some cases the concern of European authorities for industrial policy objectives did not come too late. Hence, in the field of video recorders, it is a little surprising to read in the last Report on Competition Policy, p. 204, that:

the ability to respond to specific demands in new markets is crucial for the ability to survive in the consumer electronics industry. Philips and the successful Japanese firms have maintained and developed these skills by attempting to set *de facto* standards for new products . . . Philips failed to do this for their VCR system partly because other European manufacturers elected to support Japanese standards . . . In contrast to the European industry, the Japanese industry succeeded in applying the strategy of an early anticipation of potential markets and a quick occupation of these markets through the creation of sufficient production capacities.

when one knows that a negative decision was taken in 1977 by the Commission concerning the exemption of an agreement between Philips and the main German producers in the field of video recorders on the use by the Germans of common technical norms based on Philips' patents.[13]

Without further progress in the field of political integration, there is a danger that Europe will remain essentially a free-trade area and never move towards an economic union. Europe will then be prevented from playing an active role in an international game, the rules of which become more and more complex.

Positive signs in this field resulted from the Milan summit in 1985. They materialized in 1986 with the adoption of the proposed Treaty on the European Union which extends the use of the qualified majority vote and the role of the Parliament.

NOTES

1. Optimum policies — taxes or subsidies — are very sensitive to the extent of competition in the market. See Eaton and Grossman (1983).
2. 'A Community Strategy to Develop Europe's Industry', Brussels, 23 October 1981.
3. Hence specific sectoral aid schemes always have a limit in time. In the steel industry, this has been fixed at the first of January 1986.
4. Hence, 'The compatibility of an aid with the common market must be assessed from the standpoint of the Community rather than of a single member state;. Twelfth Report on Competition Policy, 1982, p. 10.
5. See also the Thirteenth Report on Competition Policy, 1983, p. 12.
6. This interpretation is reassessed in the Thirteenth Report on Competition Policy, 1983, p. 14.
7. See Van Steenbergen et al (1983, p. 78) which states: 'in so far as the achievements of solutions require international agreements, the Community is much better placed to take part in the relevant discussions than are the member states . . . It may therefore be anticipated that, internally, the crisis will strengthen the member states, while at the same time, and sometimes in contradiction to that process, strengthening the Community externally'.
8. It was estimated in 1980 that EC spending on R & D amounted to about 1 per cent of the total (i.e. governmental and industrial) appropriations.
9. In 1986, 263 enterprises, 104 universities and 81 research institutes, which represent about 20,000 researchers, did participate in the several projects approved under the ESPRIT programme (Nineteenth General Report on the Activities of the European Communities, p. 159).
10. See Rallo, 1984.
11. The lack of interest in the last elections to the European Parliament is significant in this respect.
12. Not mentioning that the financial commitment of each member state still remains rather vague.
13. See the Seventh Report on Competition, p. 110.

REFERENCES

Commission of the European Communities, Reports on Competition Policy, Brussels.

Dixit, A.K., 1986, 'Optimal Trade and Industrial Policies for the U.S. Automobile Industry', Paper presented at the conference on 'Empirical Methods for International Trade', Cambridge, Mass., 3–4 April 1986.

Dixit, A.K. and Kyle, A., 1985, 'The Use of Protection and Subsidies for Entry Promotion and Deterrence', American Economic Review, March 1975, 139–52.

Eaton, J. and Grossman, G.M., 1983, 'Optimal Trade and Industrial Policy under Oligopoly', Quarterly Journal of Economics, forthcoming.

Hartley, K., 1984, 'The Implications of National and Community Commercial Policies for the Development of the EC's Technological Industries', CEPS Working Documents, No.7.

Jacquemin, A., 1983a, 'Industrial Policies and the Community', in P. Coffey (ed.), *Main Economic Policy Areas of the EEC*, The Hague, Martinus Nijhoff.

Jacquemin, A. and de Jong, H., 1977, *European Industrial Organization*, London, Macmillan Press.

Jacquemin, A., 1983b, '*Los Ajustos Estructurales y la Coordinacion de las Estrategias Industriales en la ECC. Problemas y Perspectivas*', in *Papeles de Economia Espanola*, **15**.

Meade, J., 1976, *The Just Economy*, London, Allen and Unwin.

Rallo, J., 1984, 'The European Community's Industrial Policy Revisited: The Case of Aerospace', *Journal of Common Market Studies*, **22**, No.3, March.

Steenbergen, J., Van de Clerq, G. and Foque, R., 1983, *Change and Adjustment; External Relations and Industrial Policy in the European Community*, Deventer, Kluwer Law and Taxation Publishers.

Swann, D., 1983, *Competition and Industrial Policy in the European Community*, London, Methuen & Co.

5

Sectoral Industrial Planning in the Andean Group

Alicia Puyana

This study discusses the case of industrial cooperation first generally and then specifically in the context of the Andean Group. It later defines the role assigned to sectoral planning in the Treaty of Cartagena and evaluates its outcome on the basis of the nature of the conflicts that have arisen between these countries.

It also discusses levels of conflict according to the relative development of the member countries, showing how this has affected industrial co-operation and the development of sectoral programmes for industrial growth, while at the same time paving the way towards the Andean Group's first crisis at the beginning of 1975, the symptoms of which can be felt partially even today. The reaction to the crisis brought its cost: the resignation of one of its member countries, Chile, as well as a relaxing of the integration agreements within sectoral planning, in tariff policies and in the treatment of foreign capital; in other words, a movement in the opposite direction of the ideas sustained by the neo-functionalist 'spill-over'.

THE NEED FOR INDUSTRIAL PLANNING

There are various causes of the concentration of industrial activities in already established centres. For example, the existence of economies of scale and external economies, or the relation between transport and raw materials costs and those of the finished product; spread effects and the development of technology which has made many production processes independent from sources of raw materials, which tends to save on labour (and not only in industry), generating a surplus labour force predominantly in crop-producing rural areas. Lastly, but of no less importance, the mobility of production factors does not produce the hoped-for levelling of costs and payments to factors.

Above and beyond the aforementioned considerations, within the framework of economic integration in underdeveloped countries, industrial planning can be justified in that: it avoids the waste of limited resources in a reduced industrial market; or, because it allows for specialization, without requiring costly duplication of investments; or due to the maximum use of economies of scale and for the need to prevent even more pronounced imbalances among countries which act as a threat to the Group's stability.

THE DISTINCT LEVEL OF DEVELOPMENT AND THE SIZE OF THE ANDEAN MARKETS

The need for centralized programming for industrial location is based on two elements: on the limitation of the market and productive resources and on the differences in the level of industrial development of the involved countries and their potential for future development. In the ALALC (Latin American Free Trade Association), the Andean Group and in the Community of the Central American Common Market two conditions could be found that required sectoral programming; in all of these there are mechanisms which have been designed for this purpose. Nevertheless, Andean Sectoral Programming has innovated industrial integration policies among developing countries owing to the fact that the Treaty of Cartagena embraces the basic principle of controlling the market up to a certain point in order to avoid imbalances among countries. This also permits a more efficient use of productive factors through full use of existing resources and an increase in productivity.

The Andean Group tended towards concentration of the Gross Domestic Product (GDP) during its first ten years of existence, which permit the deduction that there will not be significant changes in another direction. In 1978, Colombia and Venezuela produced 67.8 per cent of the Andean GDP while Bolivia and Ecuador produced 12.1 per cent. The figures for 1970 were 67 per cent and 10.4 per cent.[1] The GDP *per capita* is often used to measure the relative industrialization of a country and is a sure means for measuring its standard of living.[2] When referring to integration, this represents the 'productivity gap' and is a cause of diverging national aspirations. Countries with lower aspirations with regard to the GDP industrial value naturally wish to attain levels similar to those reached by more advanced countries which at the same time, and equally justifiably, wish to reach the levels already attained by developed countries.[3]

It is not necessary to expand upon the limitation of the effective Latin American demand for manufactured products, especially those that require significant economies of scale and for which the markets were previously freed. In general, the conclusion can be drawn, on the basis of studies of consumer structure, that only those populations with yearly incomes constantly above $1.500 since 1973 provide an effective demand for this type of manufactured product. This reduces the effective demand in decisions related to investments.[4]

For the Andean Group, for example, only 9 per cent of the total population has an income above $1.500. This means that in 1980 only 6.6 millions (in 1985 that figure will be 10 million) are an effective market for sophisticated manufactured products.[5] Nevertheless, they are not markets made up of 6 million people but rather the mathematical sum of five national markets divided by borders, with elevated transportation costs and more than precarious means of communication. The horizontal widening of markets is a partial solution to the problems of demand and indeed only allows for marginal cost reductions. Although better conditions for production are attained, these are still far from reaching international efficiency levels and the margin of utilization of economies of scale continues to be inferior to that of developed countries.

PRODUCTIVE EFFICIENCY VERSUS REDISTRIBUTIVE EQUILIBRIUM

The problems of disequilibrium within the Andean Group are severe. The initiators of the Treaty were well aware of the need for special measures to induce balanced economic growth and to prevent and correct the action of concentration effects which might threaten the stability of the Group. However, the ambiguity of the Treaty's article 32 has given rise to different interpretations of balanced development from which conflicts have arisen. The Junta interprets the basic objective of sectoral programming to be the equitable distribution of the benefits of integration and the balanced development of the countries: 'The Treaty of Cartagena is an innovation with respect to LAFTA, which makes programming the basic tool for controlling the equity of the system'.[6]

The original idea of the national representatives was to give greater emphasis to the free trade programme,[7] and to stress that the aim of the sectoral programme was to promote the efficient location of industries and savings on capital resources rather than the redistribution of benefits. The change to a strong planning orientation came about because of two elements. Firstly, there was an interest in giving concessions to Venezuela, whose entry to the group was vital, which was demanding both a change of emphasis towards programming and the reduction of the scope of the free trade programme. Secondly, there was the definite support for planning among some technical advisers, who saw clearly that only through planned allocation could the industrial development of the less industrialized countries be stimulated.[8] Both the positions of the advisers and the Junta's interpretation were reinforced by the fact that the Treaty contained no other measures for distributing benefits, revenues or financial aid, or the transfer of resources to solve chronic deficits.[9]

All the member-countries of the Andean Group joined the Pact in the hope that the enlarged demand would lead both to faster growth in the industrial sector and to the establishing of industries which would have been impossible to contemplate previously, given the size of individual national markets, or which could only have operated with excessively high social costs.[10] However, if maximum efficiency and output were the only goals, then there would be a tendency towards industrial concentration in the relatively more developed countries and a possible increase in disequilibria. But the Treaty's idea of balanced development is that the location of industry should follow a pattern of distribution distinct from that which would lead to minimum costs and maximum output. Only in this way could the less developed close the gap in industrial development. The contradiction between productive efficiency or the 'optimum' location of industry (accelerated regional growth) and the equitable distribution of benefits (preferential growth of the less developed countries) through accelerated industrial production, became evident from the outset of work on the sectoral programmes. The Junta said that sectoral programming 'is from the practical point of view, the instrument upon which the participation of all the member countries in the development of the integrated zone rests, especially in industrial activities.'[11] From this it is clear that the equitable distribution of the benefits of integration is not simply redistributive but developmental; it is a question not simply of transferring monetary resources, but rather of the mobilization of productive resources through the planned location of industrial activity.

What the principle of balanced growth, as stated in the Cartagena Agreement, really means is that the relatively more highly developed countries voluntarily give up part of the industrial growth which would otherwise be concentrated in their area. It also means that they should accept the need to absorb into their own cost structure, the costs of the industrialization induced in the less developed member countries.

THE EXPERIENCE WITH SECTORAL PLANNING

The nature of the conflicts

We analysed the Junta's records of the discussions on the several sectoral industrial development programmes (SIDPs) so far presented by the Junta. The discussions took place at technical level first of all, and then at the political level at the Commission's meetings. Our analysis showed that the following were the main problems that arose over how to measure the costs and benefits of integration, and over the equitable distribution of benefits.

(a) The measurement of the benefits of participating in an integration scheme is no simple task and requires previous common agreements and definitions. It has to take account of changes in income (in terms of social value), changes in the rate of growth, trends in foreign trade, changes in the volume and structure of employment, fiscal revenues, and the 'backwash' and 'spread' effects of industrial development. The Junta failed in its attempt to get acceptance for the regional strategy of development which might serve as a framework for establishing those criteria. The measurement of the effects over time, especially those related to externalities, is very complex, especially when the available data are unreliable, and when relative prices upon which the evaluation is made change because of the impact of the increase in investment and the restructuring of the economy under the integration programme.[12] The establishing of shadow prices is not a simple matter even at national level. Further, the definition of 'national welfare', difficult enough in any context, becomes exceedingly problematical when dealing with countries in each of which the social welfare functions may be different. One country may prefer a lower real rate of growth and a better distribution of income or an immediate increase in employment; another country may seek to maximize the rate of growth even at the cost of lower employment or immediate consumption.

(b) The second problem arises in defining the equity of the distribution of benefits. It is possible to argue that distribution is equitable when each member country receives absolute benefits either proportionate to, or equal to, its population, or to the gross domestic income, or to *per capita* income. The final criterion assumed is more political than technical. The Treaty contains no clear definition of equity, but one can gather from the articles that it is held to mean the reduction of the gap between the more and the less developed countries.[13] The existence of large disequilibria between Bolivia and Ecuador and the other four member countries, when measured in terms of GDP, industrial product, or total or *per capita* foreign trade, seems to justify giving the greatest priority to the consolidation of the union and to the narrowing of the gap between the less developed countries and the rest.

Besides the above problems, which can be classified under the political economy of integration, others arise which are of a technical nature but no less urgently in need of solution:

(a) The scope of the programme is too wide. The reserved list includes 1,800 products. Allocating and planning the investments for such a large number is a burdensome task. However, the most important problem regarding the scope of the programme is not the number of items, but the lack of differentiation with regard to the complexity of the technological process involved in their production. The Treaty sets 1980 as the date by which total free trade should be achieved in the area. Whatever the level of technological complexity, the investments have to be undertaken by the countries as quickly as possible, in order that they might have an effective monopoly and in 1980 reach such an advantage that it ceases to be attractive for other countries to set up competitive production. The compulsion to invest and consolidate the advantage granted can result in inefficiencies.[14]

(b) While the programmes may have been drawn up coherently sector by sector, inter-sectoral integration is not taken into account. Among others, the reasons for this methodology could be the priorities established by the Commission based upon the importance of the sectors, and the lack of prior definition of the subregional industrial policy. Having packages which are negotiated independently has led to interminable discussions as each country tries to obtain the maximum number of allocations in each sector. It has also made it difficult to use one sector to compensate another. A country with limited possibilities for developing petrochemicals and which is therefore given a small share of the sector cannot be compensated with a larger share of another sector in which it may be more efficient. However, while the use of multi-sectoral packages is desirable, in practice it creates difficulties. Firstly, there are no means by which the relative importance of each sector in the countries' economies can be evaluated and compared. Little is known about the external economies which come from a given project. Within the national plans, it is difficult to find a classification of industries in accordance with national priorities. Moreover, few adequate analytical tools exist to permit the measurement of the effects of an investment in one sector *vis-à-vis* another.[15] There is another reason which shows 'compensation' to be difficult. There are too few foot-loose industries and the advantage of the relatively more developed countries is such that almost every sector will be allocated in their territory. During the last two years, it was impossible to reach agreements on criteria regarding multi-sectoral programming.

(c) The tendencies which dominated the process of industrialization in previous decades continue. The objective is the substitution of imports over the subregion so that, by 1980, the group will have a productive structure similar to those of Argentina and Mexico ten years ago. The system is programmed by starting from the final product, and according to the existing capacity, assuming the rationality of the process used in the past. Not corrective elements have been introduced into the system, based for example on criteria of the abundance or scarcity of factors, the need to restructure existing patterns of consumption or the technology employed. As was noted earlier, the industries included in the programme tend to be capital-intensive and directed towards the upper segments of the market. It is therefore to be expected that the bottlenecks arising from the exhaustion of the first stage of import substitution will simply be repeated in due course. These include inflationary disequilibria, the marginalization of a large part of the population, the persistent inequality of income distribution and increasing dependence upon the export sector. The basis for this conclusion is the fact that the size of the market is not an exogenous variable, but a result of historical information. The only new factor is the enlargement of demand via the aggregation of the top end of the member countries' markets; this has not been accompanied by modifications in the income structure, in the rate of labour absorption, in the inefficiency of the agricultural sector or in the supply structure.

(d) The criterion of 'equilibrium' considers only the size of the designated market, neglecting dynamic concepts such as the generation of linkages, external economies, or technological changes: that is, those changes in the productive structure that are the final goal of sectoral programming and of economic integration. Again, the tendency for countries to try to obtain the greatest possible share of the market in each sector is reinforced; thus they lose sight of the long-term effects that may be more important. The approved programmes will suffer from inefficiencies in the form of losses of economies of scale because market criteria were applied in drawing up the plans, because national industrial priorities have not been defined, and because the prestige of the individual countries tends to be measured in terms of industrial development and diversification.

THE CONFLICTS AS REFLECTED IN NATIONAL ATTITUDES

The ambiguity of the Treaty in defining the priorities of efficiency and equity and the impossibility of agreeing on a subregional strategy of industrial development that would take account of the various national stances, meant that conflicts arose between countries. These became evident during the negotiation of each national programme. Confronted by these difficulties, especially by the poor results coming both from meetings of the Planning Committee (*Consejo de Planificación*) and from the discussions on the *Bases*,[16] the Junta avoided initiating any discussion of the contents of the programmes, or of the definition of equity, efficiency and balanced development, or of the common macroeconomic indicators to be used for drawing up and evaluating the programmes. Thus, the differences had to be resolved at the level of each individual negotiation.

The Popular Unity Government in Chile maintained a 'planning' stance within the framework of an import substitution policy. It used its membership of the Andean Group to reinforce its industrial policy, especially to argue for additional protection, and for the stimulation and nationalization of those sectors designated as the motors for development: a policy that was in complete agreement with the model implicit in the Treaty. The present absolutist government has moved to the liberal economic model, similar to that of Colombia. The two countries' strategy is based on the use of the market as the central mechanism for regulating the economy to the international market, and in which efficiency has to be measured in terms of international prices and the cost of foreign currency. This opening-up should also be the means by which distortions arising from the 'indiscriminate policy of import substitution' are eliminated. In both Chile and Colombia, the State would only intervene in strategic sectors: mining, oil, the physical infrastructure. The relative profitability on the different sectors would be determined by means of tax tariff policies, and it would be the private entrepreneur who would decide where, when and how much to invest, using the criterion of the maximization of profit.

It is clear that, for Bolivia and Ecuador, sectoral programming offers an opportunity to accelerate and strengthen their import substitution, since the tariffs in the respective programmes always grant special protection to the industries allocated to them. Thus the height of the tariff depends upon the location of industries, and not on the maximum level of subregional inefficiency previously existing. These two countries have to mobilize important public resources in order to finance investment; because private savings are inadequate, the state becomes the protagonist in carrying out the industrial development laws.[17] The industrial laws of the two countries show how priority has been given to a wide selection of basic sectors, all of which are reserved for the SIDP and towards which the policies of protection and development are directed.

Peru decided to join the Andean Group when it embarked upon a process of social change in which the state was to assume the responsibility for directing the economy and for allocating resources from the centre according to a development plan. As in the Chilean case under Presidents Frei and Allende, there was agreement on development, a strong state sector that would be increasingly active in productive investment, and a continuation of the import substitution process.[18] The government always upheld the Treaty in its declarations, and in its industrial plans it included the subregional market when drawing up the plans of key projects. It made its continued membership conditional upon the realization of the sectoral programmes. The present government has made no statements contrary to the earlier attitude, at least on matters touching on the development of sectoral programming. Some important changes of policy can, however, be seen that may lead to the relaxing of planning mechanisms and the consequent strengthening of the market. The most important here is the postponement of the implementation of certain basic industrial projects, as a part of the stabilization programme. These are precisely the projects for which the expanded markets are very important, and were the reason for Peru's firm attitude towards the priority to be granted to sectoral programming rather than to the other tools of integration. Secondly, there is a drastic tariff reduction, a liberal exchange policy and a weakening of the public sector of the economy.

Venezuela's industrial policy is of necessity based upon the possibilities of an enlarged market together with the opportunities for specialization provided by sectoral programmes. Venezuelan industrial strategy tries to shift the structure of the productive sector towards intermediate and capital goods, to make a more rational use of human and material resources, to use installed capacity more fully and to create more employment. These changes are difficult to bring about on the basis of the internal market, despite the high purchasing power of the population. Venezuela's participation in the Andean Group is not justified in terms of solving balance-of-payments problems or of conserving foreign currency. The primary export sector provides the economy with sufficient resources. The justification is rather in terms of the search for better investment opportunities in the country and the subregion, and the better utilization of productive resources.[19]

To sum up, the heart of the conflict lies in the division that runs right through the whole political economy of the integration movement. On the one hand, there were those countries that wanted to use the SIDPs primarily to reduce disequilibria and to support the protectionist conception of the new phase of industrial development, and the additional intrinsic elements of planning and state intervention. On the other side were those that tended towards greater efficiency, measured in terms of the cost of foreign exchange, and towards a greater role for market forces in their internal economic policies, and in their relations with the world market.

Regarding the negotiation of timetables, the same polarized position arose between the same two groups of countries. On one side, Chile and Colombia hoped that a large proportion, if not all, of the products on the reserved list would be moved to the automatic reduction lists, thus ending or limiting as far as possible the scope of programming. The other four countries tried to extend periods for all reserve lists, and to 'freeze', or at least, to slow down, the automatic reductions in the commercial programme until sectoral programming had been advanced proportionately.[20] The impasse was broken by the adoption of Decision No. 100 which, apart from extending the period for approving the SIDPs (and the CET, Common External Tariff) by two years, made it possible to approve SIDPs with the participation of only two-thirds of the member countries. It also sets out the conditions under which the non-participating countries can eventually join the SIDPs. For the CET, it introduced the 'tariff band'.

The two modifications represent a short-term compromise between the two conflicting camps. Chile and Colombia are able to place themselves within the lower levels of the tariff band and not take part in the SIDPs, which is in line with their policies of allocating resources according to comparative advantage, measured in world market terms. By participating in the SIDPs, other countries would withhold a part of their development from market forces and they would use the CET for allocating resources according to the SIDPs and to their economic strategies. However, this does not appear to be a wise solution.

Those countries that place themselves in the lower levels of the tariff band would have favourable balances because they would offer less protection to the products of other member countries while they would receive from them greater protection for their own exports. Countries with a lower CET would increase their imports from third countries, a factor that would make it more difficult to implement the rules of origin.

This solution is only a passing phase in terms of programming. Article 6 of Decision No. 100 states that the Commission will fix the terms and conditions for the adoption of the CET by the countries not participating in the SIDPs, and decide how they should open their markets to the products of the participants in the SIDPs. Again, such negotiations would present problems concerning efficiency and the non-participant countries would try to gain tariff reductions that would fit in with their own structures and levels of efficiency. For the participating countries this would be unacceptable because they would have been forced to develop their production within a reduced market, implying higher costs, and less benefit from economies of scale. This argument is especially relevant because of the proportion of the sub-regional market the non-participating countries might represent.

It seems unlikely that the problems can be resolved definitively, or that sectoral programming and the philosophy of the Treaty will be saved. In effect, Colombia bases its anti-SIDP position on the argument that the programmes do not lower but rather increase the costs of production. Besides, given that in Colombia there is no political decision in favour of planning the economy at the national level, there could be none for planning it at the regional level; even less so when this would mean the transfer of costs and resources prejudicial to its own position.[21] This conclusion was proved to be true during the last Commission Meeting held in Bogotá last September, whose conclusions show that the only programme to be consolidated is the commercial one. Further steps in industrial planning or in CET were neither approved nor programmed.

ACHIEVEMENTS OF SECTORAL PROGRAMMING

Four programmes have been approved: light engineering (September 1972), petrochemical (September 1975), automobile (October 1976), and the iron and steel industry (in December 1980). All of these were accepted at a time of crisis and, it could be thought, because the countries concerned wanted to show that neither the impulse towards, nor the faith in, integration had been lost.

The light engineering programme covers two hundred items (machine tools, electrical machinery and equipment, and instruments). It requires a total investment of $450 million and should generate 40,000 jobs. Its annual value of production is calculated to be $500 million (1974) and the demand in 1980 is expected to rise to $800 million.

The petrochemical programme was the subject of very prolonged discussions; presented in 1971, it was approved four years later. It requires investments of $2.620 million to generate 8,000 jobs, mainly at the higher levels of technical skill. Optimal efficiency is not guaranteed because of the multiplicity of plants. It covers fifty-six petrochemical products, some of which are exclusive to one country; others are shared by two or three.

The automobile programme was signed in September 1977. On this occasion also there was an element of drama.[22] It was possible to adopt Decision No. 12., after four years of negotiations in which the external sector played an important role, only because of the firm positions held by Venezuela and Peru, which made their membership of the Group and the continuation of the commercial programme conditional on the approval of the remaining SIDPs. The fact that the programme is very flexible suggests that it is probably not very efficient, since it allows a rather large number of plants to exist, and because of the dispersal of plants and assembly agreements.[23]

The signing of the above-mentioned SIDPs does not modify our earlier analysis, for several reasons. In the first place, we would mention the nature of the agreements. All SIDPs were approved during periods of political crisis with the intention of showing that the Treaty was alive. All are flexible enough to permit each country to develop fully its own industrial structure; and in all the principle of specialization is weakened by numerous shared allocations. Secondly, the results so far are almost negligible and represent trade in goods from already existing plants.

A rapid evaluation of what has happened to the two programmes since they were approved allows us to draw some conclusions regarding trade and investment, but not before noting that the entry of Venezuela after the signing of the light engineering programme and the withdrawal of Chile, after the approval of the petrochemical programme, have meant the reformulation and renegotiation of already approved allocations. We suggest that the approval of the respective SIDPs does not necessarily mean their success. We still see that only trade in existing production has grown while the basic agreements involved in programming have not been fulfilled. Owing to the limit on time and space of this chapter, we shall only analyse the oldest and most successful of the SIDPs: the light engineering programme.

LIGHT ENGINEERING PROGRAMME

Trade in this sector increased because thirty-three of the seventy-two units allocated were in production before the signing of the programme, at which time Colombia and Peru accounted for the greatest volume of production. During the period 1973–77, investments were made for 21.4 million dollars, basically for the expansion of existing productions.

The Junta's evaluation documents for 1975–80 showed that no investments were made in production that did not exist before the signing of the programme. According to the Junta, the main cause is that: 'The member countries are not convinced that an enlarged market actually exists, which is prejudicial to the taking of investment initiatives'.[24]

Uncertainty arises from the non-fulfillment of basic agreements, for example over the adoption of the CET and the freeing of trade in favour of those countries given allocations, and over article 33 of the Treaty, which refers to the advantages that could be given to programmed products from preferential public sector purchases. Most importantly, the agreement not to encourage production allocated to other countries has not been fulfilled. Also, it is important to take into account the difficulties of programming and locating industries in accordance with criteria such as equilibrium between countries, when the private sector is to realize the investment in an economic climate in which, theoretically, subsidies would be eliminated in the near future. Companies export only a small part of their production and they increasingly tend to locate themselves according to market demands. There is also a lack of aggressiveness on the part of exporters.

The Junta notes that in 1977 there was a stagnation of activity and that, apart from some expansion of existing production in Colombia and Peru, and one new plant in the latter, the most notable events were the closure of the plant in Bolivia and the difficulties of three Ecuadorian companies owing to problems in trading their products. The evaluation documents for 1979–80 reconfirm the earlier reports.

CONCLUSIONS

It is the differences in economic development that have made the implementation of SIDPs impossible, since the costs resulting from allocating industries according to equilibrium criteria were considered by the more developed countries to be too high.

Those same differences were the source of conflicts among the less and the more developed countries, conflicts that basically expressed themselves in terms of contradictions between the principles of efficiency and of equity. The acuteness of the contradictions is due to the characteristics of the Andean subregion and the nature of the Treaty's economic model.

There is a significant asymmetry in industrial development and effective demand between the less and the more developed member countries. This makes the policy of balanced development more costly, and means that more resources have to be transferred from one country to another. Further, the limited size of the subregional market for the type of industries for which the new stage of substitution is aimed and for the level of national value-added expected necessarily makes the subregional policy of industrialization more costly. And since other compensatory mechanisms are lacking in the Treaty, the whole weight of redistribution problems therefore falls upon the location of industry. It seems that the members are more disposed to transfer taxation revenues or to create compensation funds than to relinquish to another country production that would have been in its own territory were it not for the industrial programme.

The disagreements among countries delayed approval of the programmes, but also reduced the level of specialization among countries, with the consequent loss of economies of scale owing to the multiplication of plants in the three SIDPs so far agreed.

Trade has increased in those goods included in the approved programmes, goods that were already being produced before the signing of the Treaty. The progress in new investments is insignificant. It is valid to conclude, as we did in regard to the commercial programme, that the industrialists' main interest is only in exporting surpluses and that investments are based on prospects in the national markets. This indicates the difficulty of programming and promoting industries when the national market is not sufficient. There are risks implicit in projects directed towards export — risks that are greater when there is uncertainty over the stability or seriousness of the agreements. Certain aspects of the SIDP policy have not been complied with. We are referring to the agreements not to promote competitive production, to respect specialization programmes and so include allocated projects in national investment and production plans.

The conflicts over the criteria of equity and efficiency were apparently resolved by the weakening of the agreement on industrial specialization and industrial balanced growth. The solution was largely formal and a resurgence of the problem can be expected. Meanwhile, there have been no advances made in regard to the new programmes, and the timetable for the approval of the remaining SIDPs ran out in December 1978. One country continues to oppose the SIDPs and will not approve new ones; this means that the Treaty will lose one, if not more, of its important tools and that the problems of redistribution are still to be resolved.

INDUSTRIAL SECTORAL PLANNING AND ANDEAN MULTINATIONALS

Decision 46 about common rules for multinational corporations and treatment applicable to subregional capital was approved in December 1971. It defines Andean multinationals as those whose principal location is in a member country and whose regional capital comes from more than one member country, each shareholding country owning not less than 15 per cent of the shares. Under Decision 24, capital from one member country invested in another affords multinational status to the company so created and will be managed under the subregional system regulation capital flows, through which it will receive the same treatment granted by this system to national capital. As suggested by Kuczinsky,[25] the general rules of Decision 24 and the concept of the Andean multinational company should be seen as elements of subregional industrial policy, and constitute a serious effort to promote industrial expansion on a planned basis. The Junta has made the first attempt in Latin America to correlate regional industrial planning, regulation of foreign capital, and the removal of trade barriers. These elements are not to be found in LAFTA, which provides exclusively for the removal of trade barriers and for industrial development. The Central American Common Market provides for the establishment of integration industries in certain sectors, with rights to enter the integrated market, but there is no legislation on foreign capital, and no careful selection of industries eligible to be considered as regional.

The Andean Multinational Companies allow countries to invest in other countries' projects. These provisions were considered as an instrument to overcome concentration problems by allowing less efficient countries to invest in the more efficient. But it appears probably that the inflow of capital will aggravate the problems which it is intended to solve. The Andean Multinational Companies are in fact the type of joint companies that Hazlewood considers are the solution to the equitable efficient location contradiction.[26] However, here again the Andean Group experiences are not very encouraging. Decision 46 was not enforced regionally because member countries did not ratify it in time. Chile did so in June 1972, Venezuela and Colombia in September 1973, Bolivia a year later and Ecuador in June 1975. Peru had not ratified Decision 46 till December 1977. The reason for the Peruvian government's delay may be fear of stimulating an outflow of domestic capital to other member countries not subject to the restrictive Peruvian rules. Furthermore, no document creating Multinational Andean Companies has so far been registered in any country, Junta Evaluation documents until now come to the same conclusions. The reason given is the fact that Decision 46 was not in effect until 1976, while Decision 103, giving treatment of national capital to sub-regional capital, thus annulling the special incentives of Decision 46, had not been ratified.

The inapplicability of Decision 46 and its failure to promote the institution of Andean Multinationals made a revision of its most outstanding aspects a necessity: To eliminate the obstacles in Decision 46 for constituting companies and coordinate it with Decision 103. The proposition suggests: to eliminate official permits and other controls if the Andean Multinationals limit themselves to the SIDP. To authorize the return of capital to countries other than Andean countries (Panama) in order to attract Andean capital that had left their countries (for example, Panama); total freedom of exchange, to which countries with exchange control are opposed, although the general situation is more liberal than that which prevailed in 1970; expand from 40 to 49 per cent the participation of foreign capital in the Andean Multinationals; reduce from 15 to 10 per cent the capital subscribed by each of the member countries; authorize legal capacity and freedom of action only for the SIDP and permission to carry out activities only within the territory of member countries.

With regard to widening incentives, a general managerial claim, the solution is difficult since the Andean Multinationals enjoy the same benefits as national companies. Nevertheless, the following incentives are being currently analysed:

— Non-application of the Common External Tariff when the Andean Multinationals import capital goods or raw materials.
— Total import freedom within the subregion; in other words, a more rapid programme for lowering duties or taxes.
— The elimination of taxes for the transfer of benefits. These tend to be quite high: in Bolivia, Peru and Venezuela 30 per cent is applied. In Colombia, 32 per cent and in Ecuador 40 per cent.

Decision No. 46 on Andean Multinationals was never put into effect and to this day not one company has been created under its influence. Apparently, its incentives were scarce and were finally annulled by those created by Decisions 100 and 103, modifying the Common Treatment of foreign capital.

NOTES

1. Junta: *Indicadores socio-económicos de la subregión Andina*, Jun/di 227/rev-3, April 1980.
2. Maizels, A., *Industrial Growth and World Trade*, Cambridge, C.U.P., 1963, Chap. 1.
3. From a study by Kaiser, explaining the differences between Rumania and Bulgaria which aspire to levels of industrialization and living standards like those in Czechoslovakia, while the latter aspires to conditions like those in developed Western countries. M. Kaiser: *The COMECOM; Integration problems of planned economies*, London, Oxford, 1967, p. 205.
4. For example, in the ALALC the relation between the Gross National Industrial Product per capita in Argentina and that of Bolivia in 1978 was 7.6 per cent, while in the Central American Common Market it was 4.0 per cent.
5. Venezuela represents 50 per cent of the effective demand while Chile's withdrawal represented a 14 per cent decrease in the total population and 2 per cent in those earning above 1,500 dollars annually. The ALALC Argentina, despite its reduced population, showed a similar demand for manufactured goods. Bolivia and Ecuador offered a mere 1.9 and 5.9 per cent of the total Andean population with yearly earnings of over 1,500 dollars in 1980.
6. Junta, *Apreciación General del Acuerdo, Luego de los Cambios Producidos en 1976*, Jun/di 248 Lima, 1977, p. 10.
7. In an interview in April 1978, the Colombian ex-president, Carlos Lleras, R. said to the author that the intention was to create an integrated zone with great freedom for reciprocal trade and commercial concessions to other developing countries, which would have the capacity to negotiate with and act as a block against the United States and Europe. In the scheme, programming would be limited to a very select

group of industries which would be allocated according to criteria of efficiency. Other mechanisms, such as fiscal transfers, should be tried in order to achieve balanced development.

8. See, *Junta-Intal, Historia Documental del Acuerdo de Cartagena*, 1974, discussions of Comisión Mixta on the Cartagena Agreement.

9. The rules favouring the less developed countries are contained in the following articles of the Treaty: No. 93 grants priority to Bolivia and Ecuador in the granting of the allocation of industries. Nos. 100–194 give Bolivia and Ecuador a generous time period in which to eliminate intra-subregional trade barriers and to set up the CET. No. 55 gives these two countries a greater number of exemptions for products. No. 50 gives immediate entry to the other four markets, to a list of specific products coming from these countries. No. 106 gives Bolivia and Ecuador priority in financial activities and technical assistance on the CAF (*Corporación Andina de Fomento*).

10. Hazlewood suggests that the economic integration of underdeveloped countries becomes meaningful when they face a major industrialization project, because if investments do not count upon a market any larger than the national one, industrial development will suffer restrictions. A. Hazlewood (ed.), *African Integration and Disintegration*, pp. 11–16, and for socialist countries see J.M. Bravant, *Essays on Planning, Trade and Integration in Eastern Europe*, Rotterdam, UP, 1964, pp. 43–63.

11. Germánico Salgado, *El Grupo Andino y el Poder de Acción Solidaria* in BID-INTAL, *La Integración Latino-Américana en una Etapa de Decisiones*, p. 141. This author also recognizes that programming has to stimulate efficiency. However, while the stability of the treaty depends on ensuring the real participation of each member country, it is important to give priority to the principle of equilibrium. Also, see Junta, *Evaluación del Proceso de Integración*, 1976, Anexo II *Bases para una Estrategia . . .*, op. cit., Chap. 3 and G. Salgado, *Informe a la Segunda Reunión de Cancilleres*, 1972.

12. Morawetz analyses the technical difficulties of measuring the benefits to be derived from integration. The use of shadow prices is problematical, even if they have been passed on already in cost-benefit analysis in the use of a single country. Morawetz, op. cit., p. 74.

13. See Acuerdo, articles 1 and 2. Article 2 especially defines balanced and unified development as the reduction of the differences in development existing between the more and less developed countries. By setting up study programmes too, it says that macroeconomic elements, such as capital formation, the generation of new employment and the expansion of global exports to be gained from integration should be studied, with the differences between countries.

14. Marglin found different social costs according to the time when production began. See S.A. Marglin, *Approaches to Dynamic Investment Planning*, Amsterdam, North Holland, 1963.

15. Morawetz suggests that the negotiation of allocation by separate sectors could have led to a multiplicity of plants, and that there should be internally balanced multi-sectoral packages. However, because of the points made here and especially because of the lack of national priorities and of elements that allow for the delicate inter-sectoral (inter-country) balance, it is unrealistic to recommend these inter-sectoral packages. See Morawetz, op. cit., pp. 92–3.

16. See Junta: *Informe del Primer Seminario Interregional sobre la Planificación Integrada de los Paises Miembros, Jun/SI PL/I Informe Final*, 1974.

17. See: Ministerio de Planeamiento y Coordinación, *Plan de Desarrollo Económico y Social*, La Paz, June 1976 and Junta-UNDAT. *Situación Económica y Social del Ecuador*, 1976, pp. 20–2 and 40–1.

18. The *Ley General de Industrias*, legislative decree No. 18350 sets out the Peruvian scheme for import substitution. Besides the rules on protection according to the

nature of various industries, it establishes reforms for the distribution of income and the transformation of the system of property-holding, and reserves the state-ownership companies producing inputs for production.

19. For more details of Venezuela's interest in the GRAN and its preference for programming see: Bacha, '*Venezuela y el Grupo Andino*', *El Trimestre Económico*, **37** (1), 1970; De Blanco Iturte Eglee, '*La Estrategia de Desarrollo y la Integración: el Caso Venzolano*', Junta SI. PL/I/dt 5, No. 5 1974, p. 24, and '*Exposición de R. Figuereo Planchart, representante titular de Venezuela ante la XIX Comisión*', 10 december, 1975 Documento COM/XIX/di e. Public investment is decisive in basic industry and hydrocarbons. The country is proceeding with projects that will make Venezuela the most industrialized nation in the subregion, enlarging iron and steel capacity to 5 million tons p.a., and aluminium to 400,000 tons p.a. State investment for 1976–80 in the manufacturing sector will rise to $10,000 million, a figure approximately equal to the GDP of Colombia. See '*Segundo mensaje del ciudadano Presidente Carlos Andrés Pérez al Congreso*', March 1976, and Oficina Central de Coordinación y Planificación, *Cuarto Plan de la Nación 1970–1974*, Caracas, 1971.

20. See *Acta de la XVI Sesión Extraordinaria de la Comisión*, February–April 1976, pp. 92–8 and *Documento de Evaluación*, op. cit., pp. 1,3, and *La Exposición del Representante Titular Peruano ante el XIX Periodo de Sesiones de la Comisión*, Documento, COM/XIX/di, 10 december 1975, p. 2.

21. This was substantiated in an interview held by the author in April 1978 with the Head of the *Unidad de Planeación Global del Departamento Nacional de Planeación de Colombia*, in which he stressed that Colombia is only interested in the commercial aspects of integration and that the country will withhold the approval of or its participation in, other programmes. But as Colombia is an important member this means that there is little hope for more SIDPs to be approved.

22. During the meeting of the Presidents of the Andean countries held in Washington in September 1977 on the occasion of the signing of the Panama Agreement, they manifested the 'political will' to approve the automobile SIDP *immediately*. See, '*Declaración Conjunta de los Presidentes de los Paises Miembros del Grupo Andino*', Washington, 7 September 1977.

23. According to the *Jefe de Planeación Global del Departamento Nacional de Planeación de Colombia*, this country changed the position maintained against the programme for four years, when its meaning was changed and it was converted into a programme of co-production and assembly and not one of production. Interview, with the author, April 1978, op. cit. For a definition of the various agreements, see p. 12 in this chapter, footnote 2.

24. Junta, *Documento de evaluación*, 1975, Jun.di 1980, 196, Lima, March, 1976, Anexo VII, p. 13. The above-mentioned is confirmed in the evaluation documents published in 1979 and 1980: Junta, *Documento de Evaluación 1969–1979*, Lima, March 1979, *Anexo Técnico No. 3*, Jun/di 359, pp. 303–305; COM, *Resumen de las Situaciones de Incumplimiento y Reclamos por Materias*, COM/XXXI dt 3 nov. 14/1980 Jun/di 444/29 Enero 1980, pp. 17–19; Junta, *Apreciaciones de la Situación actual del Proceso de Integración económica del Acuerdo de Cartagena*, Jun dt 1/7, July, 1981, pp/ 10–13.

25. M. Kuczynski, *Planned Development in the Andean Group: Industrial Policy and Trade Liberalisation*, Latin American Publication Fund, London, 1973.

26. A. Hazlewood, (ed.), *Economic Integration: The East African Experiences*, London, Heinemann, 1975, p. 124.

PART 4: FISCAL POLICY

6

Fiscal Policy in the EEC

Walter Hahn

1. INTRODUCTION

Fiscal policy is a rather broad notion in the sense that it covers a wide range of the most diverse issues such as social security and regional development. Usually we subsume under the heading 'fiscal policy' all policies that directly or indirectly enter into the budget of a state. In so far as we talk about the fiscal policy of the EEC or of any other supranational organization, two different concepts have to be distinguished. Firstly, there are all those measures that primarily affect the Community's common budget. Secondly there are those decisions which, although they are taken at the Community level, do not enter into the common budget but primarily affect the budgets of the member states. The latter is generally referred to as 'fiscal harmonization', meaning the harmonization of public expenditure (e.g. subsidies), as well as of the revenue side of national budgets (e.g. taxes). If one cannot find a particular policy (e.g. environmental protection) reflected in the EC's budget, this does not necessarily mean that this policy does not exist in the Community. It could simply indicate that the policy we are looking for is pursued by means of fiscal harmonization.

A first section of this chapter is devoted to the EC's budget, emphasising the fact that the common budget on the one hand and fiscal harmonization on the other are close substitutes. We are going to analyse the three major objectives of fiscal policy (stabilization, redistribution and efficiency) and then turn to the question of how to finance the Community's budget, an issue much disputed in recent years. A second chapter will deal with tax harmonization. In particular we will have to talk about the harmonization of indirect taxes which, as part of the 1985 programme on 'Completing the Internal Market' (Commission 1985), has now moved into the center of the debate on the EC's future.

It is evident that it would need a book of a few hundred pages to discuss the EC's fiscal policy in some detail. We therefore have to restrict ourselves to those issues that are not only important for the EC's development in the coming years but that are also of general interest for economic unions outside Western Europe. Technical, institutional and theoretical aspects will hence be mentioned only briefly. Instead, the theme will be approached from a more political point of view by looking at the interaction between fiscal policy at the common and the national level and by analysing the interdependence between different common policies of the EC.

2. THE EC'S BUDGET

Stabilization

Stabilization is the first major objective of fiscal policy. By having a look at the development of the EC's budget over a number of years we cannot find any signs of stabilization policy at all. This might be surprising but it is easy to explain. First, the Community's power to borrow is very restricted. Second, the EC's budget is much to small to have any significant influence on aggregate demand in the Community. With about 28.4 billion ECU in 1985, the common budget counts for less than 3 percent of the combined national budgets and for only 0.95 percent of the Community's GDP. Therefore, from the beginning the Commission favoured a common stabilization policy by means of coordinating the national policies rather than by using the Community's own budget.

This approach, for instance, was embodied in the plans for an Economic and Monetary Union of the early 1970s. But by 1973 it had become clear that the EC would fail to implement the ambitious 'Werner-Plan' of 1970. Of course, the breakdown of the Bretton Woods System and the first oil crises had changed the international economic environment for an Economic and Monetary Union in Europe. But other reasons for the failure can be found inside the EC. There was, for example, disagreement over what should be achieved first, fiscal coordination or monetary integration. While Germany insisted on the first concept, France favoured the second (Tsoukalis, 1977). This conflict was finally resolved by establishing the European Monetary System in 1979 (Coffey, 1984). Once exchange rates are fixed or nearly fixed, monetary policy is no longer available for stabilization purposes. The EMS therefore automatically increased the need for pursuing stabilization policy by fiscal means. And since trade and factor flows are widely liberalized within the Community, it was absolutely necessary to harmonize those national fiscal policies at a common level. Although regular consultations on fiscal matters have taken place since the EC was founded, they have now become inevitable.

Redistribution

When talking about redistribution of income in a supranational context we have to distinguish two different aspects: the redistribution of income between individuals and that between the member states. It is not necessary to discuss the redistribution between the various regions of the member states as a separate issue because this can without problem be interpreted as some kind of combination between inter-personal on the one and inter-state redistribution on the other hand.

Governments use social benefits and income taxes to redistribute income between citizens. Since the idea of what has to be regarded as fair distribution varies from one country to another, the level of social benefits and taxation will also be different. If the citizens have the right to freely choose their country of residence, and this is the case inside the EC, the redistribution policy of a single government will not be very effective. Poor people will move to those states where they receive high benefits and rich people will go to places where they pay low taxes. In the end, all the poor live in one country while all the rich are united in another one. Obviously, there seems to be some need for common action.

These purely theoretical considerations do not fully apply to the EC. In fact, the mobility of people within the Community is rather low, owing to language and cultural barriers. Instead of dealing with the problems caused by people's mobility, the EC should first try to remove some fiscal barriers which also still exist. There is for instance a 1979 Draft Directive concerning the harmonization of income taxes for migrant workers (OJ 1980/C 21, p. 6), a proposal that is still waiting for adoption by the Council. Today the inter-personal redistribution of income lies within the responsibility of national governments. Redistributional policy has not yet entered into the EC's budget and it will not do so in the future. Even when people's mobility considerably increases one day there will be no need to shift redistribution policy from the member states' budgets to the common budget. It would be sufficient and much easier to follow the path of fiscal harmonization.

Inter-state redistribution of income is a quite different issue. The only peaceful way to redistribute income between the member states is to reach agreement at the Community level. But, looking at the EC's budget, we hardly find any position that is aimed at systematically redistributing wealth from the richer to the poorer countries.

Table 6.1: EC's budget (m ECU) 1983

Revenues		Expenditures	
VAT	13730	CAP-Guarantee	15788
Agricultural and		Agric. Structural Fund	750
sugar levies	2295	Regional Fund	2406
Customs duties	6989	Social Fund	1021
Other	2102	Research and Dev.	1308
		Coop. with Third World	
		countries	811
		Administration	1110
		Other	1922
Total	25116	Total	25116

Source: Eurostat Review 1974–1983, Statistical Office of the European Communities, 1985

The customs duties and agricultural levies that countries have to pay to the common budget depend on their import structure and have nothing to do with income or wealth. Admittedly, the 1.4 percent VAT that every member state contributes implies that, for instance, the Germans pay more to the EC's budget per head than the Irish. On the other hand, we have to consider that VAT is generally known as a regressive tax since the ratio of (non-taxable) saving to (taxable) consumption increases when income is rising. The CAP considerably affects inter-state distribution. Only a part of these effects are reflected in the EC's budget (e.g. subsidies for food exports to non-EC countries), while a lot of redistribution takes place in a disguised form via high food prices paid by, say, a British consumer to Danish farmers for imported food.

Although most of the budgetary activities have important distributional implications, only a few funds were established with a view to altering the inter-state distribution of income. Particularly the Regional Fund, the Social Fund and the Agricultural Structural Fund should be mentioned here. But, by accounting for less than 20 percent of the 1985 budget, they are much too small to even offset the distributional impact of the CAP. There are many ideas on how to make the EC's budget more progressive (MacDougall Report, 1977). One could, for instance, think of adding a progressive element to the VAT contributions by making the VAT that each state has to pay dependent on the GDP per head. Another alternative would be to increase the size of the Regional and/or the Social Fund. There is no lack of ideas but only a lack of political will. We therefore have to ask: should the EC attempt to transfer resources at all from the poorer to the richer states of the Community?

There are some economic reasons that make it desirable to do so. First, the success of inter-personal redistribution of income crucially depends on the assumption that the mobility of people inside the Community is fairly low. Once mobility has improved, a policy of inter-personal redistribution will inevitably fail unless it is accompanied by inter-state transfers (Buchanan, 1950). Second, different levels of economic development and prosperity make national economies react differently to changes in the world economy. Economic divergencies will therefore make it increasingly difficult to complete the Common Market or even to preserve what has already been achieved in the field of fiscal and monetary integration. But, it has to be borne in mind that a considerable transfer of resources requires a high degree of political solidarity among the member states which cannot be achieved without a minimum of political integration. Here we have a good example of the fact that the EC's budget, the Common Market and political integration have to be developed simultaneously to a certain extent. It is naïve to believe that the Community can go ahead with economic integration while leaving the political aspect aside.

Efficiency

Efficiency, or growth — which basically means the same — is the third and final goal of fiscal policy. It can be pursued by either supplying goods out of the common budget or alternatively by means of fiscal harmonization. Economic literature suggests that, in so far as we have to deal with federally organised communities, the central authority should only provide for those public goods that bear considerable economies of scale and/or regional spill-overs. Given that the EC is something similar to a federal state (or is at least on the way to it), we could expect that Brussels would be responsible for policies such as research and development, energy and transport, environmental protection, defense, cooperation with Third World countries, multilateral trade negotiations, etc. Looking at the EC's budget, we find only little about these policies. Instead, the CAP accounts for about two-thirds of all expenditure. This may indicate that the establishment of the CAP was based on political rather than economic grounds. But things are not as simple as this.

From a particular point of view, CAP can be justified with efficiency arguments. In order to do so, one has to remember that the basic goal of the EC was to provide all member states with the public good 'Common Market': the good Common Market is a public one in the sense that all member states benefit from it (provided we believe in the merits of a competitive economy), but nobody has an incentive to pay for it (since protectionism is almost always profitable to a state given that other states allow free access to their markets). The Common Market was to be based upon competition between independent enterprises. But this could not apply to the agricultural sector since the latter was highly subsidised and regulated already in the 1950s when the EC was founded. Therefore, a Common Market without a CAP was likely to enhance not competition between enterprises but competition between national governments, thus causing political unrest within the Community. Consequently, an agreement upon some form of CAP was a precondition, or say, the price, for the supply of the public good 'Common Market'.

While it was decided to transfer the agricultural policy from national budgets to the EC's budget, the member states' influence in other sectors of the economy was taken care of by means of fiscal harmonization (e.g. articles 92–94 of the EEC Treaty regulating state subsidies). During the 1960s and 70s all governments in the EC became increasingly involved in the most diverse sectors of their economies such as research and development or environmental protection. New policies first emerged in the nation states and it took some time before governments realised that they could benefit from coordinating their activities at a supranational level. Another few years were spent negotiating at Brussels. Slowly, responsibilities were shifted to the EC. The agreement on some degree of fiscal harmonization was generally regarded as the appropriate instrument to start with a new common policy. But, over time, the Council also transferred funds from national governments to the EC. Seen from a purely economic point of view, it does not really matter whether funds are kept in national budgets or whether they are transferred to Brussels. What in fact matters is the question who decides upon the funds. Is it the national parliament or is it the EC's Council together with the Commission and the European Parliament? Additionally, it is necessary to accelerate the speed by which new policies, if desirable, are shifted from the national to the Community level. Otherwise the EC will run behind actual developments in member states till the end of time, with the consequence of considerable welfare losses in every single country.

It may be added that up to now the Community's research and development and environmental policy are not explicitly mentioned in the Treaties but are based on the general authorization of article 235 of the EEC Treaty. This will change once the reform of the Treaty, decided upon in December 1985, has been put into force. The new articles 130f-t deal with the objectives and instruments of the two above-mentioned policies. But this does not mean very much. Since the new articles do not alter the principle that all decisions have to be taken unanimously, they do not bring any perceptible progress.

The EC's Finances

Having discussed the budget and fiscal policy in general, we are now going to analyse the finances of the Community in some depth. This seems to be necessary since the revenue side of the EC's budget has given rise to heated debates in recent years. And it is only a matter of months until the issue is back on the Council's agenda again.

Firstly, some historical remarks. In the early days of the EC the budget was financed by direct contributions from member states. The basis for the distribution of charges among the countries was changed several times. In 1970, the Council of Ministers agreed, after considerable pressure from France, on setting up a so-called 'Own-Resources-Scheme' of the Community, consisting of customs duties, agricultural levies and a percentage of Value Added Tax not higher than 1 percent of a commonly-defined basis of assessment. When this scheme went fully into force in 1980 the idea of own resources in the pure sense had already been given up. In 1975, the Dublin Agreement provided for a general rule for refunds from the budget, specially designed so as to meet the British 'Renegotiation' demands of 1974. In all the years since 1980, *ad hoc* decisions of the Council allowed for further refunds to the United Kingdom and to Germany. And, in all the years, continuing discussions about contributions to the budget have considerably spoiled the atmosphere in the Community.

The budgetary crises, during which the Community was in danger of going bankrupt, were settled with the so-called Fontainebleau Agreement of summer 1984. In order to free the Community from a threatening shortage of finances, the European Council increased, for the years 1986 onwards, the VAT ceiling from 1 to 1.4 percent. The British demands for reducing their financial burden were satisfied by approving a repayment to London of 1 billion ECU for 1984. For the following years, Britain was promised rebates of 66 percent of the British net contributions to the common budget whereby the net contribution was defined as the difference of the VAT contributions to and the direct returns from the budget. It has been agreed that this repayment formula will be subject to renegotiation as soon as the 1.4 percent VAT ceiling has to be raised again.

Taking all aspects into account, the Fontainebleau Agreement is nothing but a budgetary ceasefire. Since the EC will once more run out of money sometime between 1987 and 1988 (COM(86)201, 3.4.86), the quarrel about the EC's finances will soon start again. And again the political climate in the Community is in danger of getting contaminated — which in fact could mean that in all fields progress would be blocked for some time. Would it therefore not be better to call for a long-term agreement on financial contributions?

Two objections have to be considered. Firstly, if the distribution of charges is fixed, the attention of the member states will probably shift to the expenditure side of the budget. Since all decisions on the allocation of funds have distributional implications, it becomes likely that inefficient decisions prevail over efficient ones only because of their distributional advantages. Secondly, all member states have some idea about a *juste retour*, a just return from the budget, when negotiating on budgetary issues. A long-term agreement has to guarantee such a just return in order to prevail. But this is a fairly difficult undertaking since the EC's experience has proved that it is almost impossible to forecast the development of revenue and expenditure for more than one to two years. Why, one could ask, does the EC not only fix a finance rule that refers directly, e.g. to the net contribution the member states pay to the budget?

But again, problems arise. Firstly, there are quite a few common policies that do not enter into the EC's budget. Owing to a lack of information, their distributional impact is almost impossible to measure. At first sight the concept of a net contribution appears to be measurable if we restrict our analysis to the budget itself. Politicians are attracted by the idea of using money flows to and from the budget for calculating distributional effects. And even the EC's statistical office provides us with such data.

Table 6.2: Distribution of EC revenues and expenditures by countries, 1983 (m ECU)

	Revenue from	*Expenditure in*
W. Germany	6472	3825
France	4506	4255
Italy	2999	3775
Netherlands	1565	1860
Belgium	1216	1736
Luxembourg	44	6
U.K.	5084	4084
Ireland	270	1026
Denmark	480	756
Greece	378	1351
Total	23014	21674

Source: Eurostat Review 1974–1983, Statistical Office of the European Communities, 1985

Notes: 1. Expenditures are adjusted for monetary compensation amounts. 2. Some common items of expenditure are not allocated between countries.

But life is not as easy as this. Already very simple examples can prove that money flows have very often very little to do with economic advantages and disadvantages. Let us assume that a Dutch importer receives through the harbour of Rotterdam a raw material from a non-EC country. The material is afterwards delivered to a German car manufacturer who uses it to build a car which he later sells to a Danish consumer. Who exactly has to bear the customs duty that is levied at the Dutch border? Is it the Netherlands because they have to transfer the levy directly to the EC's budget? Or is it the German industry because the Dutch importer has shifted on the burden; or is it even the Danish consumer? It can easily be shown that with subsidies paid, for example to farmers, to regional development projects or to research centres, we face exactly the same problem. Neither detailed input/output tables for the whole Community nor precise shifting hypotheses are available in practice and therefore the concept of a net contribution to the EC's budget becomes, to put it forcefully, a nonsense. Unfortunately, some economists like to forget and most politicians tend not to know about it.

A straightforward solution to EC finances does not exist. The only possible way is trying to find, always in longlasting negotiations, some sort of balance between a short-term agreement on the one hand and a long-term rule on the other. Negotiations might become easier once we have dropped the illusion of being able to calculate a net contribution. The EC is not a zero-sum game and therefore it should be possible to find a solution that secures a net benefit for all member states.

3. TAX HARMONIZATION

Napoleon was one of the first to harmonize taxes in Europe by introducing a uniform tax system in some of the territories he had occupied. Since his empire did not last very long the EC had to start from scratch again. There are various reasons why tax harmonization is desirable. From the Community point of view, tax harmonization is mainly regarded as a means of preventing distortions in competition and minimising political disturbances within the EC. From the member states' point of view, tax harmonization can open markets for own exports, it can ease desirable national tax reforms, it can serve as an argument against pressures from interest groups asking for special tax treatment, and so on.

Value Added Tax

Already, since the late 1950s, the Commission has given high priority to the harmonization of general sales taxes. At that time, and this still applies today, the member states levied their sales taxes on the basis of the destination principle — which in fact means that the exporting country (the country of origin) gives a tax rebate to all goods to be exported while the importing country (the country of destination) then imposes, on the other side of the border, an import levy on all goods entering the country. Such border tax adjustments are perfectly fair as long as the tax rebate exactly compensates for the sales tax levied in the country of origin while the import levy is an equivalent of the sales tax borne by domestically produced products. But this condition was not satisfied in the late 1950s. Since all the member states (except France) made use of multi-stage, cumulative turnover taxes, it was quite impossible to determine the tax burden imposed on a particular product and the Commission was therefore unable to check whether the rate of tax rebate and import levies were justified or not. When the customs duties within the EC had to be removed during the 1960s, the member states regularly increased the rates of border tax adjustments in order to protect their national market against foreign competition. Neither the standstill agreement of 1960 nor proceedings before the European Court of Justice proved able to prevent the member states from doing so. Therefore, the Commission considered it necessary to introduce non-cumulative sales taxes in all EC-countries, which allow for a precise calculation and hence for an effective control of the rates of border tax adjustments.

But this alone did not justify the introduction of a VAT since single-stage sales taxes, as they are used today for example in the United States, were able to meet the same requirement (Neumark Report 1962). By proposing a VAT, the Commission had yet another objective in its mind. It wanted to abolish border tax adjustments altogether, sometime in the long run, so that the Community would be able to remove border checks at the internal borders of the EC. A necessary condition for the so-called abolition of fiscal frontiers was that all member states imposed the same type of sales tax. Since Germany and France at that time insisted on a VAT, there was not much choice left for Brussels. Agreement was reached in 1967 (OJ 1967/71, p/1301) and by 1973 all the old member states and the three newcomers had introduced a VAT. Meanwhile, Spain and Portugal also applied a VAT, while Greece alone lagged behind. After having been granted two postponements, the Greeks were obliged to switch over to a VAT by December 1986.

In 1970, the second round of harmonizing VAT began with the Council's decision to make VAT a part of the EC's own resources. This decision did not automatically imply a harmonization of the VAT's basis of assessment. A notional tax base would have been sufficient to calculate the member states' contributions to the common budget. But the Commission wanted to assess its part of VAT on the actual VAT base, firstly in order to establish a direct link between the EC's budget and European taxpayers and secondly because the harmonization of the VAT base was regarded as a further step on the way to the abolition of fiscal frontiers. But once VAT was introduced in the member states the latter proved very reluctant to any changes. Only after the European Parliament, together with the Foreign Affairs Council, had put considerable pressure on the Ministers of Finance and their civil servants, was a compromise finally reached in May 1977 (OJ 1977/L 145, p. 1). The so-called sixth Directive on VAT fixed a common VAT base but also allowed for 'temporary derogations' wherever agreement was difficult to find. Since then not much has happened. The Commission submitted to the Council quite a few Draft Directives aimed at completing the common VAT base. But up to now none of the more important proposals have been adopted.

Excise duties

Since the Commission was occupied during the 1960s with the general sales taxes the harmonization of excise duties had to wait for some time. In 1972 the Council agreed upon a first Directive on the harmonization of tobacco duties, saying that the tax on cigarettes should consist partly of a specific component and partly of an *ad valorem* component (OJ 1972/L 303, p. 1). Further Directives narrowed the range that was allowed for fixing the ratio of the specific component to total taxation. The latest Draft Directive (OJ 1980/C 264, p. 6) is stuck in the EP, which is unable to overcome the conflict of interest between the states of northern Europe on the one hand (in favour of a high specific component because they produce blond and therefore rather expensive cigarettes) and the countries of the south on the other (who prefer a high *ad valorem* component because they mainly produce black and therefore cheap cigarettes).

In 1972, the Commission sent five proposals to the Council dealing with duties on alcoholic drinks (OJ 1972/C 43, p. 23). This initiative turned out to be a complete failure, due in part to the fact that the 1973 enlargement of the EC made tax harmonization more difficult than it had been before. But the Commission also has to share some of the responsibility. By proposing to harmonize first the structure of the duties and to deal later with the tax rates she had chosen an approach that did not meet the real problems at all. Contrary to what we said about general sales taxes, it does not matter which type of excise duties are applied in the member states because, for the majority of all the various excise duties, it is fairly easy to determine the correct rates of border tax adjustments. Therefore, the different tax structures, seen from the member states' point of view, were of minor concern. What really mattered was to do something about the tax rates. Italy, for instance, steadily complained about the high British wine duty, keeping per capita consumption in Britain extremely low. Britain, on the other hand, was angry about the French and Italian import duty on whisky which was much higher than the internal tax on cognac or grappa, and so on. After the French–Italian 'wine-war' of 1975 the Commission felt compelled to take action. Since negotiations at Council level had ceased since 1974, Brussels went to the European Court of Justice claiming, among other things, that the British wine duty as well as the French and Italian whisky duty were not in line with article 95 of the EEC Treaty (forbidding fiscal discrimination of imports from other EC countries). Since 1980 the Luxembourg Court has come out with a number of judgments (Easson, 1981 and Easson, 1984) that resolved quite a few if not most of the urgent problems in the alcoholic drinks field.

Abolition of fiscal frontiers

Given the present state of indirect tax harmonization in the EC, neutrality in competition is more or less secured. As part of its 1985 programme on 'Completing the Internal Market' (Commission 1985), the Commission has now made clear that the time has come to go ahead with the second objective of fiscal harmonization: the abolition of fiscal frontiers. This is the goal set out in the programme and accepted by the European Council, that by 1992 all border checks at internal frontiers within the Community should have disappeared. As far as fiscal aspects are concerned, two problems have to be solved first.

Firstly, there is the question of tax rates. The rates of VAT and those of excise duties have to be aligned to a certain degree in order to prevent (non-registered) consumers from moving their purchases from their home country to other EC countries which impose lower taxes. The Commission suggests that for VAT a tax differential of up to 5 percent between neighboring countries might be _acceptable. Taking into account that going shopping abroad always involves some cost and time, this seems to be a fairly reasonable approach. But even by allowing for a 5 percent differential, there is still a lot to negotiate about (see Table 6.3).

Table 6.3: VAT rates (%), January 1986

Country	Standard	Reduced	Increased
Belgium	19	6/17	25/33
Denmark	22	—	—
France	18.6	5.5/7	33.3
Ireland	23	0/10	—
Italy	18	2/9	38
Luxembourg	12	3/6	—
Netherlands	19	5	—
Portugal	16	8	30
Spain	12	6	33
U.K.	15	0	—
W. Germany	14	7	—

Source: Commission's *White Paper* on *Completing the Internal Market*, June 1985, plus information from the Commission on later changes.

Notes: 1. Greece is obliged to introduce VAT by the end of 1986. 2. Several member states (e.g. Denmark and Britain) levy supplementary taxes on certain items like cars, TVs, etc., usually at the wholesale stage. These levies have the same effect as an increased VAT rate.

The question that is difficult to answer is whether the Community should aim at a one-rate, a two-rate or a three-rate VAT. Major problems will also be caused by the British and Irish zero-rates, not to mention the excise duties where tax rates vary even more from one country to another. Things become additionally complicated by the fact that the Finance Council, contrary to the Commission's proposal, currently seems to insist on a nearly complete unification of tax rates as a precondition for the abolition of fiscal frontiers.

A quite different issue is the question of how to deal with the trade between (registered) enterprises. In so far as VAT is concerned, two different concepts are conceivable. On the one hand, the EC could implement a clearing system: tax rebates in the country of origin and import levies in the country of destination are to be abolished; simultaneously, the purchaser gets the right to deduct VAT paid anywhere in the Community; in order to leave the original distribution of VAT revenue among the member states unchanged, a redistribution of revenue takes places via a clearing house. A second alternative is known as zero-rate notification: exports are exempted from VAT in the country of origin and the import levy gets abolished in the country of destination; on its way from the exporter to the importer the products are therefore zero-rated; the VAT of the importing country is automatically imposed on them as soon as the importer resells the products (Simons, 1981). While the clearing system causes a lot of paperwork, the zero-rate notification is said to increase the danger of tax fraud. Again, things become more difficult when we turn to excise duties. Since excises are usually levied at an early production stage, wholesalers and retailers will, in case there are marginal tax differentials, move their purchases to low-tax countries. Nevertheless, with some effort this problem can be resolved (Prest, 1983).

Given all these politically as well as technically very complicated issues, it would be unrealistic to expect fiscal frontiers to be completely abolished by 1992. But this should not be an excuse for putting hands into pockets. Instead of waiting till tax harmonization falls down like manna from heaven, the Finance Council should start from today to make border crossing inside the Community as simple as possible, given the present state of tax harmonization. There are still, as the model of the small Benelux Union proves, a few things to be done. Apart from the countries with extremely high indirect taxation such as Denmark, Ireland and Greece, there is still room to increase further the tax-free allowances granted to private travellers. And the adoption of the 1982 proposal for a Four-teenth Directive on VAT (OJ 1982/C 201, p. 5) would bring some improvement for commercial trade.

Direct taxes

Almost nothing has been achieved in the field of direct taxation. Several factors may explain this lack of progress. Firstly, from the outset of the EC, the customs union aspect of the Community was given priority over the common capital and labour market. Since the trade in goods and services was primarily affected by indirect and not by direct taxes, the harmonization of the latter automatically became an issue of minor concern. Secondly, income taxes serve as a flexible instrument for conducting a great number of the most diverse policies and therefore, understandably, member states were reluctant to give up their freedom in that field. Thirdly, as long as we do not know exactly to what degree direct taxes are shifted forward and as long as we are not able to determine what the various governments are doing with the revenue raised by direct taxes, it is rather difficult to say what form harmonization should take.

In 1975 the Commission made an effort and put forward a Draft Directive proposing the introduction of a common type of corporation income tax in all member states (OJ 1975/C 253, p. 2). Basically, the Commission suggested that member states should levy a tax rate between 45 and 55 per cent on all profits and that, for the tax paid on distributed profits, an imputation credit of 45 to 55 per cent should be granted to all shareholders inside the Community. For years now this initiative has stuck in the European Parliament. The Parliament has refused to give an opinion on the subject and, instead, asked the Commission to harmonize first the base of the corporation tax and to care about tax rates afterwards. But even if the Parliament had not refused the Draft Directive, the Council would probably have done it, given the wide range of different tax systems currently applied by the member states (see Table 6.4).

Table 6.4: Corporation tax system, rates, etc. 1986

Country	System	Corporation Tax Rate %	Imputation Credit (if relevant) %
Netherlands	Separate	42	0
Luxembourg	Separate	40 (1)	0
Spain	Imputation	35	18.57
Denmark	Imputation	50	25
Belgium	Imputation	45 (1)	40.87
Ireland	Imputation	50 (1)	53.85
France	Imputation	45	61.11
U.K.	Imputation	35 (1)	75.81
Greece	(Imputation) (2)	49	100
Portugal	(Imputation) (2)	34.2 to 47.2	100
Germany	Imputation	56/36 (3)	100
Italy	Imputation	46.368 (4)	100

Source: Information from the German Ministry of Finance and own calculations.

Notes: 1. Reduced rates are applied to low income. 2. In Greece and Portugal distributed profits are not subject to corporation tax, which is in fact equivalent to a 100% imputation credit. 3. The 36% rate is levied on distributed profits. 4. Sum of central and local taxes.

It is an illusion to think that the Germans would give up their 100 per cent imputation system, a tax which they introduced only nine years ago and a tax which is favoured by most economists because of its neutrality. Even experts from the Brussels taxation department are unhappy with the Commission's 1975 proposal. They would have preferred a 100 per cent imputation system too but they knew that this would not have been acceptable to the majority of member states. Agreement on a common tax rate and a common rate for imputation credit is not in sight. Therefore, Brussels should think about a much easier approach to the harmonization of corporation income tax: member states are allowed to decide individually whether and to what extent they want to grant an imputation credit; but member states are obliged that, if they allow for an imputation credit, they not only have to grant the credit to their own citizens but to all citizens of the EC. The obvious advantage of such an approach would be that finding an agreement in the Council would become much easier. Moreover, and this is crucial, the extension of the imputation credit to all Community citizens would be completely adequate as a first step of harmonizing corporation income tax. Equal tax treatment of all EC citizens holding shares of the same company would be secured.

At first sight it appears that the European shareholder, when deciding where to invest his money, would prefer a German company to, say, a Dutch one, simply because in Germany he gets an imputation credit. But things are not as simple, for the following reasons. Firstly, it might be that the Dutch company is able to shift corporation income tax forward. In this case net profit is not affected by taxation and therefore there is no problem for the European capital market. Secondly, it might be that the tax burden that is imposed on the Dutch company is offset by the fact that the Dutch government uses the revenue raised by corporation income tax to finance public goods (e.g. infrastructure) which are provided to the companies free of charge. In this case net profit is not affected either and there, again, there is no problem for the common capital market. The third and worst scenario would be that the Dutch companies are really disadvantaged *vis-à-vis* their German competitors. But in this case the Dutch government could easily end this situation by switching over to partial or full imputation. To do so, it does not need an EC Directive but only a unilateral decision of The Hague.

4. CONCLUDING REMARKS

The only conclusion we can draw from the above analysis is that there are still a lot of things to do. It would be oversimplified to make a mere lack of political will on the part of member states responsible for the slow progress in the fiscal field. Policy-making processes at the European level are much too complicated and varied to allow for simple statements. Admittedly, the national ministers of finance and their fiscal experts are extremely reluctant to engage in any reforms. Without being pushed hard from outside, they prefer, in most cases, to leave things as they are and to do nothing at all. Utmost caution is the crucial characteristic of every politician and civil servant who is involved in fiscal affairs because it is caution that guarantees the highest chance of survival in the dangerous field of fiscal policy. We want to end this paper on the EC's fiscal policy with a quotation taken from one of Prof. Prest's papers, a quotation that is not only nice but that also, in this author's opinion, hits the mark: 'Perhaps the most appropriate comment is the famous one by Dr Johnson on a woman preaching: "like a dog walking on its hind legs. It is not well done; but you are surprised to find it done at all." ' (Prest, 1983, p. 78).

NOTE

Dedicated to the late Prof. A.R. Prest

REFERENCES

Andel, N. (1983a), 'Direction of Tax Harmonisation in the EEC', in Cnossen, S. (ed.), *Comparative Tax Studies*, Amsterdam, North-Holland, 1983, p. 295.

Andel, N. (1983b), 'Europäische Gemeinscahften', in Andel, N., Haller, H.U., Neumark, F. (eds), *Handbuch der Finanzwissenschaft*, 3rd edn, Vol.4, Tübingen: Mohr (Siebeck), 1983, p. 312.

Berlin, D. (1980), 'Portée des dispositions fiscales du Traité de Rome et harmonisation des fiscalités indirectes', in *Revue de Droit Européen*, **16**, 1980, p. 460 and p. 635.

Buchanan, P. (1950), 'Federalism and Fiscal Equity', in *American Economic Review*, **40**, 1950, p. 583.

Coffey, P. (1984), *The European Monetary System — Past, Present and Future*, Dordrecht, Nijhoff, 1984.

Commission (1980), 'Report on the Scope for Convergence of Tax Systems in the Community', in *Bulletin of the EC*, **13**, 1980, Supplement 1.

Commission (1985), 'Completing the Internal Market', White Paper from the Commission to the European Council, Luxembourg, 1985.

Easson, A.J. (1980), *Tax Law and Policy in the EEC*, London, Sweet and Maxwell, 1980.

Easson, A.J. (1981), 'Fiscal Discrimination: New Perspectives on Article 95 of the EEC Treaty', in *Common Market Law Review*, **18**, 1981, p. 521.

Easson, A.J. (1984), 'Cheaper Wine or Dearer Beer? Article 95 again', in *European Law Review*, **9**, 1984, p. 57.

MacDougall Report (1977), Report on the Study Group on 'The Role of Public Finance in European Integration', 2 Vols., published by the Commission in 1977.

Neumark Report (1962), 'Bericht des Steuer- und Finanzausschusses', published by the Commission in 1962; English language version 1969.

Peffekoven, R. (1983), 'Probleme der internationalen Finanzordnung', in Andel, N., Haller, H. and Neumark, F. (eds), *Handbuch der Finanzwissenschaft*, 3rd edn, Vol.4, Tübingen, Mohr (Siebeck), 1983, p. 219.

Prest, A.R. (1983), 'Fiscal Policy', in Coffey, P. (ed.), *Main Economic Policy Areas of the EEC*, Den Haag, Nijhoff, 1983.

Simons, A.L.C. (1981), 'Simplification of VAT Procedures in Intra-Community Trade', in *Intertax*, 1981, p. 375.

Tsoukalis, L. (1977), *The Politics and Economics of European Monetary Integration*, London, Allen and Unwin, 1977.

Wallace, H. (1980), *Budgetary Politics, the Finances of the European Communities*, London, Allen and Unwin, 1980.

PART 5: MONETARY POLICY

7

The European Monetary System — A Possible Model for Latin America

Peter Coffey

THE BACKGROUND

The European Monetary System (EMS), which was eight years old earlier this year, is one of the real success stories of the European Community. What, then, is the EMS and why was it adopted by the Community?

First, the reasons for its creation: the EMS is the successor to a similar but different arrangement, the 'Snake' Arrangement,[1] which lasted from 1972 until 1979. This arrangement had its origins in the decision taken by the Community Heads of Governments, in den Haag, at the end of 1969, to construct an economic and monetary union (EMU) — 'provided the political will to do so existed'. This decision was taken because, by 1968, the original 'Six' founder member states of the EEC had achieved the customs union (as laid down in the Treaty of Rome), were conducting half their trade between themselves, were integrated to a large degree, had brought on-stream a Common Agricultural Policy (CAP) — which depended on stable exchange rates in order to function correctly — and were heeding French calls that the Community should have a 'common international monetary personality'.

The technical features of the 'Snake' Arrangement were a narrow band of fluctuation (2.25 per cent) within which the currencies of the participating countries could fluctuate and a common float against the US dollar. Unfortunately, the system was both inflexible (regarding exchange-rate adjustments) and not demanding enough (as far as the co-ordination of national economic policies was concerned), and, at the end of its existence (March 1979), it consisted of a small Deutsche Mark Zone.

In the last stages of the existence of the arrangement (1978), grave concern was being expressed at the lack of action by the American authorities in the monetary sphere. This concern was particularly expressed by France and Germany. Also, these same countries (together with some other Community member states) desired a re-activation of the integration process in the EEC. The result was the proposal for a European Monetary System (EMS).[2]

SPECIAL CONSIDERATIONS

Clearly, the decision to embark upon either an EMS or an EMU is no light undertaking. Thus, it is worth noting that a number of fundamental structural factors, peculiar to the European Economic Community (EEC), emphasized European concern at international monetary developments — as mentioned in the previous paragraph. Among these factors perhaps the most important one is the fact that Community countries tend to have open or very open national economies. This is in strong contrast to countries such as the United States and the Soviet Union. Common Market countries trade a substantial part of their Gross National Product (GNP). In table 7.1, this situation is clearly demonstrated. The EEC just cannot ignore international monetary upheavals. On the one hand, it is concerned (if the currencies of the Community member states appreciate) about the difficulties of selling its product abroad. On the other hand, it is equally concerned (when Community national currencies depreciate) at the danger of imported inflation.

Table 7.1: EEC: degree of 'open-ness' in national economies in 1982 (as a percentage of GNP)

	Exports	Imports
Belgium	64.0	68.4
Denmark	36.8	36.3
France	22.2	24.0
Germany (West)	29.5	28.7
Greece	14.7	26.4
Ireland	53.2	68.1
Italy	24.7	28.2
Netherlands	58.9	54.9
United Kingdom	27.1	23.9
EEC Total	29.9	30.1

Source: EEC Commission, 'European Economy', No. 12, July 1982.

Within the EEC itself, when embarking upon any form of monetary union (and bearing in mind the defects of the 'Snake' Arrangement), in the medium term, it is absolutely essential that inflation rates tend to converge. In the short run (particularly in the case of smaller countries whose currencies may be supported by their bigger partners, e.g. Denmark *vis-à-vis* West Germany), it may be possible to ride out speculation against a national currency through the adoption of a 'portfolio approach'.[3] But, sooner or later, something has to give way — that 'something' is normally the parity of the currency.

Therefore, in creating the EMS, the architects had to take into consideration a number of criteria; these were:

(i) The System would have to be more flexible (concerning exchange-rate adjustments) than its predecessor.

(ii) At the same time, the System would have to embody more constraints (or a greater degree of encouragement) on participants so that they would have to take measures leading to a reduction in national inflation rates.

(iii) To overcome the reticence of some countries towards the System, more generous credit provisions would have to be created than was the case under the 'Snake' Arrangement.

(iv) A greater role should be given to the European Currency Unit, the ECU.

(v) The EMS should encourage further integration among member states.

These are five important criteria with major implications for the EEC. To what degree, in its mechanisms and record, has the EMS met these criteria? Before making such an assessment, it is first necessary to carefully examine the precise mechanisms of the EMS. Then, the author proposes to analyse the record of the System in operation. Lastly, an assessment of the EMS, to date, will be made. Following this assessment, the relevance of the EMS as a possible model for Latin America will be examined.

THE MECHANISMS OF THE SYSTEM

The mechanisms of the European Monetary System,[4] which came into operation on 13 March 1979, clearly reflect the original aims of the System's architects — together with the subsequent refinements added thereto by the Commission. Had the old mechanism of a common band for a currency-to-currency ('GRID') fluctuation simply been adopted, the EMS would not have differed from its predecessor. However, since a further degree of convergence and integration was to be a major aim of the new System, more sophisticated, effective and responsible mechanisms had to be invented. The outcome is two bands of fluctuation running side by side. The first is indeed the old national currency to national currency (or 'GRID') mechanism, whereby a band of fluctuation (as was formerly the case with the 'Snake' System), 2.25 per cent (with a band of 6 per cent allowed for Italy), operates. However, alongside this band a much more effective ECU-national currency band of fluctuation operates. Here, the Commission had introduced a most novel system. This is the 'individualization' of the band of fluctuation for each participating currency (see Figure 7.1). This was necessary in order to prevent certain currencies from coming under unwarranted pressure on the exchange markets. At the same time, this mechanism was further refined by the very important introduction of a 'divergence' threshold, the equivalent of 75 per cent of the central part of the

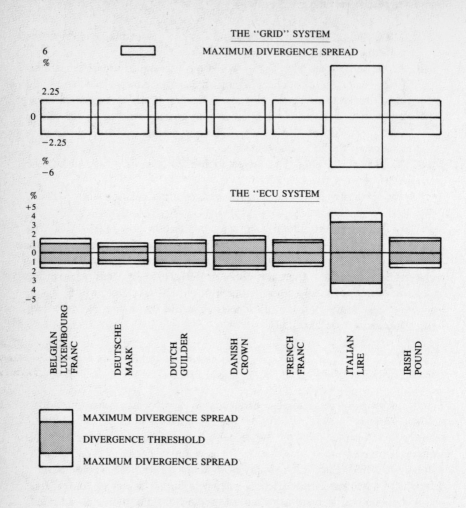

THE "GRID" SYSTEM

MAXIMUM DIVERGENCE SPREAD

THE "ECU SYSTEM

MAXIMUM DIVERGENCE SPREAD

DIVERGENCE THRESHOLD

MAXIMUM DIVERGENCE SPREAD

DIVERGENCE THRESHOLD

When a currency reaches the upper or lower limits of this band, the Government concerned must intervene in the exchange markets.

Figure 7.1

Source: Reproduced from 'The European Monetary System — Six Months Later,' P. Coffey, *Three Banks Review*, December 1979, London.

Table 7.2: The Commission's 'individualization' of maximum divergence spreads and divergence thresholds

Currencies	Maximum divergence spread *vis-à-vis the ECU*	Divergence threshold *vis-à-vis* the ECU
Belgian/Luxembourg Franc	2.03	1.52
Deutsche Mark	1.51	1.13
Dutch Guilder	2.01	1.51
Danish Crown	2.18	1.64
French Franc	1.80	1.35
Italian Lira	5.43	4.07
Irish Pound	2.22	1.67
Pound Sterling	—	—

'individualization', at which point the country concerned should take action to bring its currency into line (see Table 7.2).

Here, the responsibilities of the country concerned when the Divergence Indicator is reached *vis-à-vis* the ECU by its currency are clearly laid down by the Resolution of the Council of Ministers of 5 December 1978. These are: 'diversified intervention; monetary measures; drawing on credit facilities, and external and domestic policy measures.'

Another major innovation of the EMS is the important place given to the ECU.[5] The idea here is that the Community's unit-of-account (used for all official EEC transactions) should be the king-pin for future moves towards the implementation of an economic and monetary union. The hoped-for means of achieving this aim was to have been through a transformation of the European Fund for Monetary Co-operation (at present a shadow of a legal entity) into a more concrete organ at a second stage in the evolution of the EMS. To this end, the participating member states, together with the United Kingdom and Greece, which are not members of the EMS, have exchanged 20 per cent of their holdings of gold and dollars against ECUs.

The lack of credits under the old 'Snake' System was one of its more serious defects. This important defect has been largely made good under the EMS. Thus, the amount of credits available to member states — should they face pressures on their currencies and balance-of-payments problems — are substantially larger. In 1981, the approximate value of these credits[6] was 25 billion units of account, as compared with 11.45 billion units of account under the former system. A further refinement of the System was the setting-aside each year for a period of five years — until 1983 — of 200 million ECUs to provide interest subsidies on EIB or NCI loans for Italy and Ireland.

To the unitiated outside observer, the sharing of the responsibilities for the management of the EMS may, at first sight, seem to be unduly complex. In reality, this sharing is purely a reflection of the difficult process of economic, monetary and political integration. Actual responsibility for day-to-day intervention in the money markets to keep national currencies within the agreed bands of fluctuation naturally lies with the central banks of the participating member states. However, the overall responsibility for the management of the EMS lies with the Commission. Furthermore, this same body has the right to make recommendations about national economic and monetary policy matters to the same countries. This right emanates from the decision of the Council of Ministers concerning the attainment of a high degree of convergence of the economic policies of the member states, taken in February 1974.

Officially and legally speaking, the swaps of 20 per cent of national holdings of gold and dollars against ECUs on a three-monthly revolving basis,[7] made by nine member states, were with the European Fund for Monetary Co-operation. However, this institution is only a legal fiction consisting of a nameplate on a building in Luxembourg.[8] Thus, the swaps, like the short- and medium-term credits, are in fact managed by the Bank for International Settlements (B.I.S.), in Basle, in Switzerland. The only precondition here is that the two or three officials managing these matters should be Community nationals.

Lastly, whilst short-term credits are accorded to member states on an automatic basis, such is not the case with medium-term ones. Here, the Council of Ministers (advised by the Commission) makes policy recommendations to the country or countries receiving aid. Equally, where the Community floats loans on the international market on behalf of member states, the Council attaches policy conditions to such help.

THE RECORD OF THE EMS

To the author, the EMS has been the significant success story of the EEC since its First Enlargement. True, it has not been without its disappointments — but its successes have largely outweighed its defects. To its credit, the System has provided the world with a zone of monetary stability. On the technical side, exchange rate adjustments (with one exception) have been swift, discreet and appropriate. The question of inflation has been a more vexed one. In the first two years, things seemed to get worse and only in the United Kingdom did inflation rates fall. In France and Greece, governments pursued inflationary policies. Then things started to change. Everywhere, except in Greece (which is not a member of the EMS), member states started to pursue or to intensify deflationary policies. In both Belgium and France draconian measures were applied. In recent years, there has been a tendency for inflation rates to fall — and in a number of cases even to converge. For the first time in twenty years, all the member states of the EEC have adopted the same public economic policy choice. Without the EMS, it is doubtful that they would have done so.

But, the real success story is, without doubt, the increase in the use of the commercial ECU. Thus, for example, there has been an increase of 160 per cent between September 1984 and the end of March 1986 in ECU inter-bank assets held by commercial banks (from the equivalent of 23.9 to 61 billion US dollars). Furthermore, since June 1985, it has been possible to purchase travellers' cheques denominated in ECUs. More recently, an international clearing system for settling commercial ECU accounts between commercial banks was brought on-stream by the Bank for International Settlements on 1 October 1986.

Whilst it is possible to open ECU-denominated private bank accounts (in November 1986) without restriction in the Benelux countries, Denmark and the United Kingdom, in other countries it is only possible to do so in order to receive credits and/or loans. In West Germany, the ECU is not recognized as a foreign currency, and, consequently, it is not possible to open such bank accounts in that country. However, even in West Germany it is possible to discern a change in official attitudes (as from June 1987, West Germany recognizes the ECU as a foreign currency). Although no country has left the EMS, the System has not been without its disappointments. Thus, it was hoped that the EMS would, in March 1981, move to a further stage of integration and that the phantom European Fund for Monetary Co-operation would be transformed into a 'real' Fund. It was also hoped that a further allocation of official ECUs would be made. Unfortunately, none of these hopes have been realized, and, in fact, regarding the last point, practically none of the reserves of official ECUs have been used.

Then, the controversial issue of Britain's possible membership of the System continues unabated. Despite repeated calls by the Commission, the Deutsche Bundesbank and the Confederation of British Industry for British membership, the British Prime Minister still believes that 'the time is not yet ripe' for such a move.

A POSSIBLE MODEL FOR LATIN AMERICA?

To the author, there are no insurmountable reasons why a group of Latin American countries should not form a *de facto* monetary union — leading to an eventual full economic and monetary union. As in the case of Western Europe, the author assumes that any such move would be taken on a voluntary basis and that candidates for such a union would see clear advantages in it for themselves. Therefore, it is useful to examine the possible advantages for Latin American countries for membership of such a union, and the necessary pre-conditions and the possible candidates for a form of Latin American Monetary System (henceforth referred to as the LAMS).

THE ADVANTAGES OF A LAMS

If we take the European Monetary System as our example then it is possible to see a number of clear advantages for Latin American countries if they were to form a LAMS. The principal advantages may be the following:

    (i) A LAMS — using a common numéraire (like the ECU) as its point of reference — will be a help in controlling inflation since, if the member states do not keep their national economic houses in order, then, to paraphrase the words of Mr Louw of the Commission of the European Communities, 'the exchange market will take care of their currencies'. Inflation, until recently, has been the main problem of most Latin American countries and has, as in parts of Europe in the 1920s and 1930s, threatened their economic and political stability — and their creditability internationally. Therefore, any reasonable means of controlling inflation should be seriously examined.

(ii) One of the key elements of a LAMS would be convertibility. This factor — allied with low inflation rates — would probably lead to a greater degree of economic integration between Latin American countries.

(iii) When examining a LAMS, one is also considering, as in the case of the EMS, a common market. This implies the freeing of the movement of labour, capital and services. Such a freedom would also probably lead to a greater degree of economic integration among Latin American countries.

(iv) The increased stability of the economies of the Latin American countries — and the possible use of one or more Latin American Currency Units (LACUs) would give these countries a much greater negotiating power in international economic, monetary and trade forums — thus improving their standards of living.

NECESSARY PRECONDITIONS FOR A LAMS

There are a number of quite fundamental necessary preconditions that would have to be met if Latin American countries are to embark upon the construction of a monetary system similar to the EMS. However, as in the case of the European Economic Community, one should, in advance, consider a proviso — which is that of a monetary system of 'two speeds'. Thus, as in the case of the EMS, not all countries of a common market feel that the 'time is ripe' for membership of such a system. In the EEC, two existing member states, Greece and the United Kingdom, are only 'passive' members of the EMS, whilst the two newest ones, Spain and Portugal, do not participate in any way in the system and their currencies are not even part of the ECU. Thus, it is quite possible that some Latin American countries might not wish to join a LAMS — or perhaps they might wish to be only 'passive' members. For those countries that might contemplate full and active membership, the following basic pre-conditions would have to be satisfied:

(i) The countries concerned should be conducting a substantial amount of trade with each other — and they should preferably be quite 'open' economies. In the case of Latin American countries (see Tables 7.3–7.7), they are not conducting such a large amount of their trade with each other. This situation would have to change — otherwise the main *raison d'être* of the whole enterprise will disappear.

(ii) Apart from this trade, these countries should either already be reasonably

Table 7.3: Bolivia: imports and exports as a percentage of total, 1982

IMPORTS	%	EXPORTS	%
Andean Pact Group	3.2	Andean Pact group	3.8
Other L.A. countries	29.0	Other L.A. countries	48.0
EEC	16.3	EEC	15.0
USA	29.0	USA	26.1
Japan	11.0	Japan	1.8
Others	11.5	Others	5.3

Source: UN 1984, *International Statistics Yearbook*, Vol. 1, New York, 1986.

Table 7.4: Colombia: imports and exports as a percentage of total, 1984

IMPORTS	%	EXPORTS	%
Andean Pact Group	12.3	Andean Pact group	4.8
Other L.A. countries	6.3	Other L.A. countries	2.6
EEC	16.1	EEC	35.0
USA	34.2	USA	31.5
Japan	9.6	Japan	4.4
Others	21.4	Others	21.7

Source: UN 1984, *International Statistics Yearbook*, Vol. 1, New York, 1986.

Table 7.5: Ecuador: imports and exports as a percentage of total, 1984

IMPORTS	%	EXPORTS	%
Andean Pact Group	4.4	Andean Pact group	2.1
Other L.A. countries	12.3	Other L.A. countries	1.3
EEC	16.1	EEC	3.1
USA	30.8	USA	63.9
Japan	14.1	Japan	0.7
Others	22.3	Others	28.9

Source: UN 1984, *International Statistics Yearbook*, Vol. 1, New York, 1986.

Table 7.6: Peru: imports and exports as a percentage of total, 1984

IMPORTS	%	EXPORTS	%
Andean Pact Group	3.2	Andean Pact group	6.0
Other L.A. countries	16.3	Other L.A. countries	5.0
EEC	16.6	EEC	18.2
USA	33.3	USA	44.3
Japan	8.8	Japan	9.0
Others	21.8	Others	17.5

Source: UN 1984, *International Statistics Yearbook*, Vol. 1, New York, 1986.

Table 7.7: Venezuela: imports and exports as a percentage of total, 1982

IMPORTS	%	EXPORTS	%
Andean Pact Group	2.6	Andean Pact group	2.3
Other L.A. countries	4.9	Other L.A. countries	8.4
EEC	18.1	EEC	17.8
USA	48.3	USA	13.2
Japan	8.1	Japan	4.9
Others	18.0	Others	53.4

Source: UN 1984, *International Statistics Yearbook*, Vol. 1, New York, 1986.

integrated among themselves — or at least they should intend to construct a common market together.

(iii) They should create a system which, like the EMS, embodies flexibility in operation and policy co-ordination constraints among the members.

(iv) Adequate credits (to be given under certain specific conditions) should be available for members facing balance-of-payments problems. Equally, candidates should ensure that they have adequate exchange reserves and/or have access to adequate credits in order to enable them to ride out upheavals in the exchange markets.

(v) A common unit of account should be created in order to act as the numéraire for the operation of a LAMS and to clear transactions between the members.

(vi) Lastly, but by no means least, prospective members should have a common economic policy choice or goal which should at least include the control of inflation as one of its main component parts.

POSSIBLE CANDIDATES FOR MEMBERSHIP OF A LAMS

To the author, there are, at the time of writing (December 1986), two countries that should, within a few years, be able to form a LAMS — these are Argentina and Brazil. Then, there is a group of Latin American countries, that, given more time, and, accepting the possibility of a union of 'two speeds', could consider forming another LAMS. This latter group is the Andean Pact Group of Countries.

In the former case, the two countries have recently agreed to form a common market together. Furthermore, they have both adopted anti-inflationary policies with some vigour and have drastically reduced their levels of inflation. In both cases, the result has been an increase in their international credibility. Both Argentina and Brazil have, surprisingly, adopted the same common economic policy goal before deciding to form a common market — even the Europeans were not as sophisticated as these Latin American countries! As these countries trade more with each other and as they become more integrated, the stage would seem to be set for the creation of a LAMS between these two giants.

CONCLUSIONS

According to the Federal Trust pamphlet, 'The Time is Ripe', published in London in November 1984, the ECU, when compared with currencies such as the pound sterling, the US dollar, the Yen, the Swiss france and the Swedish krona, has been the most stable international currency. To the author, this performance is due, in part, to the competition of the ECU, and, in part, to the anti-inflationary policies adopted by EEC countries.

The attractiveness of this unit of account and the increasing use of the commercial ECU — together with the general success of the EMS — do provide certain lessons for the Latin American countries. Firstly, if at a very basic level, should Latin American countries wish to link their currencies together, they would be conducting at least a reasonable amount of trade with each other and their levels of inflation should be similar. In the former case, as we can see from Tables 7.3–7.7 — specifically for the countries of the Andean Pact Group — Latin American countries do not conduct a great deal of trade between themselves. However, in the latter case, a number of Latin American countries are making efforts to control their levels of inflation. In a number of countries, notably Argentina, Bolivia, Brazil and Peru, this has also taken the form of the introduction of a new currency unit such as the Austral in Argentina and the Cruzado in Brazil. Two groups of countries would, in the medium to long run, seem to be candidates for an eventual LAMS. One group would be the Andean Pact Group of Countries, and the other would be Argentina and Brazil.

In the former case, whilst the level of intra-group trade is still disappointingly low, the aims of the Group are those of integration and these countries do possess the institutional apparatus plus experience in co-operation that are generally lacking in other parts of Latin America. Thus, given the political will to move forwards together, these countries, among which two members, Colombia and Venezuela, do exhibit satisfactory inflation levels and international credit ratings, could eventually move towards a regional LAMS.

In the long run, however, the Common Market agreed upon in 1986 by Argentina and Brazil does offer serious possibilities for a redoubtable regional LAMS. These two countries with their relatively advanced state economic development, the size of their joint internal markets and the complementarity of Argentine agriculture linked to that of Brazilian industry — plus their combined desire to control inflation — would present a formidable regional and international force. In international trade, credit and debt negotiations, the combined force of these two giants would be enormous.

Lastly, a necessary philosophical note: when, in 1958, the original six member states of the European Economic Community started on their path of creating a Common Market, they were, in every sense of the expression, much less integrated than they are today. However, today, now that the number of member states has doubled, the economic development among them is extremely disparate — certainly at least as much so as presently seen among Latin American countries. Nevertheless, this great disparity does not prevent them from linking their currencies together in either a passive and/or an active way. This final observation is perhaps of great significance for Latin American countries.

NOTES

1. For a more detailed account of the background to and the experience of the 'Snake' Arrangement, the following works may be recommended: P.Coffey and J.R.Presley, *European Monetary Integration*, London, MacMillan, 1971. P.Coffey (ed.), *Main Economic Policy Areas of the EEC*, Den Haag, Nijhoff, 1983.
2. The original call for an EMS had in fact been made by Mr Roy Jenkins (then President of the Commission of the European Communities), in Florence, in 1976.
3. The author would define the 'portfolio approach' as being the willingness of institutes and/or governments to hold the paper of another government.
4. All the EEC member states — except Greece, Portugal, Spain and the United Kingdom — participate in the EMS. Britain and Greece have participated in the 'swap' operation — exchanging 20 per cent of their holdings of gold and dollars against ECUs.
5. The original composition of the ECU, as calculated on 28 June 1974, is as follows:

The original composition of the ECU

0.828	Deutsche Mark	3.66	Belgian Francs
0.0885	Pound Sterling	0.14	Luxembourg Francs
1.15	French Francs	0.217	Danish Krone
109.00	Italian Lira	0.00759	Irish Punt
0.286	Dutch Guilders		

On 16 September 1984, the following new composition was adopted:

The new composition of the ECU: as a percentage of the total		The new composition of the ECU: in national currencies
Deutsche Mark	: 32.0	0.719
French Franc	: 19.0	1.31
Pound Sterling	: 15.0	0.0878
Italian Lira	: 10.2	140.00
Dutch Guilder	: 10.1	0.256
Belgian Franc	: 8.2	3.71
Danish Krone	: 2.7	0.219
Greek Drachma	: 1.3	1.15
Irish Punt	: 1.2	0.00871
Luxembourg Franc	: 0.3	0.16

The main features of the new composition are the reduction in the share formerly held by the Deutsche Mark, the Dutch guilder and the Belgian/Luxembourg franc. In turn, the French franc, the Italian lira and the Irish punt have increased their share. The pound sterling and the Danish krone remain stable. The novelty is the participation — for the first time — of the Greek drachma in the ECU.
6. The new credits are divided as follows: 14 billion ECUs in short-term and 11 billion

ECUs in medium-term credit. A short-term credit is available for a maximum period of nine months and a medium-term one for between three and five years.

7. This formula was adopted in order to leave the ownership of these reserves in the hands of the member states.

8. This situation exists because, in 1973, no decision could be made about the location of the final home for this institution — the contestants being Luxembourg and London.

8

Financial Aspects of Intra-Regional Trade in Latin America

*José Antonio Ocampo**

One of the most striking aspects of the recent economic crisis in Latin America was the collapse of intra-regional trade. Until very recently, reciprocal trade was regarded as the most visible aspect of economic integration and as an important basis for a common defense policy in an eventual international crisis. Thus far, all such hopes have been completely frustrated. The central argument of this paper is that the root of the present situation lies in the structural imbalances of intra-regional trade which emerged in the years before the crisis and a system of payments which fosters policies that restrict reciprocal commerce. Thus, it seems evident that a lasting solution to the trade crisis is possible only to the extent that these problems are overcome.

The first section of the paper reflects on the growth and structure of trade within Latin America. In the second part, the LAIA payments agreement is analyzed on the basis of its functioning during the recent crisis. This analysis leads to a theoretical discussion on problems relevant to the redesigning of the system of payments. Finally, based on these theoretical considerations, alternative reforms of the current system and the major obstacles to their implementation are considered.

1. THE RISE AND FALL OF INTRA-REGIONAL TRADE

Latin American intra-regional trade flourished for the first time in the 1960s. Although part of this growth was associated with the regional integration schemes then under way, it was also part of a more general search for trade

* FEDESARROLLO, Bogotá, Colombia. This paper is a revised version of an article published in Altaf Gauhar (ed.), *Regional Integration: The Latin American Experience*, London, Third World Foundation, 1985. I am grateful to Pilar Esguerra for updating the statistical tables.

opportunities that had been overlooked both under export-led growth and in the more inward-looking models of development. This process was especially noticeable in the Central American Common Market, where intra-regional imports grew at an annual rate of 26.2 percent in 1961–70, compared to 10.7 percent for total imports from non-member countries. In the case of LAFTA (LAIA), the corresponding rates were 9.6 percent and 5.5 percent.[1] By 1970, regional trade within LAIA already made up 11.6 percent of total trade (excluding fuels) and 12.4 percent for all developing countries of America (see Table 8.1). Furthermore, manufactured goods accounted for 46.9 percent of total intra-regional trade (excluding fuels) in LAIA and 53.6 percent for the developing countries of the continent.[2]

In the 1970s, the high rates of growth of trade were sustained, based on the rapid expansion of the international economy up to 1963, and on the increased demand from the region's oil-producing countries and the boom of international capital markets. Thus, excluding fuels, intra-regional trade grew at an annual rate of 22 and 23 percent, and by 1980 it came to account for 18.9 and 18.4 percent of total trade for the developing countries in America and LAIA, respectively (see Table 8.1). Furthermore, the relative importance of manufactured goods was even more pronounced, reaching 69 percent of this trade by 1980.[3]

The network of reciprocal trade crumbled during the recent crisis. The first to weaken was Central American trade, which fell by 18 percent in 1981 and by 1982 had contracted 32 percent compared to the peak 1980 level.[4] By 1982, the crisis began to affect LAIA. Although this trade already experienced a small decline of 2.4 percent in 1981 if oil products are excluded, its collapse took place in the following years, reaching an accumulated contraction of 49 percent between 1980 and 1983. The decline of Andean trade lagged with respect to the Central American Common Market and LAIA as a whole, owing to the delay in the adoption of adjustment policies in Venezuela and the continuing high levels of imports in Colombia. Nevertheless, this trade experienced a drop of 3.5 percent in 1981, excluding fuels, and a further decline of 1.4 percent in 1982. However, the real collapse came about in 1983, with a decline of 49 percent with respect to 1982 and of 57 percent compared to the peak 1980 level.[5]

At the root of this dramatic contraction of trade lie the balance of payments policies carried out by all countries, which reserved for national production a larger proportion of aggregate domestic demands. The impact of these policies on intra-regional trade did not contribute to correct the balance of payments disequilibrium of the region as a whole. On the contrary, they proved to be counterproductive, to the extent that the decline of non-traditional exports to the region fed export pessimism in many countries. Furthermore, the contraction of trade was superfluous from the point of view of balance of payments adjustment, in so far as it centered on those segments of intra-regional exchange that were in bilateral or multilateral equilibrium in the years preceding the crisis. Nonetheless, the fact that the contraction of trade had either no effect or even a negative one on the regional balance of payments, did not mean that some

Table 8.1: Growth of trade among developing countries of America

	(1) Intra-regional trade		(2) Intra-regional trade excluding fuels*		(3) Intra-regional trade as a % of total trade, excluding fuels	
	Total	LAIA	Total	LAIA	Total %	LAIA
1970	3028	1247	1635	1114	12.4	11.6
1973	5013	2340	2938	1971	13.5	11.8
1974	9689	4006	4584	3156	15.5	14.5
1975	9616	4024	5089	3268	17.2	16.3
1976	10681	4693	5569	3661	16.2	15.1
1977	11685	5778	6651	4582	16.3	15.5
1978	12470	5911	7575	5098	16.6	15.4
1979	18350	8916	10184	7741	18.5	18.8
1980	22491	10947	11931	8830	18.9	18.4
1981	22591	11883	11211	8621	18.1	17.7
1982	21880	10402	10592	6827	16.8	16.1
1983	19799	8210	8533	4489	10.5	9.9
1984	19627	8751	8296	4915	9.8	9.3

* SITC 3

Source: United Nations, *Yearbook of International Trade Statistics*, 1970 to 1981; *Monthly Bulletin*, 1981 to 1984.

countries did not benefit from the policies adopted. Indeed, this was a feature of the adjustment processes witnessed in Latin America in the last few years. The contraction of trade within Latin America should thus be seen as a result of a Latin America version of 'beggar-thy-neighbor' policies, in the terminology of classical balance of payments theory.

The dramatic impact of the adjustment policies on intra-regional trade reflects the trade imbalances typical of the booming years. The network of Latin American trade in 1979–81 (Tables 8.2 and 8.3) reflected, in the first place, the strong surplus position (obviously excluding fuels), of Brazil with respect to each of the LAIA countries. Also noteworthy were the strong surpluses of Colombia with respect to Venezuela and of Argentina with respect to Bolivia, Mexico and, to a lesser extent, Paraguay, Peru and Venezuela. Aside from its substantial deficit position with respect to Brazil and Colombia, and its deficit with Argentina, Venezuela has also a significant negative balance with Chile. Finally, looking at non-LAIA trade and excluding disequilibria associated with fuel imports, we should mention Nicaragua's deficit within the Central America Common Market, Guatemala's and Costa Rica's positive balance within that market, Mexico's surplus with Central America and Colombia's and Peru's surpluses with Panama.

The main source of disequilibrium was Brazil's surplus position. As we will see in Section 5, the Brazilian surplus made up, in 1980 and 1981, most of non-compensated LAIA trade. In some sense, intra-regional trade was operating as a mechanism through which Brazil partially solved its serious oil imbalance. Under such circumstances, the system worked only as long as a favorable foreign exchange position was maintained in Latin America as a whole, but led to a rapid collapse when deficit countries in intra-regional trade were forced to correct their general balance of payments disequilibria. In terms of intra-regional exports, Brazil was the most affected, with sales to the region decreasing by US$2.776 million between 1981 and 1985, an amount equivalent to 57 percent of the total decline in trade within LAIA (see Table 8.5 below). Although the contraction of Brazilian exports was in most cases a direct effect of the adjustment policies adopted by other countries within the region, some indirect effects were also important. Noteworthy in this respect was the impact of the Venezuelan crisis on Colombian exports, which created an intra-regional deficit in a country that had traditionally been in equilibrium, forcing it to reduce imports from the rest of Latin America, particularly Brazil, with which it had maintained substantial deficits in previous years.

The specific form of contraction of intra-Latin American trade was thus a reflection of disequilibria present in the years preceding the crisis. As we will try to show later on, no lasting reform of the payments mechanism is possible without a resolution of these imbalances.

Table 8.2: Intra-regional trade of the main developing countries of America 1979–1981 (Annual figures in million dollars, exports f.o.b.)

Exports from/to	Bolivia	Colombia	Ecuador	Peru	Venezuela	Andean Group	Argentina	Brazil	Chile	Mexico	Paraguay	Uruguay	Rest of LAIA	Costa Rica	El Salvador	Guatemala	Honduras	Nicaragua	CACM	Dom. Rep.	Jamaica	Panama	Others	Total
Bolivia	-.-	7.5	1.1	29.4	4.0	42.0	246.1	30.8	30.6	1.4	-.-	0.5	309.9	-.-	-.-	-.-	-.-	-.-	-.-	-.-	-.-	-.-	-.-	351.9
Colombia	2.8	-.-	65.8	29.4	322.8	420.8	55.5	6.5	40.6	17.3	0.5	1.2	121.6	5.2	2.7	7.1	5.0	2.3	22.3	5.6	2.0	52.2	46.6	671.1
Ecuador	0.6	72.0	-.-	10.5	43.0	126.1	36.7	35.4	146.6	17.0	0.3	36.0	272.0	1.5	0.3	0.5	0.1	-.-	2.4	-.-	-.-	88.4	455.2	944.1
Peru	65.2	72.5	67.4	-.-	56.1	261.2	43.8	95.4	56.2	64.3	1.5	7.1	268.3	4.7	3.1	0.5	0.5	0.4	9.2	2.0	0.1	66.0	63.0	669.8
Venezuela	-.-	250.0	15.3	23.0	-.-	288.3	55.3	613.3	234.7	28.3	-.-	85.7	1017.3	69.0	96.3	108.7	58.0	80.7	412.7	222.0	165.0	149.7	4165.0	6420.0
Andean group	68.6	402.0	149.6	92.3	425.9	1138.4	437.4	781.4	508.7	128.8	2.3	130.5	1989.1	80.4	102.4	116.8	63.6	83.4	446.6	229.6	167.1	356.3	4729.8	9056.9
Argentina	126.5	47.5	16.8	92.9	109.1	392.8	-.-	748.6	188.7	172.7	180.9	184.1	1475.0	5.6	1.4	3.3	3.4	3.5	17.6	1.1	1.6	9.6	24.3	1922.0
Brazil	187.3	168.3	51.3	153.0	278.7	838.6	896.7	-.-	485.0	468.3	394.3	297.3	2541.6	16.3	4.0	13.7	15.7	13.0	62.7	16.7	6.3	35.0	94.4	3595.3
Chile	23.3	69.9	21.5	53.6	73.9	242.2	249.2	373.5	-.-	66.3	6.7	21.0	716.7	-.-	-.-	-.-	-.-	-.-	-.-	9.0	-.-	10.7	6.7	985.3
Mexico	2.7	47.0	46.7	23.0	75.3	194.7	39.0	434.7	35.0	-.-	1.0	8.0	517.7	78.7	40.3	80.3	19.3	42.0	266.6	49.0	31.7	56.3	80.3	1196.3
Paraguay	0.6	0.2	-.-	0.2	-.-	1.2	64.6	41.2	9.8	3.0	-.-	11.0	129.6	-.-	-.-	-.-	-.-	-.-	-.-	-.-	-.-	0.4	0.4	132.0
Uruguay	1.8	3.1	0.8	5.4	2.5	13.6	113.7	175.4	20.3	4.5	13.2	-.-	327.1	-.-	-.-	-.-	-.-	-.-	0.4	-.-	0.3	0.3	0.4	342.1
Rest of LAIA	342.2	336.0	137.1	328.1	539.7	1683.1	1363.2	1773.4	738.8	714.8	598.1	521.4	5707.7	100.6	45.7	97.4	38.7	58.5	347.3	75.8	39.9	112.3	206.9	8173.0
Costa Rica	1.0	3.5	5.4	1.6	2.0	13.5	1.4	2.5	1.7	6.5	0.1	0.1	12.2	-.-	47.3	65.4	26.0	82.8	224.2	3.8	1.6	40.3	8.7	304.3
El Salvador	-.-	0.7	1.8	0.1	0.2	2.1	0.1	-.-	0.2	0.6	-.-	-.-	0.9	56.2	-.-	162.6	0.5	32.1	255.4	0.6	0.1	7.3	2.3	268.0
Guatemala	0.5	-.-	1.1	0.2	1.4	3.9	0.2	0.8	0.3	33.4	-.-	-.-	34.8	72.9	192.7	-.-	53.5	65.7	384.8	6.1	0.7	15.6	2.8	448.7
Honduras	-.-	1.3	-.-	-.-	4.2	5.5	0.1	0.7	-.-	0.8	-.-	-.-	1.7	15.8	0.1	30.6	-.-	26.8	73.3	2.8	1.2	3.5	16.7	104.7
Nicaragua	-.-	0.1	-.-	0.2	0.5	0.8	0.1	0.3	-.-	2.5	-.-	-.-	2.9	32.7	12.5	16.7	13.2	-.-	75.1	0.1	-.-	2.5	0.7	83.1
CACM	1.5	5.6	8.3	2.1	8.3	25.8	2.0	4.3	2.2	43.8	0.1	0.1	52.5	177.6	252.6	275.3	93.2	211.2	1012.8	13.4	3.7	69.2	31.2	1208.8
Dominican Rep.	-.-	1.7	-.-	-.-	68.3	70.0	-.-	0.2	0.5	-.-	-.-	0.1	0.8	0.5	-.-	0.1	0.2	-.-	1.0	-.-	2.0	0.5	22.3	96.0
Jamaica	-.-	0.3	-.-	0.1	22.5	22.9	0.2	1.9	-.-	0.8	0.5	0.8	4.2	0.1	0.1	0.3	0.2	-.-	0.7	2.1	-.-	2.4	76.6	108.4
Panama	0.4	3.2	1.9	0.2	5.7	11.4	0.2	0.1	0.5	1.3	0.1	0.2	2.4	17.1	4.4	3.9	3.3	7.6	36.3	2.2	0.1	-.-	21.2	73.5
TOTAL	412.7	748.8	296.9	422.8	1070.4	2951.6	1803.0	2561.3	1250.0	889.5	599.1	653.1	7756.7	376.3	405.2	493.8	203.1	367.5	1944.7	323.1	212.6	540.7	5087.9	18717.5

Source: IMF, *Direction of Trade*.

Table 8.3: Intra-regional trade among the LAIA countries, excluding fuels 1980–1981 (Annual figures in million dollars, exports f.o.b.)

Exports from/to	Bolivia	Colombia	Ecuador	Peru	Venezuela	Andean Group	Argentina	Brazil	Chile	Mexico	Paraguay	Uruguay	Rest of LAIA	Costa Rica	El Salvador	Guatemala	Honduras	Nicaragua	CACM	Panama	Cuba	Haiti	Dom. Rep.	Total Region	Total World
Bolivia	—.—	3.8	1.2	29.4	4.7	39.1	22.7	22.1	19.9	1.9	—.—	0.3	66.9	5.0	1.4	5.3	5.5	3.0	—.—	0.1	—.—	—.—	0.3	213.2	643.1
Colombia	2.9	—.—	71.5	37.1	305.5	417.0	59.4	5.5	46.3	16.1	0.6	1.5	129.4	1.6	0.3	0.5	0.3	0.5	20.3	60.3	4.5	1.2	5.8	638.5	3370.3
Ecuador	0.6	86.6	—.—	9.6	47.1	144.0	30.9	3.8	23.8	14.6	0.3	0.8	74.2	4.6	2.6	0.3	0.2	2.0	2.4	1.1	—.—	—.—	—.—	221.8	891.3
Peru	52.9	40.7	52.8	—.—	46.3	192.6	30.3	69.0	55.6	78.2	0.4	5.8	239.3	5.8	4.0	2.9	—.—	—.—	8.4	74.2	23.3	—.—	0.1	538.0	2557.2
Venezuela	0.6	45.8	12.0	17.7	—.—	76.1	8.4	25.9	1.8	27.1	—.—	0.1	63.3	—.—	—.—	—.—	—.—	—.—	14.9	1.0	—.—	—.—	3.5	158.9	1141.5
Andean group	57.0	176.9	137.6	93.7	403.6	868.8	151.9	126.2	147.4	137.9	1.3	8.6	573.4	17.2	8.3	9.0	6.0	5.5	46.1	136.6	27.8	1.3	9.7	1663.8	8603.3
Argentina	128.5	44.6	16.8	99.2	83.2	372.5	—.—	568.0	202.2	195.5	155.8	142.9	1264.4	5.3	1.1	3.4	3.6	4.8	18.3	8.5	71.5	0.3	1.1	1736.2	8141.9
Brazil	214.5	168.0	59.4	207.0	317.7	966.6	913.4	—.—	543.4	550.9	396.4	313.9	2718.0	16.4	2.6	13.1	14.4	19.1	65.8	30.7	—.—	5.2	19.6	3806.1	20643.3
Chile	22.8	73.6	17.9	69.4	73.7	257.4	237.0	361.7	—.—	69.6	7.4	22.5	698.2	2.9	0.8	1.6	0.9	—.—	6.4	7.1	0.1	—.—	7.9	977.1	4299.2
Mexico	2.5	44.0	31.8	27.7	63.4	169.4	38.4	153.7	32.9	—.—	0.9	6.9	232.8	35.8	10.2	42.3	14.1	17.7	119.8	20.4	18.7	0.3	8.7	570.3	4865.8
Paraguay	0.8	0.1	0.3	0.3	0.2	1.5	71.3	47.0	10.9	3.2	—.—	9.6	142.0	—.—	—.—	—.—	—.—	—.—	—.—	1.2	—.—	—.—	—.—	144.9	288.6
Uruguay	1.9	3.4	0.9	7.7	2.4	16.3	127.4	180.9	26.7	5.6	13.7	—.—	354.3	—.—	—.—	—.—	0.4	—.—	0.4	0.2	—.—	—.—	0.1	371.5	1137.5
Total LAIA	428.0	510.8	264.4	505.0	944.3	2652.5	1539.5	1437.6	963.4	962.8	575.6	504.6	5983.4	77.7	23.0	69.7	39.4	47.1	256.8	204.9	118.0	7.2	47.2	9270.0	47979.8

Source: BID-INTAL: Estadisticas exportacion de los paises de la AIADA 1980–1984, Buenos Aires, 1985

2. THE LAIA PAYMENTS AGREEMENTS

The LAIA system of reciprocal credits and multilateral compensation is the cornerstone of the intra-regional payments mechanism. According to this agreement, central banks give each other bilateral credit lines to finance temporary trade deficits which may arise in either direction. These lines seek to avoid situations in which bilateral deficits give way to foreign exchange transfers between central banks prior to the multilateral compensation of balances; nevertheless, whenever a bilateral balance exceeds the credit line, the corresponding deficit must be cancelled in advance. Every four months there is a clearing of accounts through the agent bank (*Banco de Reserva del Peru*), and debtors in the compensation must make a transfer to the Federal Reserve Bank of New York payable to the agent bank, which then cancels the surplus position of the creditors. The former instruments are complemented by the Santo Domingo Agreement, which allows the concession of short-term credit to countries experiencing increases in their deficits or decreases in their intra-regional surpluses, provided they also face an overall balance of payments deficit and an insufficiency of international reserves. It should be noted that the Central America Common Market has parallel mechanisms with similar characteristics. In addition, the Andean Group has a common Reserve Fund which acts independently of subregional exchange flows. Given the relative weight of the LAIA payments agreement, our discussion will focus on the functioning of this scheme.

Since the reciprocal credit lines and the multilateral compensation of balances are mechanisms that lessen the need for actual foreign exchange transfers, they reduce the costs of intra-regional trade. Furthermore, they constitute a way to optimize the use of foreign exchange reserves in the region, by reducing the transactions demand for reserves associated with such trade. Finally, the Santo Domingo Agreement acts as a multilateral credit instrument for some countries, beyond what is established under the compensation system.

Up until 1981, the payments systems worked satisfactorily, gradually increasing its coverage of intra-regional trade and eliminating between 70 and 80 percent of foreign exchange transfers (see Table 8.1 and 8.4). However, by 1979, the insufficiency of available credit lines was becoming apparent, leading to an increasing proportion of advanced transfers. Furthermore, the inadequacy of credit lines forced some central banks into operations outside the Agreement, in order to avoid exceeding the corresponding lines. None the less, the most important difficulties were only experienced in 1982, when several countries exercised their right to withdraw part or all of their debtor balances from the multilateral compensation, thus significantly reducing the system's coverage. In effect, total transactions decreased by 30 percent in 1982 in contrast to the 12 percent decline in LAIA trade. These difficulties were associated with the impossibility of financing the debtor balances of the largest countries within the framework of the Santo Domingo Agreement, thereby inducing them to withdraw from multilateral compensation in order to obtain a forced extension of bilateral credits. Furthermore, given the characteristics of the Agreement

Table 8.4: Growth of the LAIA payments agreement (Millions dollars)

	(1) Value of compensation	(2) Anticipated Transfers	(3) Total foreign exchange transfers	(4) Total transactions*	(3) As a % of (4)
1966	31.4	—	31.4	106.4	29.5
1967	93.8	—	93.8	332.8	28.2
1968	129.5	—	129.5	376.6	34.4
1969	81.0	—	81.0	479.2	16.9
1970	94.5	15.0	109.6	560.5	19.6
1971	111.9	24.0	136.0	708.1	19.2
1972	179.9	8.7	188.6	984.4	19.2
1973	271.1	9.4	280.5	1403.1	20.0
1974	309.6	77.8	387.4	2288.3	16.9
1975	608.8	51.7	660.4	2396.3	27.6
1976	546.9	105.4	652.2	2295.5	22.3
1977	717.2	170.1	887.3	3936.0	22.5
1978	1079.2	55.7	1134.9	4459.0	25.5
1979	1329.6	300.0	1629.6	6420.7	25.4
1980	1338.6	681.9	2020.6	8663.1	23.3
1981	1684.7	868.9	2553.6	9331.4	27.4
1982	1293.6	632.9	1926.6	6553.0	29.4
1983	1181.1	309.2	1490.2	6005.3	25.0
1984	1897.0	155.0	2052.0	6780.0	24.0
1985	1399.0	62.0	1460.0	6710.0	22.0

* Not all exchanges are compensated through this mechanism.
Source: BID-INTAL, *El proceso de Integración en América Latina*, 1982 to 1985.

with respect to maturities, it was impossible to solve even the problems of the smallest countries, in particular Bolivia, thus making it necessary to design *ad hoc* mechanisms to handle the situation.[6] However, after the initial collapse, existing credit lines have been able to finance an increasing proportion of reduced trade transactions. Thus, after 1982, the share of LAIA trade covered by the payments agreement has increased and anticipated transfers have declined sharply (see Tables 8.1 and 8.4).

The main problem of the payments system was undoubtedly its complete failure to arrest the collapse of intra-regional trade. Moreover, the contraction of trade was intimately linked to the payments system. In effect, an essential feature of the current system is the need to cover multilateral deficits in hard currencies. Once the deficit countries were faced with the need to correct their global balance of payments disequilibria, they were unable to justify a preference for Latin American imports; in fact, there were important reasons for discriminating against them, since they were more competitive with domestic production and less 'essential' from the national point of view. Furthermore, even if it were deemed desirable to maintain these imports, no mechanism existed to finance the intra-regional trade deficit without jeopardizing the overall balance of payments position of the importing country.

Finally, it is important to remark that, during the recent crisis, the payments system created great incentive for bilateralism. In practice, the system is a mixture of bilateral (the reciprocal credits) and multilateral instruments (the compensation and the Santo Domingo Agreement). Nevertheless, as we have seen, no effective mechanisms exist for multilateral financing of deficit balances, and, as we will see shortly, neither is there a significant degree of multilateralism in LAIA trade. Under these circumstances, the tendency towards bilateralism that was implicit in the practice of direct import controls finally prevailed.

3. THEORETICAL PROBLEMS OF THE PAYMENTS SYSTEM

Under present circumstances, the main defense of intra-regional trade is its contribution to the generation of foreign exchange in the region. In this regard, the classic arguments in Latin America have centered on the possibility of deepening import substitution, based on the economies of scale and specialization that a large market affords.[7] However, we should not lose sight of the role that intra-regional trade can play in the generation of new exports to the rest of the world, be it by virtue of the greater efficiency associated with international specialization, of the improvement in productive processes that stems from greater competition, or the learning process that derives from using the region as a platform for launching new export sectors. These arguments, and especially those relating to the virtues of competition in export development, played a more important role in post-war debates in Europe than those relating to import substitution.[8] Nevertheless, it is important to bear in mind the possible bias against exports to the rest of the world that could be created by preferential trade mechanisms, thereby diminishing the beneficial effect of intra-regional trade on the generation of net foreign exchange.

The collapse of trade in 1982 and 1983 made evident that the danger of losing hard currencies was more important than the advantages of reciprocal trade. This point of view is understandable, to the extent that it is irrational for the deficit countries to incur the double cost of sacrificing foreign exchange and economic activity, by simultaneously covering their deficit in hard currency and accepting imports from the region to the detriment of domestic production. The current system does not represent a panacea for the surplus countries either, since the adjustment process of deficit countries has meant, in practice, that they are left without the foreign exchange and economic activity associated with the export sectors. For this reason, the recovery of intra-regional trade is possible only on the basis of changes in the payments system which greatly reduce the use of hard currencies.

In the past, this problem received attention, both in Latin America and internationally, but the restoration of orthodox thinking and economic practice, on the one hand, and the fluidity of world capital markets, on the other, relegated it to a secondary position in the 1970s. The best-known point of view on this subject was developed by Keynes in his proposals for an International Clearing

Union.[9] Such proposals were based on a diagnosis of the dangers facing the international economy under a payments system that places the entire burden of external adjustment on deficit countries. At the global level, this system has an inherently deflationary bias, since it forces the deficit countries to adopt contractionary policies, while surplus countries are not obliged to adopt expansionary measures. With respect to international trade, this asymmetry of the international monetary system embodies a double danger: on the one hand, it creates a tendency to reduce world trade, if the adjustment policies of the deficit countries affect more quickly their imports than their sales to the rest of the world; on the other, there is a stimulus for restrictive trade practices and bilateralism, which reduce the benefits of international specialization.

Confronted with the need to reconstruct international trade in the post-war era and to break the yoke of bilateralism which was a remnant of the Great Depression and of the Second World War, European discussion in the later 1940s centered on the necessity of creating a payments system in Europe which would guarantee a high level of automaticity of credits for debtor countries. The European Payments Union was a product of the controversies of the time and was converted into one of the basic instruments for the promotion of European trade as well as opening the way to the convertibility of the currencies of the old continent and multilateral trade. Its basic characteristics were: (a) the channeling of all surpluses and deficits from European trade through a supranational organisation; (b) the automatic granting of credits to the Union partly by the surplus countries and partly by the deficit ones — though limits were set to the accumulated surpluses and deficits by the former and latter countries. In the case of deficit countries, the credit component of the quota was limited to 15 per cent of its total trade with the region; (c) the channelling of a part of Marshall Aid through the Payments union — thus facilitating a greater degree of financing of the deficits of some countries (including an important aid component) without reducing the weight of the afore-mentioned financing by surplus countries.[10] This last characteristic, the complement of the expansionary conditions for the world economy and trade in the fifties, clearly helped the agreement to work. In the present circumstances of Latin America, the same conditions do not hold since an import increase in credit would promote expansionary policies in deficit countries, thus generating a global inflationary bias. This criticism, which inevitably leads to the principle of conditionality, gradually gained ground, especially in the policies of the International Monetary Fund.[11] In this way, when the problem of a suitable payments scheme for Latin American Integration was posed in the late 1950s and early 1960s, the orthodox position was dominant.[12] The problem that was posed then was similar to the one that confronts us today, but it referred more to the confidence that potential debtor countries could have in the opening-up of trade to partners in the integration process, and certainly did not have the same dimensions as the current problem, in terms of the magnitude of the intra-regional surpluses and deficits of some countries.

The arrangement that emerged did not do much to inspire the confidence of the deficit countries in the integration process, since it came close to a pure clearing union with frequent settlement of accounts in hard currencies, freedom to carry on transactions outside the scheme and, at first, no mechanism to finance the debtor balances beyond the two-month period between clearings. Thus, the payments system did not contribute in any sense to the deviation of trade. Rather, it was a relatively orthodox solution, which worked well enough, owing to the small degree of trade in the first few years and, as we saw in the previous section, to the unique circumstances of the international economy in the 1970s.

4. THE ALTERNATIVES FOR ACTION

(a) Marginal adjustment to the present system

Given the magnitude of the intra-regional trade crisis, there is a consensus on the need to stretch the possibilities offered by the current system.[13] Nevertheless, the alternatives offered by the Santo Domingo Agreement are very limited. No country presently holds substantial foreign exchange reserves and there is thus no willingness to channel multilaterally the use of the meager international assets.[14] Therefore, the resources that would permit increased coverage under the Santo Domingo Agreement would have to come from sources outside the region. It would be possible, however, to recognize explicitly that the mechanism is incapable of financing large deficit balances and, therefore, to utilize its limited resources to finance the deficits of small countries for longer periods than currently allowed. In the case of the Andean group, it is also possible to use the resources of the Andean Reserve Fund, not so much to finance the general balance of payments disequilibria, but rather the deficits in subregional trade. It should be noted, however, that Andean Reserve Fund resources are currently committed to a large extent to the former kind of financing and that, under present circumstances, a proposal of this nature would end up channelling funds to Colombia, something that might be unacceptable to the other members of the Cartagena Agreement.

Actions related to the system of reciprocal credits and multilateral compensation would be directed toward increasing existing bilateral lines and extending the length of the compensation period. Although, as we saw in Section 2, credit lines are sufficient to finance existing commercial transactions, they would again become a limiting factor if intra-regional trade recovers from its depressed levels. On the other hand, the proposal for a multilateral use of bilateral credit to avoid anticipated transfer (a mechanism that is contained in the present agreement) does not seem very efficient. In this sense, it would be more reasonable to increase bilateral credit lines, even to make them unlimited prior to compensation, so as to eliminate anticipated payments.

Of all proposals for reform within the present system, the Brazilian recommendation to allow the cancelling of bilateral balances with debt instruments which could be used multilaterally is the most ambitious.[15] According to this proposal, the present bilateral credit mechanism would be preserved, but it would permit the payment of deficit balances between two countries with debt documents, while simultaneously authorizing the receiving country to pay off its debts in multilateral compensation with those papers. This system would lead to the accumulation of payments obligations of deficit countries in the hands of surplus countries in intra-regional trade. In this sense, the proposal resembles the payments systems that we will analyze in the following section. However, its mixture of multilateralism and bilateralism is quite cumbersome. The European experience in this area indicates that the system would force the surplus countries to grant *bilateral* credit to the deficit countries, in amounts that might not be desirable to the former, given the latter's degree of solvency. For this reason, it is much more acceptable for the creditors to channel all credit through a totally multilateral entity, in which all the countries share the risk that a deficit balance may not be paid in the future.[16]

An alternative to the previous proposal would be to generalize and improve mechanisms such as the 'Andean Peso' (AP), created in December 1984. The AP is allocated by the Andean Reserve Fund to the central banks of members of the Cartagena Agreement in proportion to their share in the capital of the Fund. Countries can use these resources to cancel out balances in LAIA compensations if both subregional as well as LAIA net positions are negative. However, the initial emission was quite limited (AP$80 million, equivalent to the same amount in US dollars) and, under present rules, net debtor countries must reestablish their AP positions within three months. Thus, although potentially significant, the current mechanism has only made a very limited contribution to the short-term international liquidity of members of the Andean Group.

(b) Thorough reforms

Obviously, a marginal reform to the present system is preferable to no change at all. Nevertheless, none of the proposals considered in the previous sections represent a lasting solution to the problem which we analyzed in Section 2 and 3 of this paper: the unwillingness on the part of the deficit countries to accept a payments mechanism that implies the risk of losing foreign exchange. Thus, the restoration of intra-regional trade is only possible if the surplus countries accept soft currencies as partial payment for exports and commit themselves, in the short or long run, to equilibrate their own intra-regional balance of payments. Furthermore, an agreement of this sort would provide a great incentive for the *diversion of trade* under current conditions, and would facilitate the *creation of trade*, without the fear on behalf of each country that such trade would worsen their critical balance of payments position.

The reforms could take two different directions. The first would be the creation of a LAIA Payments Union, similar to that that existed in Europe in the early 1950s. Under this type of agreement, the surplus countries would automatically grant credit to the Union in a common currency (dollars, SDRs or an accounting unit specific to the scheme) in a relatively large proportion of expected surpluses while, in turn, the Union would grant automatic credit to the deficit countries in the same currency for a large proportion of their deficits. The share of deficits not subject to Union financing, and thus cancelled in hard currencies, would need to be carefully studied during the negotiations for an agreement of this kind. Possibly a mechanism by which the proportion to be paid in hard currencies increases with the size of the deficit (similar to the one that existed in the European Union), or one in which the rates of interest rise according to the size of the disequilibrium should be established, as an incentive for adjustment in the deficit countries. In any case, the principle of increasing deficit-associated costs should be applied to the *current* position of each country, and not to the *accumulated* deficit. The adoption of the latter alternative would produce a rapid return to the present system, in which deficit countries are forced to finance their entire current account deficit in hard currencies after a certain point. The most desirable system could be a combination of the two principles.

Naturally, the foreign exchange received by the Union would be transferred to the surplus countries. However, an essential element of the scheme is the creation of incentives for those countries to equilibrate their intra-regional balance of payments. This would be achieved by introducing the principle of increasing costs for their current as well as accumulated surpluses, through variable interest rates or proportions of the surplus to be paid in hard currencies. In order to avoid adjustments through export controls, a prior agreement should be signed requiring all countries under these conditions to adopt measures aimed at increasing their imports from the region. In addition, the possibility of adjusting the balance of payments through the capital account could be introduced, allowing surplus countries to purchase the debt of deficit countries with the Union,[17] or creating incentives for residents of the former to invest in other countries of the region.

A second alternative for reform would be aimed at allowing the deficit countries to cancel a significant share of their negative balances in their own currencies. In this case, the deficit would be reflected as a liability of the corresponding central bank *in its own currency* with respect to the Union or other central banks (in which case a larger degree of bilateralism would be maintained); the central banks of the surplus countries would at the same time accumulate assets in the currency of the deficit countries, either directly or in proportion to those collected by the Union. As in the previous case, it would be necessary to design mechanisms to ensure that a certain degree of adjustment take place in the deficit as well as in the surplus countries. Clearly, under this scheme debtor countries should guarantee that the balances in their currencies held by the Union or other central banks would not lose real value, thereby indexing the balance, either to its domestic price level or to the exchange rate.[18]

Needless to say, both systems are heterodox designs, although in either case intermediate paths may be sought, so as to make them more similar to the present agreement. The virtue of the first alternative is its similarity (though not complete) with the European Payments Union. In contrast, the second offers greater guarantees to the deficit countries, since the liabilities of a central bank in its own currency cannot be really considered part of the foreign debt of the country, while liabilities with the Payments Union in the first case are clearly so. In any case, there are difficulties of implementation, not only in terms of overcoming the criticisms of orthodox schools of thought, but also the real problems that must be resolved in order for these schemes to function. These problems will be addressed in the following sections of the paper.

5. THE DIFFICULTIES

(a) Orthodox criticisms

As their theoretical and practical predecessors, the schemes set out in the previous section will be criticized by orthodox economists for inducing undesirable adjustments in the deficit countries. When considering such criticism it is necessary to bear in mind the facts. The orthodox position has left its mark in Latin America in the traumatic balance of payments adjustments of the 1980s and the collapse of intra-regional trade. Although the proposed systems are certainly sub-optimal in the aseptic world of neo-classical models, they are valid options, even from a neo-classical perspective, considering the 'imperfections' that characterize the actual working of international trade and payments.

Furthermore, one should not lose sight of the fact that the intra-regional deficit or surplus scarcely constitutes a fraction of the global disequilibrium facing a specific country. It is thus unlikely that a government would consciously incur the risks of a *global* deficit in its balance of payments in order to take advantage of this kind of agreement. Of course, exceptions do exist, such as the case of countries whose intra-regional deficit accounts for a large share of their external disequilibrium (See Table 8.5). In dealing with such cases, the design of the system could include the setting of limits on the amount that a deficit country may borrow as a proportion of its exports.

(b) Chronic debtors and creditors

The theoretical literature as well as the practical experience of the European Payments Union indicate that the basic problem with a multilateral compensation system is the existence of countries that are far from an equilibrium position in intra-regional trade.[19] Furthermore, the system gains effectiveness in direct proportion to the degree of multilateralism in trade. From both perspectives, the Latin American trade environment in the early 1980s was not especially favorable for an agreement of this sort. Excluding fuels, most of the intra-regional trade was balanced on a bilateral basis. Between 1980 and 1983 multilateral balancing represented only 10 to 13 percent of total trade.

Table 8.5: Intra-regional trade, LAIA (million dollars)

	(1) INTRA-REGIONAL EXPORTS						(2) TRADE BALANCE						(3) INTRA-REGIONAL EXPORTS EXCLUDING FUELS				(4) TRADE BALANCE EXCLUDING FUELS			
	1980	1981	1982	1983	1984	1985	1980	1981	1982	1983	1984	1985	1980	1981	1982	1983	1980	1981	1982	1983
Argentina	1871	1741	1514	1025	1381	1120	−227	−5	−23	−389	−188	155	1747	1526	1368	932	13	182	231	−83
Bolivia	366	409	462	433	392	231	−61	−36	229	242	116	169	132	73	64	42	−292	−352	−167	−149
Brazil	3456	4216	2862	2056	2829	1440	742	1254	−217	44	811	663	3318	4051	2697	1912	1621	2874	1469	1138
Colombia	550	565	522	263	282	688	−202	−349	−427	−552	−457	−373	537	555	509	254	53	19	−85	−147
Chile	1105	823	717	451	537	730	−238	−490	−93	−282	−270	−194	1094	819	698	449	190	−206	208	−18
Ecuador	446	316	517	188	89	336	135	147	223	−75	−218	−189	219	225	198	66	−78	−14	−50	−130
Mexico	665	1052	1000	876	823	590	−150	−88	482	631	320	8	409	394	310	221	−400	−722	−172	20
Paraguay	144	147	165	108	127	353	−446	−494	−323	−224	−313	−238	144	147	165	108	−429	−406	−252	−168
Peru	575	417	369	241	324	417	131	−146	−124	43	−59	−92	540	337	295	231	113	−239	−190	−47
Uruguay	393	348	314	247	244	244	−313	−346	−169	−3	−36	−12	393	348	314	247	−126	−142	29	63
Venezuela	1439	1643	1599	1072	1022	638	628	554	442	566	296	92	139	139	114	57	−665	−994	−1020	−480
Total	10980	11677	10041	6960	8052	6787	±1636	±1954	±1376	±1258	±1543	±1086	8672	8614	6732	4519	±1989	±3075	±1936	±1221
Energy-Exporting countries*	2916	3420	3578	2569	2326	1795	553	576	1376	1363	515	81	899	831	686	386	−1435	−2082	−1050	−740
Brazil	3456	4216	2862	2056	2829	1440	742	1254	−217	44	811	663	3318	4051	2697	1912	1621	2874	1469	1138
Other non-energy exporting countries**	4608	4041	3601	2335	2897	3552	−1294	−1830	−1159	−1407	−1323	−754	4455	3732	3349	2221	−185	−792	−60	−399

* Bolivia, Ecuador, Mexico and Venezuela.
** Argentina, Colombia, Chile, Paraguay, Peru and Uruguay.
Source: BID-INTAL, *Estadísticas de Exportación* . . , op. cit.

Table 8.6: Balance and unbalanced trade of LAIA, excluding fuels (million dollars)

	1980	%	1981	%	1982	%	1983	%
Total trade, excluding fuels	8.676		8.614		6.734		4.519	
In bilateral balance	5.772	66.5	4.404	51.1	3.971	59.0	2.701	59.8
In multilateral balance	915	10.5	1.135	13.2	827	12.3	597	13.2
Compensated trade	6.687	77.1	5.539	64.3	4.798	71.3	3.298	73.0
Non-compensated trade	1.989	22.9	3.075	35.7	1.936	28.7	1.221	27.0
Brazilian surplus	1.620	18.7	2.874	33.4	1.469	21.8	1.138	25.2

Source: Calculations by the author based on BID-INTAL, *Estadisticas de exportación* . . ., op. cit.

Furthermore, a relatively large proportion of trade was neither in bilateral nor in multilateral equilibrium. What is more, over 80 percent of this disequilibrium was associated with the Brazilian surplus (see Table No. 8.6). Even so, the conclusion that was arrived at in Section 1 of this study is inevitable, namely, that a readjustment in the region's system of payments requires a lasting solution to the Brazilian imbalance.

An equally significant problem, particularly in 1982 and 1983, was the global surplus of energy-exporting countries (See Table 8.5). Although the decline in oil prices and the success of import-substitution of energy in Brazil significantly reduced the surplus of these countries in 1985, the significant positive balance of fuel exporters indicates that a major problem in the negotiation of agreements such as those suggested lies in defining what proportion of oil and gas trade would be included within the scheme. If this trade is totally excluded, Brazil's participation may not be viable. On the other hand, the inclusion of energy products in the payments agreement would create an incentive for the region's importers to channel all their fuel and gas purchases through the system. It would also create an absurd situation for the fuel-exporting countries, since they would have to grant automatic credits to their intra-regional customers or to receive soft currency payments, although in the case of oil they have the option of selling it outside the region for hard currencies.

The energy trade problem thus demands careful attention. However, there are various ways of approaching the issue, two of which will be mentioned here. The first would consist in defining *ex-ante* all bilateral oil and gas transactions to be included in the agreement, i.e. establishing a quota system to be negotiated by the interested parties. The second would be to uniformly establish a larger hard currency component for the payment of all intra-regional energy trans-actions.

(c) The hard currency component of intra-regional trade

The previous section illustrates a more general problem: the payments agreements that we have reviewed assume that most of the transactions are not convertible into hard currencies. However, there are at least two elements of partial convertibility in intra-regional trade. The first is associated with that part of the regions' exports that could be sold outside the region. The second is tied to the imported component (from the rest of the world) of intra-regional trade.

The existence of this convertible component of trade has two important corollaries. The first is that, in agreements such as those proposed in this paper, it would be wrong for member countries (with the possible exception of chronic debtors) to create incentives for exports to the region. In such a case, the country runs the risk of losing hard currencies, both from that portion of exports that could have been directed to the rest of the world, as well as from the imported component of exports to the region. At a global level, this means that intra-regional trade incentives should be granted mainly to the *importers* and not the exporters in each country.

The second corollary has to do with the need to maintain a minimum degree of convertibility in intra-regional transactions. This is especially true of the imported component of trade aimed at import substitution for the region as a whole. At the national level, the substitution process has always been faced with the need to channel foreign exchange to the leading import-substitution sectors at certain times. At the international level a mechanism must be found to channel at least the imported component of these sectors' exports; in the opposite case, the absurd situation could arise whereby a system that is largely designed for joint import substitution would force the countries that could lead this process to restrict their intra-regional exports.

(d) Fluctuations in real exchange rates

Since the 1960s, the problem of unstable real exchange rates has constituted one of the central themes in discussions of alternative LAIA payments systems.[20] Recent experience has confirmed this difficulty. The most complex issue is associated with sudden devaluations that only temporarily change the real exchange rates, without achieving lasting changes in the direction of trade flows. This greatly complicates the establishment of stable commercial networks.

The design of specific exchange rate systems for intra-regional transactions is extremely difficult, and does not really contribute to a lasting equilibrium in intra-regional trade flows or to greater stability of real exchange rates. Furthermore, it should be borne in mind that instruments other than the exchange rate exist for equilibrating intra-regional trade flows, among them payments systems like those proposed here and the management of tariff and quota restrictions. However, it might be desirable to complement these instruments with mechanisms that compensate sudden fluctuations in real exchange rates (especially through a system of compensatory taxes and subsidies) and in this way stabilize commercial networks in the region.[21]

6. CONCLUSIONS

The last few years have been tragic for Latin American economic integration. The collapse of intra-regional trade has not only led to a rapid disintegration of the most visible aspect of this process, but has nullified its supposed creative effects in the midst of a critical phase for the region as a whole. As this paper has shown, this crisis is related to the inefficiency of the current system of payment in the region and to the imbalance of intra-regional trade during the boom years. Therefore, action must be taken on both fronts if the advantages of integration are to be enjoyed. This paper has highlighted the need for a system of payments that provides a guarantee for intra-regional deficit countries that their disequilibria will not contribute to a worsening in their already critical balance of payments conditions. This requires the automatic granting of credit for a significant proportion of their deficits or allowing them to cancel their debts in their own currencies. Without concealing opposition by the orthodox schools of thought to the proposed system or the real difficulties implied in its design and negotiation, we are convinced that the current situation in Latin America will not be overcome with easy solutions that may be put forward nor with recourse to continuity.

NOTES

1. BID-INTAL, *El proceso de integración en América Latina, 1968/71*, Tables 11–1 and VII–8.
2. SITC 5–8. See United Nations, *Yearbook of International Trade Statistics*, 1981.
3. Ibid.
4. BID-INTAL, *Estadisticas de exportación de los paises de la ALADI, 1980–1984*, Buenos Aires, 1985.
5. Ibid.
6. Alfredo Echegaray Simonet, *'El proceso de revisión de los mecanismos financieros de la ALADI'*, *Integración Latinoaméricana*, No. 83, September 1983, pp. 19–29.
7. See, for example, *El Pensamiento de la CEPAL*, Santiago: Editorial Universitaria, 1969, Chap. 5 and José Antonio Ocampo, 'New Development in Trade Theory. and LDCs', *Journal of Development Economics*, June 1986.
8. See the works quoted in footnote 10.
9. John Maynard Keynes, *Shaping the Post-War World: the Clearing Union, Collected Writings*, Vol. 25. For a more recent view of this problem, see Paul Davidson, *International Money and the Real World*, New York, John Wiley & Sons, 1982.
10. Robert Triffin, *El caos monetario: del bilateralismo a la casi convertibilidad en Europa*, Mexico: Fondo de Cultura Economica, 1961, Chaps. III–V. William Dielboid, *Trade and Payments in Western Europe, A Study in European Cooperation*, New York, Council of Foreign Relations — Harper and Brothers, 1952, Part.I: W.M.Scammell.
11. See, for example, Sidney Dell, *'El Fondo Monetario Internacional y el principio de condicionalidad'*, *Revista de la CEPAL*, No. 13, April 1981, pp. 149–61.
12. Barry N. Siegel, *'Sistema de pagos de la Asociación Latinoaméricana de Libre Comercio'*, in Miguel A. Wionczek, *Integración de América Latina: Experiencias y Perspectivas*, Mexico: Fondo de Cultural Económica, 1964, Chap. 14.

13. Echegaray, op. cit.; Guillermo Maldonado, *et al.*, *'América Latina: crisis, coopera-ción y desarrollo'*, *Revista de la CEPAL*, No. 20, August 1983, pp. 77–102; JUNAC, *Bases para una estrategia de financiamiento, inversiones y pagos*, Lima, October, 1983.

14. The proposal for a Guarantee Fund is subject to the same problem, since it is, in fact, a kind of common reserve fund.

15. Echegaray, op. cit., p.26.

16. Triffin, op. cit., pp. 147–8; Diebold, op. cit., pp.22–4.

17. This system existed in the European Payments Union and proved to be very useful.

18. See, for example, José Antonio Ocampo, *'Esquema de un sistema de pagos para el Grupo Andino'*, *Coyuntura Económica*, No. 50, June 1983.

19. R.F. Kahn, *et al.*, 'The Contribution of Payments Agreements to Trade Expansion', in P. Robson, *International Economic Integration*, Chap. 12, Penguin Books, 1971.

20. Sidney Dell, *A Latin American Common Market?*, London, Oxford University Press, 1966, pp. 164–9; Gonzalo Cevallos, *Integración Económica de America Latina*, México, Fondo de Cultura Económica, 1971, pp. 221 and 237. As this last author states, the problem was not severe in Central America, given the traditional stability of the exchange rates in that region.

21. Eduardo Conesa (*'Un mecanismo equilibrador de las balanzas comerciales reciprocas entre paises que desean integrarse económicamente'*, *Integración Latinoaméricana*, No. 82, August 1983, pp. 38–43) has proposed a system of certificates, applicable to intra-regional transactions, which exporters would sell to importers of the same country on the open market. In the case of deficit, the value of the certificate would operate as a surcharge on reciprocal trade. As the same author recognizes, the maximum amount of the surcharge is the margin of preference from the region. However, the system is not symmetrical in the case of surpluses and relies on adjustments that come about as a result of small variations in effective exchange rates.

PART 6: THE INSTITUTIONS

9

The Andean Group Institutions

Ciro Angarita

INTRODUCTION

It is well known that the frustrations and conflicts encountered within the Latin American Free Trade Association (LAFTA) owing to the concentration of advantages for a minority of its members, led the governors from some countries with insufficient markets and a lesser degree of development to work towards the creation of a different integration scheme, on a more reduced geographic scale and with more far-reaching and diversified economic goals.[1]

Thus, the so-called Declaration of Bogotá, signed on 15 August 1966 by the Presidents of Colombia, Chile and Venezuela, as well as personal representatives of the heads of state of Ecuador and Peru, recommended that within the framework of the Treaty of Montevideo an agreement be drafted among less developed countries with insufficient markets, with advantages that would not be extended, at least temporarily, to non-member countries.

To examine the measures that would be required, a Mixed Commission was set up which, at its third meeting held in Caracas in August of 1967, adopted the 'Basis for a Sub-Regional Agreement'.[2] The document was submitted to the Council of Ministers and to the LAFTA Conference of Contracting Parties and duly approved by them (Resolutions 203 and 222 respectively), after it had been ascertained that it was in keeping with the guidelines set out for regional agreements both by the Declaration of the Presidents of the Americas, issued at Punta del Este on 14 April 1967, as well as by Resolution 202.

In this connection, the legal mainstay for the Andean Group, that is to say the Cartagena Agreement, was signed in Bogotá on 26 May 1969 and became binding on 16 October of that same year. The Agreement seeks to promote the balanced and harmonious development of the member countries, to accelerate growth by means of economic integration, to facilitate participation in the process of integration foreseen by the Montevideo Treaty, and to create conditions that would enable LAFTA to operate as a common market. All these goals were to make their contribution towards the improvement of the living standards of the peoples of the subregion.[3]

The implementation of the previously mentioned objectives was entrusted to the main institutions such as: (i) the Commission; (ii) the Junta, and (iii) the Andean Court of Justice, as well as auxiliary bodies such as (iv) the Andean Council; (v) the Andean Parliament; (vi) the Consultative Committee; (vii) the Advisory Committee for Economic and Social Affairs; (viii) the Coordination Councils; (ix) a financial body called the Andean Development Corporation; (x) the Andean Reserve Fund, and (xi) a number of technical agreements and institutions.

The experience gained so far, as well as the results obtained from this complex institutional structure, have given way to certain possible reforms, as was only to be expected (xii). As briefly as possible, because of the limited scope of this chapter, a description will be provided of the institutional structure of the Andean Group.

1. THE COMMISSION

(a) Nature and composition

It represents the highest political authority, responsible for stating and implementing the national interests of the members of the Group. It is made up of plenipotentiary representatives of each of the governments of the Andean countries who may, on occasion, enjoy ministerial rank.

(b) Functions

Among the most important functions are those of drafting general policy and adopting whatever measures are needed to implement it. Taking into account the nature of its activities, the Commission is primarily a legislative body which expresses its will by means of *decisions*. It also carries out administrative functions when called upon to implement community instruments.[4]

In spite of its ranking, the Commission is under the obligation to review any proposals made by the Junta, either to adopt, reject or modify them. The Commission designates the members of the Junta, imparts instructions, and grants approval to its annual operational budget. It is also responsible for promoting economic international relations among the members of the Group and, in particular, whatever action is needed as a result of international trade, as well as assuring participation in organizations and meetings of an economic nature.[5]

2. THE JUNTA

(a) Nature and composition

It is the Group's foremost technical body responsible for defending the common interests of the subregion. It is made up of three members who are appointed, as has already been mentioned, by the Commission.[6]

(b) Functions

The Junta ensures that the Agreement is complied with and that the Commission's decisions are fulfilled. To do so, it is empowered to take autonomous decisions by means of Resolutions approved unanimously. These are, of course, of lesser ranking than the decisions adopted by the Commission.

Its regulatory and supervisory functions are primarily expressed as part of the liberalization program and power to apply the safeguard clause or to temporarily suspend the application of the minimum common customs tariff schedule.[7]

On the other hand, it should also be pointed out that the Junta also has legislative functions, together with the Commission, which are exercised by making proposals to the Commission aimed at facilitating or ensuring fulfillment of the Agreement. Such proposals in recent years have become the basic input for decisions adopted by the Commission.[8]

3. THE ANDEAN COURT OF JUSTICE

(a) Origin

The need to ensure strict compliance with all commitments, either directly or indirectly stemming from the Agreement of Cartagena, the complexity of its structure and the need to safeguard the system by means of a legal instrument at the highest level, independent from governments and other bodies set up by the Agreement, led to the creation of the Court by means of a public treaty signed by the five Andean countries on 28 May 1979 in Cartagena, which became binding on 20 May 1983.[9]

In accordance with Article 81 of the Operational Statute of the Court (Decision 184), this new body took up activities in its official headquarters of Quito on 2 January 1984 with the approval of the Minister of Foreign Affairs of Ecuador.

(b) Nature and characteristics

The Court is one of the Agreement's main bodies, which means that it is of equal importance with the Commission and the Junta. Its functions are both legal and supervisory.[10] It is endowed with international legal capacity since it is empowered to negotiate the immunities and privileges of the appointed Judges, Secretary and Court officers when appointed as international staff members, as well as agreements with the member countries to grant the necessary facilities to ensure full independence on the part of those who ordinarily take part in legal proceedings. Furthermore, the Treaty that led to its creation grants the immunity recognized internationally and, in particular, by the Vienna Convention on diplomatic relations.[11] It should also be pointed out that its judgments are legally binding in the member countries and, as a result, do not require either confirmation or exequatur.[12] The Treaty also provides the Court's full autonomy *vis-à-vis* the member countries.[13]

(c) Organization and composition

The Court abides by the Treaty signed to set up this body, the Operational and Legal Procedures Statute which is found in Decision 184 of 19 August 1983, and its own internal rules of procedure which were enacted on 15 March 1984. The Court is made up of five judges, citizens of the member countries, with the highest moral attributes and able to exercise in their own countries of origin the highest legal functions or legal experts of acknowledged competence. They are legally banned from carrying out any professional activities, whether paid or unpaid, aside from academic activities, and should abstain from any action incompatible with their functions.[14]

Judges are designated for six-year terms and re-election is possible only once. Each judge will have two alternates who will replace him, in the proper order, if definite or temporary absences so require it or in cases of challenges or impediments. The alternate judges should be endowed with the same qualities as the main judge. On the other hand, whenever necessary, the Treaty foresees that the number of judges may be altered by unanimous decision of the members of the Commission. The Court may also create the post of General Counsel, with similar functions to those carried out in the Court of the European Communities.[15]

(d) Jurisdiction

The Court has jurisdiction to deal with nullity and non-compliance actions, as well as pre-judicial consultation proceedings and review of judgment for non-compliance. Its jurisdiction is, consequently, quite restricted and of a mixed nature.[16] In instances of non-compliance that may affect individual parties, they may call for an action to declare void, request a pre-judicial consultation, or appeal to national judges.[17] Together with the Junta and national judges, the Court uses its special jurisdiction to enforce, within the limits imposed on it, the Andean legal system.

(e) Experience and results

After two years, the Court judges recognize openly and explicitly that the Court has suffered from a frustrating inertia, resulting in part from the crisis that the Andean integration process in general is undergoing.[18]

4. THE ANDEAN COUNCIL

(a)

By means of an agreement reached in November of 1979, the Ministers of Foreign Affairs of the region set up this new body.

(b) Nature and composition

It is a political advisory body set up to guide the activities of the institutions that make up the Andean system and to issue recommendations to contribute to the proper functioning of the integration process. The Council is made up of the Ministers of Foreign Affairs of the Andean nations. It is convened whenever circumstances so warrant it.

(c) Functions

Its main task is to draft common foreign policy for the member countries and to identify the ways and means to implement it. It should also issue guidelines to facilitate integration and effective coordination of all the agreements that are part of the system.

It is precisely for this reason that it has been pointed out quite correctly that the Council represents a mechanism that coincides with the main purpose sought by integration, by arranging for meetings to enable the ministers to gain information on the course of integration and issue recommendations which they may feel are necessary rather than an attempt to work towards political integration, as some might feel.[19]

(d) Experience

In recent months, the Council has been predominantly concerned with measures aimed at overcoming the current crisis in the integration process. Since June 1984, the Junta prepared a protocol to modify the Cartagena Agreement which has been examined and discussed at a number of meetings. It is anticipated that it could possibly be signed in May of this year (1986). A brief reference will be made to this important document at the proper time (xii).

The purpose of providing the Andean process with a new political thrust, as evidenced by the Council's declaration issued in Cartagena on 15 September 1985, for example, has led some authors to note a clear trend to 'shift the direction of the process from technical to political bodies, enhancing the authority and initiative of the Andean Council in comparison to that of the Commission of the Agreement or of the Junta itself'.[20]

5. THE ANDEAN PARLIAMENT

(a) Origin

As a reflection of the growing degree of democratization that the region has experienced, the member countries agreed in October 1979 by means of a special treaty, to set up this new institution which is part of subregional integration.

(b) Nature and composition

At present, it is mainly a 'parliament of parliaments' without legislative jurisdiction which belongs, as has already been pointed out, to the Commission. Its role is advisory in nature, as well as in the defense of integration, freedom, social justice, democracy, and human rights. It is made up of representatives from the Congress of the Contracting Parties. It should be stressed that the Treaty whereby the Andean Parliament was set up provides for the election of its members by direct and universal suffrage once an additional protocol is adopted ten years after the entry into force of the Treaty.[21]

(c) Functions

Among the functions of the Parliament are the review of the subregional integration process by means of the analysis of annual reports submitted by the various Andean agreements in order to make proposals and suggestions to bring the legislatures of the countries of the subregion closer together. It should also endeavor to improve all integration schemes, enhance democracy, and protect human rights. By means of the proper use of its right to receive information, the Parliament would be able to exercise political control over the direction and execution of the process, to censure any technical deviations or administrative irregularities.[22]

(d) Experience and results

The officers of the Andean Parliament meet at regular intervals to review matters that require action on their part. As of 1985, the Executive Secretariat operates in Bogotá. Its opinions take the form of recommendations. Throughout its existence, it has expressed its wish to play a role more in keeping with its popular origins and with the functions it should carry out within the integration process.[23]

Its ties with the European Parliament have become of an institutional nature by means of the creation of delegations responsible for maintaining permanent contact. The inter-parliamentary conference which brings together the European Community and Latin America is perhaps the most important event in these relations. Up to now, seven meetings have been held (Bogotá, 1974; Luxembourg, 1975; Mexico, 1977; Rome, 1979; Bogotá, 1981; Brussels, 1983; Brasilia, 1985). The main topics at these conferences have been democracy and human rights, relations between the Community and Latin America, industrial, technical and cultural cooperation, the Contadora process, the foreign debt, and environmental protection.

6. THE CONSULTATIVE COMMITTEE

(a) Nature and composition

It is a subsidiary body, to liaise with national authorities made up by representatives of the countries of the subregion. It is specifically mentioned in the Agreement of Cartagena.[24]

(b) Functions

Its tasks are carried out not only by providing a link between the member countries and the Junta but also by advising and contributing to whatever studies and reports the Junta may require, at its request, and by participating in the legislative process through the analysis of proposals.

7. THE ADVISORY COMMITTEE FOR ECONOMIC AND SOCIAL AFFAIRS

(a) Nature and composition

It is a subsidiary body, specifically foreseen in the Agreement,[25] made up by representatives from the private sector and labour organizations from each Andean country who are designated by their own organizations in equal numbers.

(b) Functions

Provides assistance to the main bodies that are part of the Agreement at their request. It may also submit its own opinions on the manner in which the integration process is advancing.

8. THE COORDINATION COUNCILS

(a) Origin

Up to now, the following coordination councils have been set up: planning, currency and exchange rates, financing, fiscal policy, foreign trade,[26] tourism, social affairs, health, and physical integration.[27]

(b) Functions

These councils are responsible for the coordination of development plans and the harmonization of the economic and social policies of the Andean countries in order to facilitate joint planning efforts.

9. THE ANDEAN DEVELOPMENT CORPORATION (CAF)

(a) Origin

The Declaration of Bogotá provided, among other things, that a development institution would be set up to study, promote and finance projects undertaken to advance integration. The charter whereby the Corporation was created was signed in Bogotá on 7 February 1968 by representatives of the governments of Bolivia, Ecuador, Chile, Peru and Venezuela. It took effect as of 30 January 1970 and began operations on 8 June of the same year. Its headquarters are located in Caracas.

(b) Functions

In coordination with the Commission and the Junta,[28] CAF is the institution that provides a financial instrument to the Andean integration process in order to carry out priority projects in keeping with goals and objectives which foster the subregion's development. In the exercise of its functions, CAF channels available internal and external resources to finance integration programs and projects. By means of the creation of the so-called Andean Trade Financing System (*Sistema Andino de Financiamiento de Comercio (SAFICO)*) in August 1974, it has made a real contribution to strengthening subregional trade and to enable regional enterprises to reach world markets.

On the other hand, CAF supports any activities that take advantage of the opportunities and resources within its area of interest by means of the creation of productive or service enterprises and through the expansion, modernization and conversion of existing enterprises in order to further rational specialization and a more equitable distribution of investment in the subregion.

(c) Experience and results

It should be highlighted that, during its past history, CAF has given approval to projects amounting to US $706 million (not taking into account loans provided by SAFICO). A total of US$561.2 million has been tapped from subregional sources, as well as sources outside the region. Through SAFICO, trade loans have been granted for a total of US$157.6 million.[29]

10. THE ANDEAN RESERVE FUND

(a) Origin

The Fund was set up by virtue of an agreement signed in Caracas on 12 December 1976 which entered into effect in June 1978. It has been recognized as having international legal capacity and its headquarters are located in Bogotá.

(b) Functions

By granting loans or underwriting certain credit transactions, it gives support to the balance of payments schemes in the countries of the subregion while also contributing to a greater harmonization of exchange, monetary and financial policies in coordination with the Commission and the Junta in order to provide greater liquidity in the investment of their international reserves.

To fulfill its goals, it is authorized to receive deposits, loans and securities, to issue bonds and notes, and to give loans to stabilize the balance of payments.

(c) Experience and results

As a result of a proposal put forward by Peru, as of September of 1984, the Executive President of the Fund has been looking into the viability and advisability of issuing some type of security to be used by the Andean central banks as a subregional means of payment, thus contributing to the financial integration of the area.

The outcome of this effort was a multilateral agreement signed on 17 December 1984 in Lima by the central banks and the Fund which provides that the participating banks agree to 'accept payment in *Andean pesos* from other central banks, at their face value for unpaid balances resulting from intra-subregional trade according to settlements made within ALADI's payments scheme'.[30] Responsibility for this mechanism, that is to say the 'Andean peso', was given to the Fund.

Initially, the Fund was authorized to issue a total of 80 million Andean pesos which are currently equivalent to one US dollar. This currency unit is only used for payments made through the Fund to authorized holders.[31] By setting up this financial instrument it is hoped to reduce the cost of transactions among the countries of the region and to make a contribution to Andean trade.[32]

11. AGREEMENTS AND SPECIAL INSTITUTIONS

By means of a number of special agreements with undeniable social implications and through the creation of specialized institutions, the Andean group has attempted to channel and rationalize its joint efforts in several areas. Thus, for education, science and culture, the Andrés Bello Agreement has been signed (1970); in the field of health, the Hipólito Unanué Agreement (1971); the Simón Rodríguez Agreement in connection with labour aspects (1976); the José Celestino Mutis system has been designed in the areas of agriculture, food, security, and environmental protection (Decision 182, 1983).

To strengthen integration in the areas of technical administrative cooperation, to improve services and execute future projects such as the Andean satellite, the telecommunications computer program for the Andean system, and the production of telecommunication equipment, the Association of Government Telecommunication Enterprises (ASETA) was set up in July 1974.

According to the Cartagena Mandate and to explicit provisions adopted by the Commission, a Technical Coordination Committee was set up in 1983, made up by the highest echelon directors of member bodies (Junta, CAF, FAR, ASETA, the Court of Justice). As its name would indicate, the body coordinates the operational programs of these institutions and assesses the manner in which they have evolved. By way of institutional back-up, each of these agreements and special institutions relies on two basic bodies, namely the Council of Ministers in each sector and an Executive Secretariat.

12. POSSIBLE REFORMS

The Junta of the Agreement of Cartagena, in compliance with a clear mandate, submitted to the Commission a draft additional Protocol to the Cartagena Agreement in June 1984. Since that time, the document has been reviewed and debated extensively, but it is too early to say if it will be adopted or not. Its forty-seven articles basically attempt to adjust the features or modalities of certain mechanisms that are part of the integration program to current circumstances and, as a result of the experience gained during the time it has been implemented, to adjust certain aspects to make it possible for the program to be executed and to remedy certain vacuums that stem from now obsolete legal aspects of the LAFTA system.

The Junta has summarized the contents of the additional protocol as follows:

in addition to extending the terms as needed, [it] suggested a new approach by introducing new operational modalities, by giving added flexibility to existing mechanisms, foreseeing special agreements whenever necessary, ensuring ways to participate for [all] social sectors, and creating economic and social cooperation channels. All this would be achieved in a balanced manner in keeping with ordinarily divergent positions and with no other purpose than working for the common interests and objectives of the sub-region.[33]

It is clear, then, that the Protocol does not modify the essence of the economic integration scheme which was adopted at the outset. Nevertheless, we feel that the time has come to raise a few aspects contained in this document which would have implications as far as the institutional system of the Andean Group is concerned.

(a) The main bodies

The Commission retains the same structure and the same functions as those given to it by the Cartagena Agreement. As far as the Junta is concerned, during the forty-fourth session of the Commission held in Cartagena, Colombia, from 8 to 13 April 1985, the delegation of Ecuador reasserted its proposal in terms of modifying this body in such a manner as to make it a unipersonal body, not mandated to make proposals. To do so, it would be necessary to amend articles 13 and 14 of the Agreement.[34]

It has been noted, and not without reason, that a reform of this type would disrupt the needed equilibrium between national and subregional interests and would do away with the body responsible for seeing to it that the Agreement is complied with. It would also lose certain functions that represent a first instance before appealing to the Andean Court of Justice.[35] The fact is that to date at least articles 13 and 15 of the Agreement have not been modified in any manner whatsoever and, as a result, the Junta retains its original structure and functions.

Regarding the Andean Court of Justice, the Protocol simply includes it as one of the main bodies of the Agreement.[36] On the other hand, the judges who have experienced the frustrating inertia of the past two years do not hesitate to recognize that the overall weakening of the integration process, reflected in the greater flexibility of its mechanisms, the retrenchment of its original objectives, and the effort to strike a balance between bilateral and community interests, makes it necessary to rely on an operational legal body. It is essential to choose between alternatives such as the elimination of the Court and the return to classical systems of control and settlement of disputes, maintaining the Court as a final instance or as a body to be used occasionally, or to strengthen it and grant it additional powers to justify its ongoing existence.[37] A review of the documents issued at the various meetings does not seem to show that these warranted concerns have had sufficient echo.

(b) The auxiliary bodies

The Protocol recommends[38] a substantial modification of article 22 of the Agreement in as much as it refers to the Advisory Committee for Economic and Social Affairs as follows:

there shall be an Entrepreneurial Advisory Council and a Workers' Advisory Council made up in each case by four top-level delegates, directly elected by representative organizations of the employers and labour sectors in each of the Member Countries and accredited by the liaison institutions mentioned in paragraph (i) of Article 15 of the current Agreement.

The Advisory Councils will be called upon to render opinions to the Commission or the Junta either at their request or by their own initiative on those programs and activities of the process that may be of interest to the employers and labour sectors.

Each Advisory Council will draft its own rules or procedure.

(c) The subsidiary bodies

The Protocol assigns this classification to already existing councils or to those created in the future by the Commission in accordance with Article 29 of the Agreement. It is well known that, according to this provision, the Commission adopted Decision 22 on 31 December 1979, whereby several councils were set up and integrated by high-level representatives of national institutions who were entrusted with the responsibility of designing and implementing development plans and issuing recommendations to the Commission and cooperating with the Junta.

(d) The settlement of disputes

Article 23 of the Agreement which empowered the Commission to negotiate, to propose its good offices, mediation and conciliation if discrepancies arose in connection with the interpretation or implementation of the Agreement, has been replaced by another provision that specifies that the settlement of disputes will be subject to provisions contained in the Treaty whereby the Andean Court of Justice has been created.[39]

(e) The Andean Parliament

The Parliament has been insisting on the need to include it as one of the main bodies of the Agreement and to be assigned the functions of control and supervision both on budgetary questions and on political matters. Some of these functions would be the approval of annual budgets, the review of budget accounts of the other bodies of the Agreement, and the possibility of summoning members of the Junta and the Commission to provide explanations to the representatives of the peoples of the subregion.[40]

(f) Coordination of institutions

The Protocol replaces article 24 of the Agreement by another version which imposes on the Commission and the Junta the obligation to maintain close links not only with CAF but also with the other institutions for subregional integration created by other international instruments.[41]

(g) The near future

Whatever hopes there may have been for the speedy adoption of the possible reforms and their obvious implications for existing institutions seem to have been dashed as a result of the languid outcome of the meeting of ministers responsible for integration in the member countries that was held in Caraballeda, Venezuela on 13 and 14 February 1986. In effect, to coincide with the Regular Meeting of the Council of Ministers of Foreign Affairs of the Andean Group, the ministers responsible for integration were invited to set down the basic guidelines that would apply to the drafting of the modifying protocol of the Agreement. Their functions are closely linked to the fate of integration in the future but, on this occasion, they confined themselves to analyzing the evolution of the process and to identifying areas of full agreement as well as those where it was necessary to continue to hold consultations to reach a definite consensus.[42]

NOTES

1. INCOMEX, *De la ALALC a la ALADI: Un propósito de integración latinoaméricana*, Bogotá, Colombia, Abril de 1982, p. 39.
2. Antecedentes del Acuerdo de Integración Subregional Andino, *Comercio Exterior*, **1**, No. 1, Julio 1969, p. 11.
3. Acuerdo de Cartagena, article 1.
4. Ibid., article 6.
5. Alcalde Cardoza Javier, *Hacia una caracterización de las negociaciones en el Acuerdo de Cartagena, En el derecho de la integración en América Latina, 1979–1982*, Tomo I BID-INTAL, Buenos Aires, 1983, pp. 49, 50.
6. Acuerdo de Cartagena, article 13.
7. Alcalde, op. cit., p. 50.
8. Ibid., p. 51.
9. Sáchica Luis Carlos, *Introducción al Derecho Comunitario Andino, Colección de estudios del Tribunal de Justicia del Acuerdo de Cartagena, número 2, Artes Gráficas señal, Quito*, 1981, pp. 134, 144.
10. Tratado Constitutivo, article 6; *Estatuto de Funcionamiento*, Decisión 184, article 2.
11. Tratado Constitutivo, article 13; Decisión 184, article 82.
12. Tratado Constitutivo, article 32.
13. Articles 7, 8, 13.
14. Ibid., article 11.
15. Ibid.
16. Ibid., articles 17, 18, 23–27, 29.
17. Ibid., articles 17, 19, 27, 29.
18. Sáchica, op. cit., p. 153.
19. Ibid., p. 74.
20. Ibid., p. 182.
21. Tratado Constitutivo.
22. Sáchica, op. cit., p. 74.
23. Salazar Santos Felipe, *El Régimen Institucional del Grupo Andino, Ponencia, Seminario sobre el Grupo Andino, Cámara de Comercio de Bogotá*, Febrero 4–7 de 1986, p. 13.

24. Tratado Constitutivo, article 5.
25. Article 5.
26. Decisión 22.
27. Decisiones 36, 39, 68, 71.
28. Acuerdo de Cartagena, article 24.
29. CAF, *Memoria y Estados Financieros 1984*, p. 7.
30. *Convenio Multilateral entre Bancos Centrales miembros del Acuerdo de Cartagena y el Fondo Andino de Reservas*, article 1.
31. Directorio del Fondo Andino de Reservas, Acuerdo No. 83, Diciembre 17 de 1984, article 1.
32. Ibid., segundo considerando.
33. Junta del Acuerdo de Cartagena, *Exposición de Motivos del Anteproyecto adicional al Acuerdo de Cartagena*, Doc. JUN–Di.820, 26 de Julio de 1984.
34. 'Comisión del Acuerdo de Cartagena, cuadragésimocuarto periódo de — sesiones extraordinarias', *Acta final*, 8 a 13 de Abril, de 1985, Cartagena de Indias, Colombia, p. 3.
35. 'Consejo Directivo del Instituto Colombiano de Integración', *El Grupo Andino: Proyecto de Reforma, Ponencia, Seminario sobre Grupo Andino, — Cámara de Comercio de Bogotá*, Febrero 4–7 de 1986, p. 32.
36. Proyecto de Protocolo, 13 de Marzo de 1985, article 5.
37. Sáchica, op. cit., pp. 154, 155.
38. Cfr. Proyecto de Protocolo, 13 de Marzo de 1985, article 5.
39. Ibid., article 23.
40. Salazar Santos, op. cit., pp. 12, 13.
41. Proyecto de Protocolo, 13 de Marzo de 1985, article 24.
42. Junta del Acuerdo, JUN./Di. 975, *Acta de la reunión de Ministros*, Caraballeda, Venezuela, 13 y 14 de Febrero de 1986, p. 1.

10

Crisis And Problems: A Test For The Institutions

Richard H. Lauwaars

1. INTRODUCTION

The European Communities have been established by three different treaties: the Treaty establishing the European Coal and Steel Community,[1] the Treaty establishing the European Economic Community[2] and the Treaty establishing the European Atomic Energy Community (Euratom).[3] Each of these treaties provides for four institutions: a Council of Ministers; an executive organ; a Court of Justice, and a Parliamentary Assembly. Although one would, therefore, expect the Community to comprise twelve institutions, in fact there are only four; that is, the result of two separate treaties:

— *Convention on certain Institutions common to the European Communities* (Rome, 25 March 1957), which provides for one Parliamentary Assembly and one Court of Justice, and
— the so-called *Merger Treaty* of 8 April 1965, which replaced the three Councils by one 'Council of the European Communities', and the three executive organs by one 'Commission of the European Communities'.[4]

It should be noted that the Communities themselves have not been merged. Each institution exercises the powers that have been conferred on it in each of the respective Community Treaties.

Sections 1 to 5 (inclusive) are the text of a paper which was presented to the EEC-Latin American Seminar, held at the University of Los Andes, Bogotá, in July 1984. Section 5 contains an updating of the period 1984–1986. The author wishes to thank Mr. Howard Gold, a librarian at the Europa Instituut, who prepared the footnotes to this chapter.

Aim of This Paper

The object of this paper is to give a general description of the institutional structure of the EEC, and its decision-making process. I shall limit myself to the three political institutions: Council, Commission and Parliament. Although the Court of Justice fulfils an essential role in the whole of Community life, it has its own, rather specific characteristics which cannot easily be dealt with in this paper. I shall also leave out of account the ECSC and Euratom Treaties.

2. COMPOSITION, TASKS AND POWERS OF THE INSTITUTIONS

(a) Council of Ministers

(i) Composition and presidency. According to article 2 of the Merger Treaty, the Council consists of representatives of the member states. Each government shall delegate to it one of its members. Its actual composition depends upon the subjects that have to be treated. Besides the Council of Ministers of Foreign Affairs (the so-called 'General Council'), the Council may consist of the Ministers of Agriculture, Economic and Financial Affairs, Social Affairs, Transport, Energy, etc. Each of these Councils exercises the powers that have been granted by the Treaties to the Council of the European Communities.

Since 1975, the Council has also met at the level of heads of state or government, together with foreign ministers, the so-called 'European Council', a continuation in institutionalized form of the former summit conferences. The office of president is held for a term of six months by each member of the Council in turn.[5] Up to 1 July 1987 it was held by Belgium; during the second half of 1987 by Denmark.

(ii) Tasks. The Council is the legislative organ of the Community. Its task is to adopt the fundamental provisions in the field of, for example, agriculture, transport and commercial policy. The Council is further empowered to conclude on behalf of the Community agreements with third countries or other international organizations.[6] The Council, finally, has a dominant influence in budgetary matters.

Although the European Council, when it acts in matters within the scope of the European Communities, does so in its capacity as a 'Council of the European Communities',[7] prefers to define its own tasks and not automatically follow the rules of the Treaty. During its meetings of 29 and 30 June 1977, in London, it agreed that it should have:

— 'informal exchanges of view of a wide-running nature held in the greatest privacy and not designed to lead to formal decisions or public statements;
— discussions which are designed to produce decisions [of the] normal Councils, and

— [the task to] Settle issues outstanding from discussions at a lower level [the European Council as a] body of appeal'.

In evaluating the above definitions one should not forget that the European Council also plays an important role in the framework of *European Political Cooperation*, i.e. cooperation between member states in the field of foreign policy. This subject falls outside Community Treaties. Statements in this field are not made by the 'European Council', but by 'Heads of State or Government' or, in brief, the 'Ten'.

(b) Commission

(i) Composition. According to article 10, para. 1, of the Merger Treaty, as amended by the last Act of Accession, the Commission consists of seventeen members, two from each of the large member states and one from each of the others. The members of the Commission shall, in the general interest of the Community, be completely independent in the performance of their duties (article 10, para.2). They are appointed by common accord of the governments of the member states (article 11).

(ii) Tasks. The most important tasks of the Commission are:

— to ensure that the provisions of the Treaty and the measures taken for its implementation are applied;
— to exercise its *right of initiative*. In almost all cases in which the Council has been empowered to take an implementing act, it may only do so on a proposal from the Commission. This right is *exclusive*: the Commission is the only one that can make such a proposal and it decides whether and when it will do this.
— to effectuate its *decision-making power*. In some cases the Commission derives this power directly from the Treaties, for example in the fields of competition policy and the management of the customs union. However, in most cases this power is delegated to it by the Council, for example in the field of agriculture. It is, finally, the Commission that negotiates on agreements with third countries or international organizations (these agreements are, as already mentioned, eventually concluded by the Council).

(c) Powers of the Council and Commission

Neither the Council nor the Commission (nor the other institutions) possess a general decision-making power. Their powers are particularly attributed to or conferred upon them in the various fields of application designated by the Treaties (so-called *principle of attributed powers*). This principle is to a certain extent weakened or softened by:

— the rule of article 235 of the EEC Treaty, and
— the doctrine of 'implied powers'.

(i) Article 235. This article provides for a supplementary decision-making power in the event that Community action is necessary to achieve a Treaty objective and the Treaty has not provided the required powers. Article 235 has been applied in the fields of, for example, processed agricultural products, the harmonization of customs policy, monetary policy, social policy, and environmental policy. It has also been used to establish new organs, for example, the *European Fund for Monetary Cooperation*.[8]

(ii) Implied powers. The doctrine of 'implied powers' plays an important role in the law of international organizations. It deals with the interpretation of treaties and offers an auxiliary instrument to achieve a useful interpretation of treaty provisions. It has been described by the Court of Justice of the EC as follows: 'the norms established by an international treaty or by law imply those norms without which the former would not make sense or would not permit a reasonable and useful application' (First Publication of Transport Tariffs Case, Case 25/59 of 15 July 1960).[9]

The difference between implied powers and article 235 is that the former have to be derived from an *explicit power* and article 235 refers to the *objectives of the Treaty*. In other words, article 235 may only be applied if the Treaty does not provide the necessary, express or implied powers. The doctrine of 'implied powers' is particularly important in the field of the external relations of the Community.

(d) European Parliament

(i) Denomination. The Treaties use the term 'Assembly'. The Assembly itself adopted in its Resolutions of 20 March 1958 and 30 March 1962, the denomination 'European Parliament'. Although the European Parliament does not possess the legislative, supervisory and budgetary powers that the national parliaments of the member states have obtained, it has since become general usage to follow this new, self-chosen terminology.

(ii) Composition. Since 1979 the members of the European Parliament have been directly elected. The legal bases therefore are article 138, para 3, of the EEC Treaty and the Act concerning the election of representatives of the Assembly by direct universal suffrage of 20 September 1976.[10]

As from the accession of Spain and Portugal (1 January 1986),[11] the directly elected Parliament has 518 members. The members are not divided according to nationality, but on the basis of *party-groupings*. In the present Parliament, the following eight groupings have been constituted:

Socialists	172
Christian-Democrats	118
European Conservatives	63
Communists	46
Liberals	42
Progressive Democrats	34
Rainbow Group	20
European Right	16
Non-attached	7
	518

The members of the directly elected Parliament hold office for a five-year term. Although the Treaties prescribe that the elections should be held 'in accordance with a uniform procedure in all member states' and the Parliament prepared a draft *European Electoral Statute*, such a Statute has not yet been established by the Council. The second direct elections have, therefore, again been held on the basis of the national electoral statutes. They were held between 14 and 17 June 1984.[12]

(iii) Powers. According to Article 137 of the EEC Treaty, the European Parliament shall exercise the advisory and supervisory powers that are conferred upon it by the Treaty. The Parliament further has important budgetary powers.[13]

— *Advisory powers* In many instances the Council has been obliged by the Treaty, before the adoption of a decision, to consult the Parliament about a proposal from the Commission.[14] The absence of this consultation results in the illegality of the act involved, which may be declared null and void by the Court of Justice. The Parliament may also on its own initiative express its view on all subjects that fall within the scope of its activities. However, all statements of the Parliament, whether they concern an opinion on a proposal or a resolution on its own initiative, are *non-binding*. The Council is, therefore, not obliged to follow the Parliament.

— *Supervisory powers* The supervisory task of the Parliament relates to the Commission and its policy. The most drastic instrument in this respect is the *motion of censure*. If such a motion is adopted, the Commission shall resign as a body.[15] However, the procedural requirements for its adoption are so heavy that the motion is not in practice a very appropriate instrument. Another reason for its lack of effectiveness is that it would be directed against the wrong body; as earlier observed, it is not the Commission but the Council of Ministers that is the main decision-making body in the Community.

Another instrument to effect its supervisory task is the right of Parliament and its individual members to pose written or oral questions. According to article 140, para 3, of the EEC Treaty,[16] the Commission is under a duty to reply to such questions. Parliament, finally, has the opportunity to scrutinize the Commission's policy during the debate on the annual general report.[17]

It appears from the above that the Parliament has no means of supervision of the *Council*. In the view of the authors of the Treaty the individual members of the Council should be responsible towards their respective national parliaments. However, as has recently been confirmed by the Declaration of Stuttgart of 19 June 1983,[18] the Council and its members will respond to oral or written questions and 'resolutions concerning matters of major importance and general concern, on which Parliament seeks their comments'. According to the same Declaration (point 2.1.4), the European Council will address a report to the European Parliament after each of its meetings; this report will be presented by the President of the European Council.

— *Budgetary powers* It is only in this field that Parliament obtained a considerable extension of its powers. As a consequence of the introduction in 1970 of the Community's own financial resources, Parliament acquired real influence on the budget of the Community. According to article 203, para. 9 of the EEC Treaty,[19] the budget is adopted by the President of the Assembly. However, if there are 'important reasons', Parliament may also reject the draft budget and ask for a new one (article 203, para. 9). This occurred for the first time in December 1979, when Parliament rejected the draft budget for 1980, *inter alia*, because of the fact that the cost of the Common Agricultural Policy was not sufficiently reduced by the Council. Subsequent rejections occurred in 1982[20] and 1984[21]. In spite of Parliament's new budgetary powers, the situation is still far from satisfactory. First, the Council in fact still has a dominant influence on a large part of the Community's budget, notably on the establishment of the so-called *obligatory expenditure*, that is to say 'expenditure necessarily resulting from this Treaty or from acts adopted in accordance therewith' (mainly consisting of the expenses of the CAP).[22] This expenditure is not susceptible to Parliamentary amendments (unless it rejects the draft budget in its entirety). Second, as already mentioned, Parliament has almost no influence at all on the establishment of the Community's legislation; however, it is this legislation that lies at the bottom of the Community's budget. We are here again confronted with a *substantial defect* of the institutional structure of the Community, i.e. the lack of a co-legislative power of Parliament.

3. DECISION-MAKING PROCESS

The main lines of the decision-making process have already been indicated.

— the Commission submits a proposal to the Council;
— the Council consults the European Parliament on this proposal;
— the Council takes a decision on the basis of this proposal.

In a more elaborated way, we could say that the whole procedure starts with the preparation of a proposal by the Commission, after consultation with experts and representatives of the unions and the employers' organizations. During the second stage the Commission on its own responsibility adopts the proposal and submits it to the Council. During the third stage the Council asks the European Parliament and the Economic and Social Council, an auxiliary organ,[23] for their opinion, which they address to the Council. During this stage — and, as a matter of fact during the whole decision-making process — the Commission has the right to modify its original proposal, 'in particular where the Assembly has been consulted on that proposal'.[24]

When in this way all necessary data have been collected (proposal from the Commission and the respective opinions of EP and ESC) — in the fourth stage — official preparation of the Council's decision-making will commence. This official preparation is effected by the *Committee of Permanent Representatives* and its *working groups*. The Committee of PR, the so-called 'Coreper', consists of the ambassadors of the member states to the EC. Its task is to prepare the work of the Council and to carry out the tasks assigned to it by the Council.[25] The working groups consist of officials of the national ministries, and each deals with a specific area of the activities of the Community.

If, at the level of 'Coreper', full agreement between the member states has been reached, the Council will adopt the proposal without debate (the so-called A-point on the Council's agenda). But, in most cases, proposals will figure on the Council's agenda as 'B-points', i.e. they will be fully discussed by the ministers, members of the Council.

It is during this stage — the fifth — that a number of 'artificial means' may be applied in order to promote the adoption of a decision by the Council. It may happen that the Council does not close its meeting before a decision has been adopted — so-called 'marathon-sessions'. This device is applied in particular during the annual establishment of agricultural prices. Another artifice is the establishment of a 'package deal', i.e. a combination of several subjects, each of which contains some attractive features for at least one of the member states. There is, finally, the possibility of asking for a statement by the *European Council* (in this instance acting as a 'body of appeal', referred to above).

One means of decision-making that is seldom used is *voting*. In many instances, for example, in the fields of agriculture and the common commercial policy, the Treaty prescribes that the Council may take its decision by qualified majority. This majority is a weighted, qualified majority. According to article 148, para. 2 of the EEC Treaty,[26] each member state has a certain number of votes (the large member countries ten or eight, the medium-sized five and the small member countries three or two votes) and a decision requires fifty-four of the seventy-six votes. However, in practice the Council continues its discussion until all members agree. This is a consequence of the so-called *Luxembourg Agreement*[27] of January 1966, which states as follows:

I. Where, in the case of decisions which may be taken by majority vote on a proposal of the Commission, very important interests of one or more partners are at stake, the Members of the Council will endeavour, within a reasonable time, to reach solutions which can be adopted by all the Members of the Council while respecting their mutual interests and those of the Community, in accordance with Article 2 of the Treaty.

II. With regard to the preceding paragraph, the French delegation considers that where very important interests are at stake the discussion must be continued until unanimous agreement is reached.

III. The six delegations note that there is a divergence of views on what would be done in the event of a failure to reach complete agreement.

IV. The six delegations nevertheless consider that this divergence does not prevent the Community's work being resumed in accordance with the normal procedure.

It is this Agreement, that has recently been confirmed by the *Declaration of Stuttgart*,[28] which in practice is applied by all member states, at all levels of the decision-making process and with regard to almost all decisions.

4. CRISES AND PROBLEMS

Turning now to a discussion of the crises and problems in the institutional and budgetary field, it is again the Agreement of Luxembourg that has first to be dealt with, followed by the lack of delegation by the Council to the Commission, the British budgetary problem and the enlargement of the Community's own resources.

(a) Agreement of Luxembourg

This Agreement, which is not a real agreement, but a summary of conclusions established at the end of an extraordinary meeting of the Council held in Luxembourg on 28 and 29 January 1966, has had a paralysing effect on the decision-making process. It is also based on a wholly incorrect view of the role of majority voting. As the Commission states in its Report on 'The Institutional System of the Community':

Majority voting does not mean that a vote is taken in every case where majority voting is possible, for the simple reason that it is always preferable for Council decisions to be acceptable to all Council members. However, even if unanimity is out of the question, it should be possible to avoid deadlock. Majority decisions should therefore be seen as a last resort, but one which cannot be abandoned without seriously jeopardizing the workings of the Community.[29]

The Agreement has, finally, weakened the position of the Commission and, thus, of the European Parliament also.

In the course of the years, several proposals have been made to improve this deplorable situation. Thus, the 'Three Wise Men' in their report on the European Institutions[30] suggested that in cases where the Treaty did not call for unanimity and where no member state's vital interests were at stake, a vote should be taken after a certain amount of time had been devoted to the search for a generally acceptable solution. Any member state that wanted to avert a vote because of an important national interest would have to say so clearly and explicitly and take responsibility for the consequences on behalf of its government. On an earlier occasion the Commission had already made a similar proposal.

None of these proposals had any concrete result. As has already been mentioned, the Agreement of Luxembourg was more or less confirmed by the Declaration of Stuttgart of June 1983. Let us hope that President Mitterand's speech before the European Parliament on 24 May 1984,[31] where he appeared to be in favour of a narrow interpretation of the Agreement of Luxembourg, in this way leaving more room for majority voting, marks the beginning of a new and more profitable era in this respect!

(b) The lack of delegation

In its report on 'The Institutional System of the Community', the Commission further observed that the strengthening of the intergovernmental element within the Community also finds expression in 'the Council's refusal to delegate important administrative and managerial functions . . .. to the Commission, even when the Treaties explicitly state that the Commission is to perform such functions, as, for example, under Article 205 of the EEC Treaty[32] with reference to the budget' (ibid., at 3). In spite of the explicit provision of article 155, last item, of the EEC Treaty, which specifies that the Commission 'exercises the powers conferred upon it by the Council for the implementation of the rules laid down by the latter', the Council prefers to keep its powers in its own hands, albeit at the cost of its own overburdening and further weakening of the role of the Commission.

In the Declaration of Stuttgart,[33] the Heads of State or Government 'confirm the value of making more frequent use of the possibility of delegating powers to the Commission within the framework of the Treaties'. It was not the first time that the Heads of State or Government had made such a statement; they had already said the same in December 1974 on the occasion of the Second Paris Summit Conference.[34] Perhaps the Declaration of Stuttgart will lead to better results than the former.

(c) The British budgetary problem

The third problem to be mentioned is that concerning the British contribution to the Communities budget. This problem had already been mentioned during the first European Council meeting in March 1975, in the framework of the 'renegotiation' of the conditions for membership of the United Kingdom of the

EC.[35] On that occasion agreement was reached on a so-called *corrective mechanism*, i.e. a mechanism to prevent the weak economies of member states from carrying a disproportionate burden regarding the financing of the Communities. However, the mechanism did not work and was no solution to the British budgetary problem, i.e. the discrepancy between the part of the budget to be financed by 'British' money (about 20 per cent) and its share in the Community's gross national product (about 10 per cent). This could be explained by the stringent conditions for its applicability and, in particular, the linking of its operation to the gross amount of a member state's contribution instead of the net amount.

In 1979 the problem was again — and now in very strong words — brought to the fore by Mrs Thatcher, the British Prime Minister: 'I want my money back!' The European Council of June 1979 requested the Commission to submit a reference paper describing the financial consequences of the budgetary system for each member state. It appeared from this that in 1980 the United Kingdom would indeed be the largest contributor. The problem was (provisionally) solved in two different ways. On 30 May 1980 the Council first agreed that the United Kingdom would receive a refund for 1980 and 1981 by virtue of the 'corrective mechanism' mentioned above and by means of 'additional measures in the U.K.' (infrastructure and coal exploitation). The Council, secondly, charged the Commission with a 'mandate' to prepare a report on *structural changes* which should in the future prevent the occurrence of similar problems, in particular 'unacceptable situations'. This report was submitted by the Commission to the Council on 24 June 1981.[36]

However, the 'structural changes' that the Council had asked for and which the Commission had broadly proposed in the report mentioned above, have as yet not been effected (the so-called 'new policies'). In fact, for each of the years following 1981, the system of refunds has been continued, the amount of the refunds being the result of lengthy and tiresome negotiations. In respect of the refund for 1982, the European Parliament rejected the Draft Supplementary Budget which provided for this payment, but the Commission nevertheless remitted the amount due. The European Parliament placed the refund for 1983 in Chapter 100 of the budget (Reserve); the release thereof — an exclusive right of the Parliament — depends upon the definitive solution of the 'British problem' which the Heads of State or Government will hopefully find at their meeting of 25 and 26 June 1984 at Fontainebleau (France).[37]

It is obvious that the definitive solution of the 'British problem' is closely connected with two other outstanding questions, namely: the introduction of budgetary and financial discipline; and the establishment of a new method of financing the Community, mainly intended to prevent 'budgetary imbalances' from occurring again in the future.

(d) Creation of new own resources

Although the European Council, held on 19 and 20 March 1984 at Brussels, could not achieve final agreement, Heads of State or Government were in principle prepared to increase the part of VAT that is assigned to the Community to 1.4 per cent in 1986 and 1987, and to 1.6 per cent from 1988.[38]

5. SOLUTIONS AND NEW PERSPECTIVES: THE EUROPEAN COUNCIL MEETING OF JUNE 1984 AND THE 'SINGLE ACT'

During the years 1984–1986 some of the above-mentioned problems were solved. For other problems solutions became visible by the agreement that the member states reached at the end of 1985 about the text of the Single European Act, i.e. the Treaty amending the existing Community Treaties and on European Political Cooperation (II.A(2), supra, hereinafter 'the Single Act').

(a) The European Council Meeting of June 1984

(i) The British budgetary problem. At this meeting, held on 25 and 26 June 1984, at Fontainebleau, Heads of State or Government in fact reached agreement on the amount of compensation to be granted to the United Kingdom to reduce its contribution to the Communities' budget.[39] The basis of the agreement was as follows: in 1984 the United Kingdom was to receive a lump-sum compensation of 1,000 million ECUs; in subsequent years it would receive two-thirds (66 per cent) of the difference between what it payed in VAT and what it received from the Community budget.

As regards of the two connected problems (the introduction of budgetary discipline and the prevention of the occurrence of new 'budgetary imbalances' respectively), the following decisions have been taken:

— At the beginning of the budget procedure the Council of Ministers will have to define a 'reference framework', i.e. the maximum level of expenditure that it considers it must adopt to finance Community policies during the following financial year (see also the Conclusions of the Council on the measures necessary to guarantee the effective implementation of the conclusions of the European Council on budgetary discipline.[40]
— Any member state sustaining a budgetary burden that is excessive in relation to its relative prosperity may benefit from a correction at the appropriate time.

(ii) Creation of new own resources. During the same European Council meeting it was decided to create new own resources by raising the VAT ceiling to 1.4 per cent on 1 January 1986; a further increase to 1.6 per cent on 1 January 1988 has been provided for, but will depend on a unanimous decision of the Council and approval by all the parliaments of the member states. At that time the Council will have to deal again with the British compensation, as the length of

the correction mechanism has been linked to the duration of the 1.4 per cent VAT rate.

(b) Single Act

The Single Act was signed on 17 and 28 February 1986; owing to opposition in Ireland it has not yet entered into force. The Act is the outcome of a process, which was initiated by the adoption of the Declaration of Stuttgart in June 1983 and which also comprises the draft Treaty establishing the European Union, adopted by the European Parliament in February 1984, and the report of the Dooge Committee of March 1985 (Bull. E.C. 1985, pp. 102–11).[42] The main purpose of the Act is, according to its preamble, 'to improve the economic and social situation by extending common policies and pursuing new objectives, and to ensure a smoother functioning of the Communities.' In this chapter only the institutional provisions of the Act will be treated.

(i) The powers of the European Parliament. The European Parliament — which will henceforth be so designated by the Treaties — will receive a modest extension of its advisory powers. In a certain number of cases the consultation of Parliament, as described above, will be replaced by a 'cooperation procedure'. This very complicated procedure in essence amounts to the grant to the Parliament of a *right to a second hearing*, i.e. that Parliament will have the chance to discuss the Council's position on a Commission proposal and on its own opinion as issued at the end of the first hearing. In the event that the Commission joins the Parliament in its view on the Council's position, the latter may only unanimously deviate from the Commission's proposal. The Parliament will further have to *approve* any future association, or accession treaties.

(ii) Delegation of powers. According to article 145 of the EEC Treaty[43] the Council will have to confer on the Commission the powers that are necessary for the implementation of the rules laid down by the former. In this way the drafters of the Act tried to solve the problem, described above, of the lack of delegation. However, by virtue of the same article, the Council may also retain these powers of implementation. It may moreover impose specific procedural requirements on the exercise by the Commission of its delegated powers.

(iii) Majority decisions. A basic feature of the Act is that it will also replace in a number of instances the requirement of unanimity by a qualified majority. However, the Act is silent in respect of the notorious 'Agreement of Luxembourg'.[44] In that respect — and the same applies to many other articles of the Act — one will have to wait for the future decision-making practice of the Council; only then will one know whether the member states are indeed prepared to improve the Community's decision-making process.

NOTES

1. Treaty establishing the European Coal and Steel Community, Paris, 18 April 1951.
2. Treaty establishing the European Economic Community, Rome, 25 March 1957.
3. Treaty establishing the European Atomic Energy Community (Euratom), Rome, 25 March 1957.
4. 'Merger Treaty', 8 April 1965. See 'Official Journal'.
5. Merger Treaty, 8 April 1965, article 2, para.2.
6. See note 3: article 228, para. 1.
7. Solemn Declaration on European Union, Bulletin No.6, 1983 (known as 'Declaration of Stuttgart', 1983): para. 2.1.3.
8. See note 2.
9. Reports of Cases before the Court, Luxembourg, 1960.
10. *Official Journal*, Luxembourg, 1976, No. L278/5.
11. Spain and Portugal. See Bulletin EC, No. 6, 1985.
12. *Official Journal*, Council Decision of 2 June 1983, Luxembourg, 1983, No. L155/11.
13. See note 2: article 203.
14. Ibid.: for example articles 43, 56 and 100.
15. Ibid.: article 144.
16. Ibid.
17. Ibid.: article 143.
18. See note 7: point 2.3.3.
19. See note 2.
20. Second Draft Supplementary Budget, 1982, e.g. 1982, C11.
21. Draft Budget for 1985, e.g. 1985, ch.2, p. 207.
22. See note 2: article 203, para. 4.
23. Ibid.: articles 4, para.2 and 193 to 198.
24. Ibid.: article 149, para. 2.
25. See note 4: article 4.
26. See note 2.
27. *Bulletin of the EC*, No. 12, Brussels, 1966.
28. See note 7.
29. *Bulletin of the EC*, Suppl.3/82 at 7, Brussels, 1982.
30. *Bulletin of the EC*, Suppl.11, Brussels, 1979, points 1.5.1 and 1.5.2.
31. *Agence Europe*, No. 3857, Luxembourg.
32. See note 2, p. 3.
33. See note 7: point 2.4.
34. *Agence Europe*, 9–12 December 1974, Nos. 1648–1650, Brussels, 1974.
35. *Bulletin of the EC*, No.6 Brussels, 1975.
36. *Bulletin of the EC*, Suppl. 1981/1. Also published in Gijlstra/Völker, *Materials on the Law of the European Communities*, Deventer, 1983, pp. 28–39.
37. *Bulletin of the EC*, No. 6, Brussels, 1984.
38. *Agence Europe*, No. 3814, 21 March 1984, No. 3814, Brussels, 1984, p. 3.
39. See note 37, pp. 10–11.
40. *Bulletin of the EC*, No. 12, Brussels, 1985, pp. 102–11.
41. *Bulletin of the EC*, No. 3, Brussels, 1985.
42. See note 2.
43. See note 27.
44. Swann, Dennis, *The Economics of the Common Market*, 4th edn., Penguin, Harmondsworth.

PART 7: CONCLUSIONS — THE FUTURE

11

The Andean Pact — Problems and Perspectives*

Germánico Salgado Penaherrera

THE CARTAGENA AGREEMENT: BASIC PRINCIPLES, EVOLUTION, ACHIEVEMENTS AND PROBLEMS

The Cartagena Agreement, which unites the countries of the Andean Pact, was signed in May 1969 in Cartagena, Colombia. The Council, the Pact's administrative body, was immediately constituted and began to function alongside the Commission — the decision-making body, made up of government representatives — towards the end of 1969 in Lima, Peru, which was chosen as the headquarters for these institutions. They have now been in existence for fourteen years, a long enough period of time to be able to make a serious evaluation of the long-term perspectives for this attempt at regional integration.

The Cartagena Agreement was a direct outcome of the frustration felt by some members of the Latin American Free Trade Association (LAFTA) over the way that that form of regional integration had worked in practice. The countries concerned were those of medium economic importance within the LAFTA (Colombia, Chile, Peru and Venezuela), and two of the so-called relatively less developed countries (Bolivia and Ecuador). The LAFTA was created in 1960 with the aim of achieving within the space of twelve years a free-trade zone according to the classical definition.

As might have been expected given its structure, the system worked to the advantage of those countries in a more advanced stage of industrialization, which, because of their larger internal markets, had been able to go further in the import-substitution process. These were Argentina, Brazil and Mexico. The benefits of the system to them are shown by the figures for the expansion of trade, and participation in complementarity agreements, in the vast majority of which these three countries were involved. As a result, negotiations within the Association stagnated, with the weaker countries (the small and medium-sized) blocking any advance.

Of these countries, the Andean nations wanted to form a group that would bring about more rapid and complete integration, without leaving the LAFTA — thus they called themselves a 'subregional' group. The aim was to give the group as a whole sufficient weight to be able to negotiate on more equal terms with the major countries in the LAFTA (Argentina, Brazil and Mexico). This implied a more ambitious form of integration than what had been achieved so far, despite great efforts, through the Association: emphasis on the industrial sector, through joint planning in areas of major concern (consumer durables, intermediate products and capital goods), and a system that would ensure 'harmonious and balanced development' for all member states, which basically means first of all the existence of effective preferential treatment for the weaker countries in the group.

The initial responses to the frustration caused by LAFTA, and the need to reconcile the different interests of the more and less developed nations in the group determined the basic features of the structure of the system of integration which was built into the Cartagena Agreement. To give a brief summary, its original characteristics were:

(1) The creation within a period of ten years of an economic union of a new kind. This was more than a customs union, since it involved harmonizing policies in fields such as technology, foreign investment, and industrial policies. Nevertheless, it could not be called a common market, since there were no specific provisions for the free movement of productive factors.

(2) The basic aim was to create economic conditions and the necessary means for joint industrial development. It was not simply a question of coordinating the industrial policies of member states, but of drawing up an industrial strategy and policies for the subregion which would also have to be planned or 'programmed'. This planning would have to take into account the need both for justice and effectiveness.

(3) Two systems were used to create a market, involving the removal of internal barriers to commercial exchange, and the erection of common protective barriers against third parties. The first was the automatic and lineal liberalization of tariffs, accompanied by a two-stage process of progressively building up a common external tariff; the second involved joint industrial planning, which also used the mechanism of liberalization — common external tariffs, but in this case to support the distribution across different countries of industrial projects, through the sectoral programmes for industrial development.

(4) The principle of balanced and harmonious development should be respected throughout the process of integration and in the operation of the main programmes. An entire chapter of the Agreement was dedicated to the question of support for the weaker countries (Bolivia and Ecuador). This chapter established a series of favourable conditions for these countries, including a longer list of items excluded from the

common tariff policy, a longer period in which to liberalize tariffs and bring themselves into line with the common foreign tariffs, etc. But the chief mechanism fo the Agreement for evening out differences in the level of development of the member states was the sectoral programmes for industrial development.

(5) A number of objectives for the coordination of economic and social policies were specified. In so far as policies directly affecting trade were concerned, the terms and nature of the coordination were defined very precisely. The Agreement did not set terms and was less precise in relation to other areas, with one very important exception: policies towards foreign investment were to be drawn together and a common position established within a year.

(6) The creation of a set of strong institutions which would have a real influence over the development of the process of integration. Firstly, there was the Commission, the decision-making body, which was composed of ministers of the member states. Then there was the Council, whose powers represent one of the most important innovations differentiating the Agreement from the LAFTA and other forms of integration. The Council has virtually exclusive power to put forward proposals, as well as the power to make resolutions regarding certain issues, and to ensure that the Agreement is observed. It never carried out this last function, since it was clearly the role of a judicial agency, whose creation became necessary because of subsequent developments which demanded a means of resolving disputes: this agency, the Andean Court of Justice, has now been set up, and will begin to function in 1984.

(7) In the Agreement the member states did not state a preference for any one political system. The Agreement was purely economic, and was considered to be compatible with different political systems.

During the first years after the Agreement came into force, there was tremendous vitality. The governments of the member states showed political will, and the process of integration moved forward, meeting the demanding deadlines laid down in the Agreement. Trade between countries multiplied, and despite all the difficulties that arose during the negotiations, the first Sectoral Programme for Industrial Development, dealing with the metal-working industry, was agreed in 1972. Venezuela, which had initially remained outside the Pact, asked to join, and this was negotiated during 1973.

However, there soon emerged the difficulties which led to the Andean Pact's current problems. To summarize, these are the main problems that have faced the Andean Pact, and which explain the progressive loss of vitality in this attempt at regional integration:

(1) Radical changes in the economic policies of some member states in relation to the openness or liberalization of their economies to foreign interests, particularly in the case of Chile who eventually withdrew from

the Pact. Even among those governments that did not take a neo-liberal position, there were growing differences in approach to economic policy in relation to levels of protectionism and the priority given to import-substitution: the kinds of economic policy pursued by members became more varied.

(2) Repeated failure by all members to observe the articles of the Agreement, either because these had not been incorporated into national law, or because those articles that had become law were not observed. Initially, the problem only arose in relation to specific issues; it took on massive proportions after 1980, and became especially acute more recently with the reduction in trade caused by the international economic crisis.

(3) Difficulties in the preparation and negotiation of the Sectoral Programmes for Industrial Development. Although the Council tried from the start to put forward programmes covering broad fields, that offered potential for all countries, there were exceptional problems in negotiation. In more than one case this led to solutions being found that were unsatisfactory in terms of increased efficiency. Only three programmes have been agreed: the programmes for the metalworking industry (1972), for petrochemicals (1975) and for the automobile industry (1979), as well as the outlines for an iron and steel programme, which has not progressed enough to allow any action to be taken. Two of these three programmes have been partially put into practice. All three have had to reformulated, one in order to bring in Venezuela, who was not a member of the Pact when the metalworking programme was agreed, and the other two because the international crisis and the increase in petrol prices have profoundly altered the economic and technological characteristics of the petrochemical and automobile industries. The changes in these two programmes have still not been agreed. In fact, at the present moment the balance between the different systems that the Agreement had anticipated has been destroyed, with the automatic reduction of tariff barriers taking precedence: this can be seen clearly in the unwillingness of the weaker nations to complete the reduction of tariff barriers and the establishment of common external tariffs.

(4) Political and territorial disputes between member states. Political differences came to light when Andean integration gave itself a politically democratic character, while developments in one member state went against democratic principles. In practice, this country was not involved in negotiations for several months. A territorial dispute, with the serious problems that this entails for economic integration, occurred when there was armed confrontation between Peru and Ecuador. The international situation in recent years has had a negative and quite significant influence at every stage.

THE PRESENT SITUATION AND PROPOSALS FOR REACTIVATION

The effect of these problems has been to bring key negotiations between the Andean Pact countries to a total standstill over the definition of the market (common external tariff, liberalization and industrial programmes). Although there has been progress in other fields, there is a general feeling of discouragement and more recently a real reduction in trade that has made the sense of crisis more acute.

Member states have drawn up a candid and precise analysis of the present situation under the title 'Plan for a Reorientation of the Process of Andean Integration', which was recently approved. The report states:

The Andean Pact is at present being affected by a number of disruptive factors, which are clearly holding up its development, and are now putting at risk the community structures we have worked so hard to build. Today we can see problems over the issue of freeing trade, difficulties in putting into practice programmes for joint industrialization, a lack of definition over questions like the common external tariff, and the failure of member nations on many occasions to respect their obligations under the legally-binding statutes of the Cartagena Agreement.[1]

Many of the major problems have remained unresolved for a number of years, despite the ongoing and determined efforts of the agencies of the Agreement, in particular the Council which has prepared evaluations, drawn up programmes of action based on these, and most recently put forward for consideration by the Commission, the 'Plan for a Reorientation of the Process of Andean Integration' mentioned above, and following on from this a series of strategy documents.[2] The Commission has not ceased to function, except during the turbulent period following Bolivia's temporary withdrawal and the inevitable interruption of business caused by the conflict between Ecuador and Peru. Since May 1979 the Heads of State of the member nations[3] have met six times, and on each occasion one of the main themes has been how to reactivate the process.

It is a measure of the stubbornness and difficulty of the problems facing the Andean Pact that these have not been resolved in spite of this ongoing institutional activity, and the influence of another group of institutions which in their own way are demanding solutions to these problems; i.e. the Andean Parliament, the professional, employers' and workers' organizations, etc. Objectively, one cannot deny that the Pact has made progress even in this period of growing difficulties. It has a long list of achievements in a number of spheres; negotiations over foreign affairs with the United States and the EEC, the coordination of positions in other international forums, among them the ALADI itself, serious efforts to work out joint action in the sensitive field of agricultural policy, real achievements in technological policy, and even joint investigations which offer great promise for the future.

But the failure to make progress in the main areas of policy regarding the creation of an open market and joint industrialization has detracted from the effectiveness and importance of what has been achieved in other fields, has aggravated a crisis mentality, and has increasingly weakened faith in the future of the Pact. Moreover, as has been mentioned, events contribute to deepening concern and discouragement. Trade between member countries, which for the first ten years of the Pact's existence grew at an average annual rate of 28.2 per cent[4] showed virtually no increase after 1979, and in the first few months of 1983 showed symptoms of severe contraction. The serious financial crisis that all members are experiencing has brought not only devaluations, which have radically altered the relationship between prices, but even the imposition of restrictions which violate the Agreement; these restrictions, according to the Council, today affect 40 per cent of trade between member countries.[5] All of the countries have been affected by the reduction in trade within the group, but for the countries with less relative development, this reduction in sales comes on top of their dissatisfaction with the results of the industrial programme, and contributes to a feeling that they are suffering comparative disadvantage and damage, which is precisely what the founders of the institutions of the Agreement of Cartagena had sought to avoid.

Faced with this complex situation, the agencies of the Agreement have put forward the 'Plan for a Reorientation of the Process of Andean Integration', which will be put into practice through the agreement of strategies for each of the so-called 'major areas for priority action'. It is probable that the method of carrying this out will be for the elements of these strategies that are approved to be formulated as decisions of the Commission. Three strategies have already been approved (those relating to farming, industry and the creation of an open market) and others are being discussed. According to the Plan, there are eight priority areas[6] and we will try to provide at least some indication of the principal points of the proposals and their objectives, with the exception of those three areas in which the key problems of this process of integration arise, as we have indicated above. These three fields are trade, industry, and the special terms for Bolivia and Ecuador, the two relatively less developed countries, which receive preferential treatment under the terms of the Agreement. Here it is essential to go in depth into the proposals in order to understand the possibilities they offer of resolving the central problems in the Agreement. These three areas will be examined in the following section; the remainder will be briefly discussed afterwards.

PROPOSALS FOR ACTION IN CRITICAL AREAS

Formation of a larger market and strengthening of commercial activities

Emphasis is put on completing the programme for the freeing of the market, extending some time limits, making the treatment of excepted areas more flexible, and regulating the use of safeguard clauses. In relation to the adoption of a common external tariff, the aim of the first stages is reduced to 'revising or adjusting' the levels of the common minimum external tariff, with the creation of a common tariff with upper and lower limits left until a later stage, and the period in which it is to be carried out unspecified.

Clearly the idea of perfecting the customs union has been abandoned, at least in the short term. This is reflected in the greater flexibility that is proposed for harmonizing policies which directly affect the common external tariff, such as non-tariff measures, traditional rules, and industrial development legislation, and in general, all exceptional tariff systems. Given this relative softening of the terms of the Agreement in relation to the classical means for developing an integrated market, the strategy puts significant emphasis on less orthodox means of increasing trade, which are referred to as 'new forms of commercial exchange'[7] (agreements over state purchases, regulated commerce, such as compensated exchange, and trade in agricultural surpluses and shortfalls), and in general on the promotion of trade, and the increase in trade relations with third countries. This is symptomatic of the desire that exists today to go beyond the limits of the purely formal integration process and make better use of its potential for joint action. Later we will assess how far this is possible, and its likely value.

Integration in the industrial sector

This is the sector in which we can see most clearly the change in the objectives of the Cartagena Agreement over the years. As has been mentioned, the high priority given to industrialization in the Agreement is well known. This was the basic motivation behind setting-up of the Andean Pact, and can even be seen in the lack of formal rigour[8] with which other areas of activity are treated in the same text of the Agreement. Furthermore, according to Article 32, the aim was to 'embark upon a process of industrial development in the sub-region, through joint planning', that is, introduce a common industrialization policy, in which for a number of reasons the sectoral programmes for industrial development were to play a vital role.

The documents we are now discussing show a considerable change from this concept. In the 'Plan for the Reorientation of the Andean Process of Integration' the importance of industry within the Andean process is mentioned alongside other factors: while it is not denied, its status is reduced.[9] The document is still more explicit about the character of the industrial policy when it states that 'it is not the intention of the strategy to establish a uniform or all-encompassing pattern of development for the Andean Pact countries'. It subsequently adds that 'New actions taken at the sub-regional level must take into account national programmes and priorities, identifying the common denominators of national policy as the basis for joint initiatives.[10]

This pragmatic approach is undoubtedly the result of past experiences, but it is a clear indication of the possible irrelevance of mechanisms of joint planning, and especially the sectoral programmes for industrial development, given the new approach which the strategy proposes for the Andean integration process. In fact, only one, and as we shall see, not the most important of the areas covered by the industrial strategy refers to this sectoral programming. The central aim in this area is to 'adjust and perfect the sectoral programmes for industrial development', but this involves only those programmes approved so far (metallurgy, petrochemicals, automobiles and steel). The reference to 'new possibilities for planning' which is also included in this section of the strategy covers only the mandatory (under the terms of the Agreement) allocation to Bolivia and Ecuador of some industrial projects which have been taken from the list of the so-called 'goods not in production', which are normally areas of little economic importance, or which are technologically difficult to introduce. In general, the emphasis in planning is on the project and not on the sector as a whole, and there is a desire to limit the allocation of projects to the two weaker countries, and then only in a restricted field and on a once-off basis.

The emphasis on the project and the omission of any reference to the idea of distribution within the sector is seen in a second part of the strategy entitled 'Areas of new industrial opportunities', although here priority sectors are established (agro-industry, capital goods production, electronics and communications).[11] Of the three parts of this strategy that remain to be covered, the first and clearly the most important in relation to the overall approach of the document is the 'consolidation of existing industry by improving its competitiveness and encouraging its development'. The focus is on those sectors that are going through crises, and quite rightly, the immediate priority is seen as being to regain and extend markets, with countries outside the Pact as well as member states. Emphasis is also put on the importance of the rationalization programmes which were included in the Cartagena Agreement but which have not yet been put into practice, mainly because of the lack of trading mechanisms (such as preferential tariffs, common external tariffs, etc.) which could be incorporated into the PSDIs.

Finally, the strategy puts forward proposals for actions to support industrial development, through studies, analyses and the preparation of projects, a policy for business and technological development, horizontal cooperation with third countries, etc.

Application of the special rules for Bolivia and Ecuador

In the preceding pages, we have already described the special function within the Agreement of the preferential treatment for Bolivia and Ecuador. The most effective means of achieving this was intended to be the industrial planning and the direct allocation of industries by sectors which this entailed. Analysis shows that the results of the application of this treatment have been negative, and the agencies of the Agreement have not attempted to hide this.

The Plan for a Reorientation states plainly that 'the results achieved have not lived up to early expectations'.[12] The Council of the Agreement's document 'Principles for a strategy for the application of the Special Rules for Bolivia and Ecuador' attributes these results to the 'limited' application of the joint industrial programme.[13]

One of the most serious aspects is that among the reasons for this limited application which has not produced satisfactory results, the failure of other countries to carry through their commitments, even in the sphere of industrial planning, bears a major responsibility, as the Council itself has said in the document recently quoted.[14] This led to the liquidation of a number of enterprises, and the consequent loss of credibility by PSDI. There have also been other problems, stemming from the internal conditions in the relatively less-developed countries, such as their limited capacity to initiate and carry through projects; nevertheless, it is reasonable to conclude that even given this last limitation, if the other countries had met their commitments in terms of joint planning and freeing of trade, this would have encouraged investments and a significant flow of trade, which would undoubtedly have lessened the sense of frustration of the weaker countries.

As might have been expected, the relatively less-developed countries have in their turn been unwilling to comply with their obligations to introduce an automatic and linear freeing of tariffs, and have requested the Commission that this tariff removal be postponed. Their frustration has increased the difficulties in negotiating other measures, such as the Common External Tariff, and the two countries are taking the attitude that it is not advisable to proceed with the creation of a larger market while this system of preferences, which has proved to be so weak in practice, remains. As in the case of many attempts at regional integration of developing countries, differences in the distribution of costs and benefits have become the main force blocking the process of integration.

This is why it is so important for the Andean Pact countries to reorientate and improve the system of preferences. Without for the moment making any judgment about its success in achieving this, this is the aim of the strategy put forward by the Junta. This includes systematic references to the nature of the preferential treatment that will be given in each of the areas of joint action that make up the process of integration. The treatment basically consists of commitments to take preferential joint action (technical support, carrying out of studies, drawing up projects, access to greater resources from the CAF and the Andean Investment Fund, emphasis on promotion, etc) in order to enable projects to be carried out, or to encourage the solution of certain problems such as Bolivia's lack of a coastline. By their very nature, these are fairly general commitments which reflect intentions rather than definite obligations which have to be carried out in a specific way. The exceptions are in the spheres of trade and industrial integration.

In the programme for the removal of restrictions, the postponement by the two weaker countries of their participation is made formal; the mechanism established for this programme is the partial removal of tariffs, whose continuation will be dependent on future evaluations. The mechanisms for implementing the trading policy are also made more flexible — among these are the lists of exceptions and the application of national regulations.

In industry, preference in joint action follows the pattern discussed above of making general commitments to provide support through joint action (through the identification and encouragement of projects, technological and institutional support, financial assistance, priority in rationalization programmes). There are specific references to the 'preservation of viable allocations and cooperation in achieving these', and to the 'establishment of reserved markets'. This second question would have to be explained in detail in order to give an idea of its effectiveness; the first clearly refers to existing allocations under the PSDI and those items in the list of goods 'not yet in production'.

We should remember that in the industrial strategy it is argued that in modifying the PSDIs already approved, preferential allocations should only be retained for 'viable and priority' areas of production in Bolivia and Ecuador. This question has already been discussed in the Commission of the Agreement, in relation to the programmes for metallurgy, petrochemicals and steel, following consultations by the Council with member states. These consultations[15] and the subsequent discussion of the issue by a Working Party of the 39th Extraordinary Session of the Commission which did not lead to any firm agreements[16] indicate the considerable problems that will be faced in determining which are the 'viable and priority' projects for Bolivia and Ecuador.

It is apparent, therefore, that given the present attitude of members, little can be expected from the PSDIs approved so far for the Special Rules for Bolivia and Ecuador, since the difficulties of reaching meaningful agreements will be still greater, if such a thing is possible, in the case of the automobile programme, for which no proposal for modification has yet been put forward.

PROPOSALS FOR OTHER AREAS OF JOINT ACTION

As well as the proposals mentioned above, the Plan includes suggestions for other areas in which joint action might be worthwhile. Put together, these make up a long list of proposals, simply to name which would take up several pages. Here we will only mention the spheres of action, and make a few comments on their importance, because unlike the three areas discussed so far, these do not constitute the basic problems for the integration of markets which have led to the present stagnation of the Andean Pact. These proposals would undoubtedly be very beneficial if they were put into practice, but in our opinion, they represent secondary forms of cooperation, and if progress is made in the task of integrating markets, there should be little problem in introducing a good many of the ideas proposed. There is one exception, and that is the area of transportation, and road transport in particular. The Andean Pact has not been able to take any significant measures in this sphere. It is obvious that if the problems in the negotiations between the countries are resolved, the expansion of the Pact's trade will make it necessary to find immediate solutions to all the issues involved in the improvement of transport, which is one of the areas of the strategy that we wish to mention in this section.

The other areas are: foreign relations; the integration of farming and fishing; investments, finances and payments; science and technology. The Pact countries have already done some work in all these areas, and the foundations have been laid for more concentrated activity in the future. In one area — that of investments, finance and payments — joint institutions have been created (the Andean Development Corporation and the Andean Reserve Fund) which have provided support for the Pact. Now these institutions need to increase their own resources to prove their ability as financial intermediaries by arranging loans on a scale adequate to meet the demands of the present situation.

In the sphere of foreign relations, the plan represents an attempt to systematically employ the strength given by negotiating in conjunction. This has already been carried out in the agreements with the United States and the EEC, and now it is necessary to extend these kinds of agreements and to diversify the range of countries with whom they are made. The natural priorities for this area must be ALADI, the organization which succeeds LAFTA, and a number of other Latin American countries.

In the spheres of both science and technology and the integration of farming and fishing, the Andean Pact countries have done some useful work. Now they must increase their work in these fields. In relation to the first, the Andean Pact was the first attempt at integration in the developing world to give serious consideration to the question of technology, making a systematic investigation of the field, and even carrying out its own research projects (the Andean Programme for Technological Development). Today the aim is to put into practice a genuine policy for shared technology. In relation to the integration of farming and fishing, there is good reason to call for a form of horizontal cooperation which will allow each country to introduce farming and fishing policies of its own, which will help to ensure a 'secure food supply'. The question of trade in farming and fishing products is mentioned in the strategy, but clearly without any hope that these suggestions will be carried out shortly, or to any significant extent. Instead, there are many other areas in which joint action or mutual support could be beneficial without creating conflicts (regulations on animal and vegetable hygiene, campaigns to eradicate infections, research, training, etc).

THE IMMEDIATE FUTURE FOR THE ANDEAN GROUP

I feel some disquiet in embarking on this final section, which will inevitably have to combine arguments or recommendations with predictions. This implies being able to give an answer, which may be extremely arbitrary, to many questions about the immediate future internationally and in each of the member countries, as well as making a subjective evaluation of the experiences and interests of each of them. The risk of arbitrariness is unavoidable here, since any option will be based on the perspectives and possibilities of the Andean Pact.

The atmosphere for negotiations within the Pact is today, in spite of frustrations and suspicions, a positive one if judged in terms of the work carried out and the concern of the countries to find a solution to this stagnation and deterioration. Even accepting that there is a generally *positive* attitude of concern to overcome this 'impasse', it has to be said that the overall context of the negotiations is difficult, both because of objective factors, and because of the evaluation made by each member of their experiences during the lifetime of the Andean Pact.

One of the most important objective factors accentuating the problems of the Andean Pact, and a consequence influencing the climate of negotiations, has been the international scene, with the particular repercussions this has had for the Latin American financial crisis and the crisis in the balance of payments. The contraction of the economies of the industrialized nations between 1980 and 1983 has had, as is generally recognized, a devastating effect on Latin America and, therefore, on the Andean Pact countries.

Even if the economic recovery in the United States is consolidated this year, and that brings in its wake a recovery in the other industrialized countries, a development which is probably, but not certain, the economic and financial problems in Latin America and the Andean Pact countries will continue to be pressing and urgent for several years because of the heavy financial obligations of the region. We may foresee a continuation of policies designed to restrict imports and predict that the instability of international exchange rate will be reflected in devaluations on a large scale, given the relationship between these measures and inflation, which shows no signs of falling significantly in the near future. Such a situation is clearly not ideal for negotiations over the integration of markets and production. Experience shows that these require a minimum space to enable medium- and long-term objectives to be identified.

I know that my opinion goes against current expectations about the response to the crisis that can logically be expected from our countries. This response would favour closer cooperation between Latin American countries which would enable them not only to reduce the effects of the present situation, but also to give their national economic policies more autonomy. This view has been put forward in a recent series of regional economic meetings which culminate in the Latin American Economic Conference which is taking place while these words are being written. But despite this, I believe that at least in the immediate future these calls for closer links of integration and cooperation will nevertheless carry little weight when it comes to making decisions over crucial problems in the Andean integration process. In taking these decisions, the traditional positions of member states, coloured to some extent by the experiences of the past and the restrictive situation created by the international situation, will be of more importance than arguments about the clear benefits of future cooperation. This is not to deny that the logic of cooperation may be followed in many areas (financial questions, the administration of trade, relations between countries, etc.) and below we shall indicate some of these areas; but I am not convinced that this logic now prevails to the extent of creating a climate for negotiations that would allow the reconciliation of differences which is crucial if the Andean Pact is to advance in the process of regional integration according to the basic principles of the Cartagena Agreement. I believe that the crucial issues contained in the

Plan for Reorientation, which have been briefly examined in preceding pages, will be discussed and decided upon without the above-mentioned response to the crisis having a significant influence.

The Plan for Reorientation is, as our summary suggested, really a list of everything that could reasonably be done jointly by a group of countries that have already gone some way towards integration. The Cartagena Agreement's original objective was to achieve a far-reaching integration of markets and production. It is worth asking, therefore, which aspects of the Plan are essential for this level of integration. This will allow us to assess if, in the form in which it is set out, the Plan will in the first place lead to the kind of integration that the Agreement had intended, or to a process with different characteristics; and secondly to see whether its proposals are viable given the present situation in which the Cartagena Agreement finds itself. Once we have an answer to these questions, we will be able to risk an opinion on the viability and significance of the other measures of cooperation.

Earlier in this paper, we gave a summary of the proposed strategy in three areas which we consider crucial in continuing the process of integration, and it is not surprising that these are also the areas in which we find the most difficult problems for negotiation. These three areas are: the creation of a larger market, integration of industry, and the special regulations for Bolivia and Ecuador, the two weaker countries, or those with relatively less development.

The proposals for the creation of a larger market — which, it should be said, represent a realistic identification of those areas in which, in the best of cases, there may exist a possibility of agreement — imply a considerable softening of the terms of the Agreement, both in respect of the time in which these must be carried out, and of the area to be covered by the tariff reduction, at least during the initial period. The same thing can be seen in relation to the common external tariff, an instrument of integration which to begin with will be simply a common minimum level, which will later move within the so-called 'margins' — that is to say, will move between maximum and minimum levels. In both cases, the Plan for Reorientation suggests, in vague terms and clearly as a distant goal, a later stage when progress will be made towards a complete removal of tariff barriers between nations, and the countries will agree on a single common external tariff, which were the initial goals of the Agreement.

In real terms Andean integration will no longer aim for the special brand of economic unity which we talked of at the beginning of this paper. Its aspirations now lie in an intermediate path between a partial free-trade zone and a customs union. The concept of a 'margin' within which the foreign tariff will operate is particularly worrying, because in order for it to exist, a series of regulations will have to be introduced which will cause conflict during negotiations (over traditional tariffs, and over rules of competition, etc.) and will be extremely difficult to make effective. Given that integration will take this form, with differences remaining between countries in the level of protection imposed against the products of countries from outside the Pact, it will moreover be virtually impossible to deal with certain questions which, at least from a technical point of view, are unavoidable in a process of integration, such as the minimum harmonization of monetary and exchange policies. The programme mentions these questions, but this is quite obviously merely a formal gesture.

The aim of the Cartagena Agreement was undoubtedly not this kind of integration, but that is not to deny that its achievement would be an important step forward. The real question is whether even this lesser form of integration is viable in the present situation. One can only give an answer — which in any case inevitably risks being subjective — when one has made an analysis of the three key areas, which of course are closely linked.

The second area is that of industrial integration, the most precisely defined aspect of the integration of production contained in the Cartagena Agreement. Here the application of the new strategy would mean a major shift away from the original approach of the Cartagena Agreement, as we have already pointed out. We see to begin with a desire to reduce the importance given to industrial development within the process of integration; the strategy goes on to state plainly that it will not attempt to impose a 'uniform and all-embracing' policy, that is, a common industrial policy of the kind foreseen by the Agreement, but rather to find 'common denominators' within national programmes, which will provide the basis for measures to increase integration, Finally, despite assurances that sectoral planning for industrial development will continue, it is apparent that it will virtually cease to involve the larger countries, and will play merely a residual, almost formal role in relation to Bolivia and Ecuador.

I believe that this formal shift in priorities should be understood first and foremost as an effort to widen the sphere of joint action, and prevent excessive emphasis on a sector which up to now has proved the most difficult and prone to conflict. We should just make one rather obvious comment, that the motivations for the integration of developing countries, like those of the Andean Pact, lie basically in the desire to enjoy the advantages of large-scale production for industrial development, and that the results of the process will be evaluated principally by looking at the indicators for trade in industrial products, investment and technological change. If industry has been an area of conflict within the Andean Pact, that is because expectations have focused on this area, and it is here that the first real effects of the integration of markets and production have been felt. Farming has not been a problem up to now, because there have been no real expectations for this sphere, and the mechanisms of integration have not been employed in it. Had this not been the case, farming would have caused more conflict than industry, as is happening in the EEC, even despite the fact that in developed economies agricultural production has relatively considerably less importance than in countries with a large primary sector. We could go so far as to say that in practice the change in priorities is merely formal, and that in fact Andean integration will continue to be assessed by its members principally in terms of its achievements for industrial development.

The other two changes in the original approach of the Agreement are far-reaching and deserve a closer critical examination. The decision to abandon the goal of a common industrial policy and the use of sectoral programming of industrial development as a means of achieving this goal means that, at least for the three largest countries, Andean integration will return to the old pattern of integrating markets and production by using the market as the single means of distributing resources. As we have said, the Cartagena Agreement was originally based on the decision to reserve an area of industrial development — at that time expected to cover those industries of greatest complexity and potential — for control by a special mechanism which would determine where development would take place, and consequently the allocation of investment. The disappearance of this area removes from the Agreement a mechanism that in the first place had been intended to neutralize to some extent the natural advantages or disadvantages of member countries and to prevent or reduce the scale of the classical conflicts that occur in any attempt at integration among developing countries. It deprives it in the second place of a way of rationalizing, as far as possible, industrial development within the new economic unit. As we said above — and we will now see that this is equally true for the relatively less-developed countries — it is market forces that decide not only the flow of trade, but also of investment. Naturally, this will not be either a wholly open market, nor one that is uniformly protected, but instead will be a market with much more limited scope than had originally been intended, yet which will nevertheless have exclusive control over the distribution of resources.

We believe that these are the fundamental aspects of the proposals for industrial strategy which need to be borne in mind. The rest of the proposals — rationalization programmes, support for projects offering new opportunities in industry using advanced technologies or in priority areas, joint investment, or the use of Andean multinational enterprises as a means of advancement — involve horizontal cooperation, which could theoretically occur without integration, even though in practice they would be more effective and equitable as part of a dynamic process of integration.

Numerous worthy reasons can be given for this change in the principles of the Cartagena Agreement. We do not intend to repeat here what has already been said about the tremendous difficulties confronted in negotiations over the PSDIs or the disruption which the negotiations caused in the efficiency of the programmes; but I feel that the countries should at least try to salvage those programmes already approved, with their considerable powers of allocation, as far as possible improving them and making every effort to carry out their resolutions.

The position of the two relatively less-developed countries and the whole body of preferential treatment established for their benefit are also affected by this change of principles. The strategy proposes that some of the areas of production allocated to them under the PSDIs already approved should be retained. The discussion within the Commission of specific proposals for changes is clear proof of the difficulty in reaching significant agreements over particular points. The terms of negotiation are totally different from those of the original programmes, and today negotiations take place over isolated projects that will benefit individual members. This brings all the irritation, and in the long run little of real importance, as usually happens where negotiations are one-sided.

We have already discussed the implications of the preferential treatment for tariff removals and the common external tariff. The proposed strategy takes a flexible approach towards the two relatively less-developed countries as regards their removal of tariffs, and probably also their adoption of the two types of common external tariff. If these proposals were accepted by the Commission, this flexibility could help to some extent to counterbalance the concern that Bolivia and Ecuador may feel at the virtual annihilation of the system of industrial planning in the areas that offer most potential for them. But, at the same time, the preferences given under the trading rules may make the other countries much less sympathetic to the aspirations of these two countries and less concerned to act in their favour, either in the allocation of the few projects in the PSDIs already approved, or in the other areas of preferential treatment that depend basically on unilateral decisions by other members to offer their cooperation. In fact, despite the potential breadth of the system of preferences proposed in the strategy — there is practically no area in which no mention is made of some kind of measure to benefit the two countries — in only very few cases is there a clear and firm requirement that members put these preferences into practice, as had existed with the PSDIs or the commercial preferences. The implementation of the other measures of support will depend on the goodwill of the rest of the members and their ability to offer effective cooperation, which is frequently doubtful. In the past, support has been given in financial matters, and a few other fairly isolated cases; but their own problems and limitations make it very unlikely that a system of preferences could be made to work on this basis. Looking at the expectations and concerns that exist today, it is clear that neither of the two relatively less-developed countries see this as sufficient compensation for removing virtually all the industrial planning powers, which they had quite understandably considered the essence of the system of preferences. This explains their insistence on including the allocation of industrial projects within the packet of support measures which are under negotiation at present.

With all modesty, we believe that this analysis provides the basis for making a realistic evaluation of the future of the Andean Pact. We start from the premise that today it is more important than ever to keep alive the movements for integration that have appeared in Latin America. For a number of different reasons, they face a difficult situation, and there may be circumstances in which the only way to keep them 'alive' is to leave them ticking over until better times arrive. I hope that this will not be the case for the Andean Pact. The Cartagena Agreement could be implemented less energetically than was originally hoped, yet still be of use to all the members. It is essential that the benefits be shared by all. If the Pact is going to work at half strength, as appears inevitable, it will be disastrous if the process of integration deepens contradictions between members. The distributive effects of the process should be monitored more carefully than ever to prevent any of the members, whether or not these are the relatively less-developed countries, from being marginalized from the development taking place in the more dynamic sectors, and to prevent them from feeling that they are bearing unjustifiably high costs in relation to the benefits received. Some difficult decisions will have to be left until conditions have improved, and the Pact returns to a system that is more able than at present to find ways of compensating for the sacrifices it demands.

Finally, it is vital that the Andean Pact regain what could be called its 'credibility'. The creation of the Court of Justice is a new development which should allow violations of the Agreement to be drastically reduced. To keep the Pact alive for the moment demands above all that commitments be kept, once, as the Council has proposed, their irrelevant or inapplicable clauses have been removed.

These considerations are particularly important given the nature of the change in direction proposed by the Plan for Reorientation and the strategies that we have discussed above.

The first proof of viability must be the completion of the negotiations at present going on in the Andean Pact. As we have seen, the Gordian knot can be found in the three key areas of creating a larger market, industrial development, and the special rules for Bolivia and Ecuador. Because of the terms under which the negotiations are taking place, they are likely to be extremely laborious and to demand substantial concessions by members, especially in the allocation of industrial projects of real relevance and importance to Bolivia and Ecuador. To fail to make these concessions would be like limiting the integration process to the biggest countries. This is an alternative that cannot be ruled out, since the larger countries are certainly a more homogeneous group, but it is an alternative that would have very serious political and economic costs, and that would have to be considered carefully by all members. For the moment, we will not even consider it, on the basis that the aim is to maintain the present structure of the subregion.

Even if the negotiations are completed, the challenge will remain of making the process of integration described schematically above function. There are two aspects of the process that should be borne in mind. First of all, it is a process that will use the mechanism of the market both in relation to the flow of trade and in the allocation of investments. Given the great differences between members, the effects of this will tend to concentrate benefits. In the second place, this market mechanism will operate within a fragmented or limited space (where there are exceptions, sensitive products, safeguard clauses), where competition is likely to be distorted because of the lack of a common external tariff. These factors will limit the tendency to concentrate benefits mentioned previously, but will equally create numerous possibilities of conflict and will demand complex administration. Here the speed and efficiency of the Andean Court of Justice will be put to the test. The survival of the Pact will be conditional on its work.

In short, we believe that the integration of markets and production can proceed using this system; but the need to maintain a minimum balance and reduce conflicts over routine activities will be reflected in serious limitations on the extent and pace of the process of integration. I believe that the Andean Pact's Plan for Reorientation has taken this inevitable result into account, and that is why it is emphasizing a range of complementary measures for cooperation or joint action in areas that go from foreign relations to science and technology. As long as the core of the process of integration of markets and production is maintained, it will be much easier to arrange cooperation between members and to draw third parties into negotiations. If this does not happen, and the present stagnation and frustration with the process of integration continues, it is very unlikely that even the most worthwhile attempts at cooperation will be carried out.

It is not the place here to examine one by one the long list of tasks that come out of the strategies. In every sphere it would be possible to make progress on a number of the ideas put forward. In some cases it is essential for the process of integration that progress should be made, as in the case of transport. In other areas, like financing, a relatively developed form of organization already exists and could be made to work more energetically. Finally, there are other areas like science and technology in which the increased degree of cooperation implied by the proposals would provide the process of integration, which by now is lacking in fresh ideas, with new goals and aspirations. In almost all of these areas, the Andean Pact could also encourage action at a Latin American level. Great potential undoubtedly exists, but if this is to be realized, the process of integration must first of all be salvaged; without neglecting other areas, this must for the moment be the Andean Pact's main focus.

NOTES

* This article first appeared in *Regional Integration: The Latin American Experience* published by Third World Foundation for Social and Economic Studies, London, and who hold copyright.
1. Council of the Agreement of Cartagena, 'Our Nation is America', 1983, p. 15.
2. The principles and main arguments of the strategy documents referred to are given in the following documents which the author has been able to consult: Jun/dt. 205/Rev.2; COM/XXXIX-E/dt. 7; June/dt. 212; Jun/dt. 204. This last document is dated September 1983, and the others, November 1983.
3. Exceptionally, the place of one or other Head of State has been taken by a delegation of officials, with the status of personal representatives.
4. 'Our Nation is America', op. cit., p. 40.
5. Ibid., p. 40.
6. They are as follows: (1) foreign relations; (2) farming; (3) trade; (4) industry; (5) financing and payments; (6) trade and technology; (7) physical integration, boundaries and tourism; and (8) special terms for Bolivia and Ecuador.
7. Document: 'Outline for a strategy for the formation of a larger market and the strengthening of commercial activity', JUN/dt. 205/rev. 2, p. 37.
8. Less precise measures relating to commitments, or no indication of the time-scale within which these are to be adopted.
9. 'It is thus vital to move towards a more balanced integration of trade, farming and industry', p. 23.

10. The Plan for the Reorientation of the Andean Process of Integration.
11. Outline for a subregional strategy for integration in the industrial sector'. COM/XXXIX-E-dt 7, November 1983, p. 32.
12. Op. cit., note 10.
13. JUN/dt.-213, November 1983, p. 7.
14. Ibid. 'Failure to respect the commitment agreed by the other countries under the Pact, which affected both the exclusive nature of the allocations granted to Bolivia and Ecuador and also the freeing of trade', p. 12.
15. 'Reports on consultations with member states on the modification and completion of the PSDIs. COM/XXXIX-E/dt 5; November 1983.
16. 'Report of the Working Party of the Commission on the adjustment and completion of the PSDIs in metallurgy, petrochemicals and steel', COM/XXXIX-E/dt 6, November 1983.

Index